THE SECRET LANGUAGE OF
MONEY

HOW TO MAKE SMARTER FINANCIAL DECISIONS AND LEAD A RICHER LIFE

DAVID KRUEGER, M.D.
with JOHN DAVID MANN

New York   Chicago   San Francisco   Lisbon   London
Madrid   Mexico City   Milan   New Delhi   San Juan
Seoul   Singapore   Sydney   Toronto

The **McGraw·Hill** Companies

To Carly

1 2 3 4 5 6 7 8 9 0 DOC/DOC 0 1 0 9

ISBN: 978-0-07-162339-1
MHID: 0-07-162339-6

This publication is designed to provide accurate and authoritative information in regard to the subject matter covered. It is sold with the understanding that the publisher is not engaged in rendering legal, accounting, or other professional service. If legal advice or other expert assistance is required, the services of a competent professional person should be sought.

> — *From a Declaration of Principles Jointly Adopted by a Committee of the American Bar Association and a Committee of Publishers and Associations*

McGraw-Hill books are available at special quantity discounts to use as premiums and sales promotions, or for use in corporate training programs. To contact a representative, please e-mail us at bulksales@mcgraw-hill.com.

This book is printed on acid-free paper.

CONTENTS

ACKNOWLEDGMENTS

I want to express my deepest appreciation to the invaluable contributors who made this book possible.

Carly Jennings, my best muse and brilliant perturbator, tirelessly brainstormed concepts and constructs with me.

John David Mann, who first worked with me as Editor in Chief at *Networking Times* when I had a regular column there, has richly influenced and advanced the craft, story, and content of the project. Dan Clements, John's writing partner, contributed illuminating narrative and detail to this final realized version of *The Secret Language of Money*.

Margret McBride and Donna DeGutis, my amazing literary agents, believed and encouraged, for which I am ever grateful.

Mary Glenn and Morgan Ertel, our brilliant and attentive team at McGraw-Hill, midwifed the project lovingly and expertly from manuscript to finished product.

I also want to express my appreciation to my coaching clients and students who have taught me so much over this last decade of collaboration together. The continued creative learning is always stimulating. I am especially grateful to Will Craig, visionary founder of Coach Training Alliance, and to my fellow faculty colleagues and staff for their extraordinary support and inspired collaboration.

INTRODUCTION

A well-known therapist once observed, "Money questions will be treated by cultured people in the same manner as sexual matters, with the same inconsistency, prudishness and hypocrisy." The year was 1913. The therapist was Sigmund Freud, early explorer of the secretive, unspoken side of the human psyche.[1]

Today, nearly a century since Freud wrote those words, most of us have come to speak far more openly about sex, yet we remain embarrassed and conflicted when it comes to talking about our money. If you doubt this, ask the hosts of your next dinner party what their annual income is. You probably won't be on the guest list for their next event. Ask how much debt they have, and you may not see dessert. That's the nature of our relationship with money: silent, forbidden—and unexamined. It may be true (as Freud himself is alleged to have said) that sometimes a cigar is just a cigar—but even Freud might have agreed that a $500 *cigar* is something else altogether.

Our relationship with money is strange, to say the least. It certainly goes well beyond the simple numbers it takes to tally up what we earn and what we owe. If money were about math, none of us would be carrying any debt. The numbers are simple. What's complex is what we do with money: *we give it meaning*. We breathe life into money and give it emotional value. We make it bigger than it is. We use money to do things money isn't designed to do, and that's where things get complicated.

Money is a magnifier. Like adversity, it reveals and exaggerates character. For a problem drinker, money creates more drunkenness. For the habitually insecure, money can make them paranoid. In the hands of the caring and generous, it engenders philanthropy. But it doesn't simply magnify who we are: it also amplifies who we hope to be, fear we might have become, or regret that we may never be. It gives form to our fantasies and shape to our compulsions. We don't simply earn, save and spend money: we woo it, flirt with it, crave it and scorn it, punish and reward ourselves with it.

We invest money with a totemic power it doesn't truly possess and then live our lives under the thumb of that dictatorial rule. Like the master of a runaway band of mad marionettes, money runs us in circles and beckons us down dead-end paths, inflates our dreams and dashes our hopes—and all the while it is we ourselves who hold the strings that make the puppets move!

It is not money but the *love* of money that Saint Paul identified as the root of evil. It is not wealth and possessions or even the chase after these that creates problems in our lives: it is when we lose ourselves in the chase. And when do we lose ourselves? When we imbue money with meaning it doesn't really have, and then keep that meaning a secret even from ourselves—thus holding ourselves hostage to our own *money story* without even realizing we were the ones who made it up it in the first place.

For three decades—two as a psychoanalyst, one as an executive coach—much of my work has been focused on exploring the hidden side of money and helping people successfully change their money stories. Whether top CEOs and the ultra-rich or the average middle-class family, the clients I've helped over the years have all shared one thing in common: their problems with money are not about the money. They're about the story they try to tell with it.

What follows is a journey to understand the architecture of *your* money story: how you use money to shape the world around you, and how it shapes you back.

One thing we'll discover is that the brain and mind are not always in agreement. While one part of us says, "We should be planning for retirement," another says, "Hey, let's have that second cognac and order the plasma TV!" Each part struggles over the same dollar, and unless we understand the secret language of money, the results can be disastrous. In these pages we'll explore both the brain and the mind, looking through the lens of leading-edge scientific research from such fields as psychology, neuroscience and behavioral economics, along with case studies from my thirty years in the trenches of psychoanalysis and executive coaching. We will apply these insights to help you strategically rewire your brain, reprogram your mind and reshape your habits, so that you can begin using money to say what you want it to say, and create the life you want to be living.

The Secret Language of Money is not really about your income, expenses, assets and investments, although it will change how you view and manage all of these. It is about your *relationship* with money and how it affects everything in your life, including your financial success. It is an unblinking examination of the running dialogue inside your head about money—about how much you think you're worth, and how much you feel you deserve; about what you believe your money says about you, and how much of it is enough. This book is a rare glimpse into the secret conversation you hold with yourself about the meaning of money in your life—and therefore, about your life itself.

Money does talk—but what is it really saying? Or more accurately, what are you saying through money? This book is about finding the answer to that question.

Note

1. "On Beginning the Treatment (Further Recommendations in the Technique of Psycho-Analysis: I)," in The *Collected Papers of Sigmund Freud*, 2:351; 1913.

Part I

YOUR MONEY STORY

one

MONEY TALKS—BUT WHAT IS IT SAYING?

If there's something strange in the neighborhood,
Who ya gonna call? **Ghostbusters!**
If there's something weird and it don't look good,
Who ya gonna call? **Ghostbusters!**

—Theme song to *Ghostbusters*,
music and lyrics by Ray Parker, Jr.

Something strange was going on, all right. When Alex Popov set off for San Francisco's PacBell Park that morning, softball glove in hand, it had seemed like a good plan. It just didn't turn out that way.

Two nights before, the San Francisco Giants had played well past midnight in the longest nine-inning game in Major League history, only to lose to the L.A. Dodgers. Today, on Sunday, October 7, 2001, in their last game of the season, the Giants came back with a 2-to-1 victory. But that wasn't what made history that day. No, the epic moment came in the first inning, when Barry Bonds hit a knuckleball from the Dodgers' Dennis Spring and sent it clear over the fence into the arcade, setting a new all-time record by swatting his seventy-third home run in a single season.

When Bonds hit his homer into the stands, the fans went wild—and in this instance, that is not a figure of speech.

Anticipating the smash hit and knowing that Bonds tended to favor right field, especially enterprising fans had packed that standing-room-only area hoping for a serious shot at the record-breaking ball. And exactly two fans—Popov, owner of a Berkeley health-food restaurant, and a software engineer named Patrick Hayashi—got their wish. As the ball hit Popov's glove, he was instantly tackled, thrown to the ground and buried in a swarm of determined fans. In the ensuing mayhem, Hayashi came up, ball in hand. Eyewitness testimony (later disputed) would claim that Hayashi bit a teenage boy and even grabbed Popov's crotch in an attempt to get control of the ball. A cameraman's videotape of the entire fracas proved inconclusive.

The court battle between Popov and Hayashi raged for months—the two as fierce as litigants in any custody case—until 20 months later, in June, 2003, a judge decreed that the ball be auctioned off and the two fans split the proceeds. The ball was eventually purchased at auction for $450,000 by Todd MacFarlane, creator of the *Spawn* comic book series, netting Popov and Hayashi each a cool $225,000—which didn't even come close to covering court costs. In fact, Popov would have needed to net more than twice that amount just to cover his legal expenses. To make matters worse, the two men owed taxes on the entire auction income of $450,000.

After nearly two years of legal brawling, Popov and Hayashi were both heavily in debt, and MacFarlane had his slightly used baseball for the bargain price of $450,000.

And here the story goes from odd to odder still.

That single-season record Bonds broke had previously been set by Mark McGwire, who hit his seventieth single-season home run in 1998. That winning baseball had also been purchased by MacFarlane for $3.2 *million*—which represented "most of his life savings," as he told newsmen.[1] In a previous deal, costing him about $300,000, MacFarlane had also purchased the first, sixty-seventh, sixty-eighth, and sixty-ninth home run baseballs of McGwire's 1998 season.

Each ball had cost about $5 to manufacture.

What happened here? Something strange indeed; something that defies normal logic. And while Popov, Hayashi, and MacFarlane's story may seem a little extreme, it's really not so different from the stories of people we know well.

A single mom of 38, Barbara is in a tough spot. Recently divorced, with custody of her two teenage children, she is approaching middle age and struggling to make ends meet. Her fixed salary and meager child-support payments are barely adequate to support her family's basic needs. Money is tight, at best, and Barbara's financial prospects look grim.

Barbara has a strategy for dealing with her subsistence lifestyle, which, if not the most logical course of action, has the dubious advantage of simplicity: *She shops.*

Despite her precarious finances, Barbara goes on frequent spending sprees. On one day's forage alone, she brought home a $250 silk blouse, a $175 silver ring, and a pair of $825 silver earrings. With every day that passes, with each shopping spree, Barbara is inching herself and her family ever closer to the precipice of utter financial meltdown. And the closer to the edge she gets, the more she shops and spends.

Robert's story begins on the opposite end of the money spectrum from Barbara's: Where she started in a tight spot, Robert set out from a place of affluence.

It was only 12 years ago that Robert found himself an unusually wealthy man. When his father died, Robert inherited $20 million, enough to ensure his financial security for a lifetime. Yet by the time I met him, Robert had managed to spend nearly every penny.

Distant and emotionally isolated, Robert's father had lavished him with money and expensive gifts all his life. Robert recognized his father's financial magnanimity as an expression of guilt, a poor proxy that scarcely compensated for his absence in his son's life. Robert now sustained his anger at his father, as he described it, "by pissing away my father's money, gambling and making bad investments." The bad investments piled one upon the other. Robert's poker losses became larger and more frequent; he lost several thousand dollars in a single session.

Having attained complete financial independence, Robert now seemed determined to spend his way to bankruptcy.

> *Something strange in the neighborhood.*
> *Something weird, and it don't look good.*

Money, Money Everywhere

Over the first five decades following the close of World War II, something remarkable happened: We grew steadily richer. A *lot* richer. During the second half of the twentieth century, more wealth was created in the United States alone than had ever before existed on the planet. By the new millennium, even America's poor had reached a standard of living higher than the middle class of the 1950s. Our homes were larger, our cars more luxurious than ever, and necessities such as food and water were cheap, abundant, and close at hand. Any measurement of life using the wealth yardstick during those times told us exactly what we love to hear: *Life is good and getting better.*

Yet underneath the glitter, something was amiss.

Our perennial competitors, the Joneses, may have looked good on the outside, but the numbers revealed a different story. Despite our growing levels of apparent affluence, savings rates had dropped to an all-time low, and debt had climbed to an all-time high. By 2001, Americans owed more than $1.7 *trillion* in consumer debt—almost three times the value of all the U.S. dollars in circulation—and bankruptcies began to skyrocket.

By 2008, the onrush of affluence seemed to have slammed into full reverse. Corporate scandal, bad debt, collapsing housing markets, and shifting international demographics had launched the first genuinely global financial crisis in history. The ride, at least for the moment, was over.

And what a strange ride it's been. After winning what might best be described as an economic jackpot, we seemed to be shedding our gains as quickly as we'd gotten them. Stranger still, we've somehow managed to spend our personal happiness along the way: Our internal lives have become as troubled as the state of our finances. After peaking in 1957, the number of Americans who rank themselves as "very happy" has steadily declined. A diagnosis of depression today is 10 times more common than it was a half century ago. Our physical health, our sense of connection to others, our time spent engaged in our communities — factors which might arguably be seen as indicators of a truly rich life — are on the same precipitous downward trend.

It's puzzling. The more money we have, the more financial trouble we seem to find. Our standard of living is better, yet our *lives* seem worse. For all its apparent importance, more money seems to deliver only more problems, as we increasingly act in ways that make no rational sense. We spend beyond our means. We agonize, argue, litigate, and divorce over money. We fall victim to scams and cons, sometimes repeatedly. We gamble to the point of destruction. We sink deeper and deeper into a morass of money-related misery that threatens our health, our families, and our survival.

Why do we do these things? Clearly the *quantity* of money is not what we lack. In fact, the opposite seems to be true: The more of it we have, the worse things seem to get. But if that's true, is there then no solution? Is the pursuit of both wealth and happiness a doomed quest?

Fortunately, the answer is "no." There is a path through the money minefield, and it's one we can walk with joy and satisfaction. There is a way to pursue increasing our wealth *without* decreasing our success; to build financial value, eliminate debt, and relieve crushing fiscal strain without sacrificing those things that are most important to us, such as our health and happiness, our families and friends, communities and careers—in other words, without sacrificing our *lives*.

Finding that path starts with a simple question: What *is* money?

The Rest of the Iceberg

On the surface, money is something quite simple, a tangible thing we can readily measure. It's a carefully manufactured piece of paper or shiny coin, a set of digits on a computer screen, a printed number on a paycheck. At its most basic, money is a *thing*, and in these days of abundant information, we understand money the *thing* fairly well. We can invest it and calculate interest, and we can spend it and make sure we have correct change. We have banks and software developers, investment companies and financial advisors, radio stations, television shows, and money gurus galore. There are entire industries dedicated to ensuring our full understanding of money the *thing*.

Yet despite all this knowledge, we still struggle with money. We can't seem to get it right: We spend when we should save, buy when we should sell. We trade away our time, and sometimes our health and relationships as well, in the pursuit of money in the hopes that it will eventually buy back some of the very time we traded away.

No matter how much we know about money, we still do some very strange things with it. Picture this scenario:

You are at an auction, surrounded by a sophisticated-looking group of perhaps six dozen. The auctioneer holds up a $100 bill and carefully explains the scenario about to unfold: "Bids will move in five dollar increments. The highest bidder wins the bill. The second highest bidder pays his or her bid, but gets nothing in return. And this is real money, people."

Within seconds, the bids pass $100, and soon they are up to $300. Two participants get into a bidding war. When it's over the victor earns the right to pay $465 for the $100 bill, and the runner-up pays the auctioneer his high bid of $460 and receives nothing in return.

You are thunderstruck. How could reasonable, intelligent people pay over four times more for something than it's worth?

You might conclude that these people must be suckers with little or no experience in the real world of money. But in this you would be quite mistaken.

This is not an imaginary scene: The auction actually took place at Harvard's John F. Kennedy School of Government. The auctioneer was Professor Max Bazerman; the participants were a group of investment specialists and economic gurus. Some of the brightest financial minds around won $100 bills by paying three and four times their worth.

And not just once. This experiment was repeated *over 600 times.* Commented Professor Bazerman, "I've never seen the bidding stop below $100 in any of the over six hundred times I've done it."

If money is so simple, why is it so complicated? Because when we look at money, we're seeing the *thing*. But money the thing isn't the whole story. The whole story is an iceberg-sized tale, and the part we pay attention to—the cash or debt in hand—is only the tiniest tip visible above the water's surface. The rest of the story lies invisibly submerged beneath the surface of appearances and events. Just because we don't see it doesn't mean it isn't there, or that it can't sink our lives when we run up against it, just as surely as the Titanic. Just ask Barbara and Robert.

That vast, hidden side of money's story has nothing to do with money the *thing*. It has to do instead with what we *tell* ourselves about money, and for many of us, it's a whopper.

A successful business owner once described her money conundrum to me like this:

> "It's a way I use to soothe myself. I'll go into my study and think about how much power I've created for myself. I can do anything I want. I think about my successful, demanding business that's become my life, and calm myself by saying, "I can get out of here. I can leave." Now, the only thing I can enjoy is getting away on vacations. But even then, I can't

relax. Chasing money has taken over. I make all this money so I won't ever again feel helpless or controlled by someone else.

"Once I put money into investments, I don't do anything. I neglect it. Money equals power. I want to have the power, but then I avoid the money so it doesn't have control over me.

"I don't even know how much money I have."

This woman was so far removed from money the *thing* that she literally could not even count it. Her full-time occupation was to use money to generate meaning, to create an emotional state.

We say, "Money talks," but what does it say? The remarkable truth is: *It says whatever you tell it to.* The wonder of money is that it can represent anything. It's a stand-in for what we idolize and desire yet fear and lack, for what we covet, crave, spurn, chase, or follow. We use money to show how much we care, or how little. We use it to measure success and buy happiness—or try to. We use it to bolster our self-esteem. We use money to *communicate*.

The challenge is that much of this given meaning is hidden. We may have a perfectly logical reason (or so it seems to us) to want or even *need* this particular new car, but beneath the surface, an invisible, inaudible, richly nuanced dialogue is weaving a broad tapestry of meaning as to what getting that car (or *not* getting it) says about us.

Money *does* talk. It whispers in our ear, often just below the level of our conscious awareness. Money speaks to us as confidante, seducer, adversary, protector, or drug. Money serves as a tangible container for such subjective matters as hope, ambition, love, and disappointment. Money whispers of caring, of success, of power, of *happiness*. Money can become a currency of caring, a symbol of success, a measure of power, a promissory note for happiness, or a filler for a sagging sense of self.

The trick is that the secret language of money is just that: a secret, hidden and often inscrutable. And because we don't speak the secret language of money—the mental, psychological, emotional language that weaves our outward lives—we do very strange things where money is concerned. We make money mistakes, driving ourselves into debt, despair, and depression. We overspend, under-save, and deceive ourselves. We covet what we don't really want, and don't want what we truly need.

Why do we make these tragic errors? We make money mistakes because we use money to accomplish nonfinancial goals. We seek to use money the *thing* to do what no "thing" can: regulate our moods, increase our self-esteem, and control others. We use money to try to soothe emotional pains and buy the respect of others and ourselves. In doing so, we take money the thing and turn it into something more. We give money *meaning*. We breathe life into it, give it emotional value, build a relationship with it, and make it bigger than it is.

And then something strange happens.

The moment we begin to make money more than the simple, tangible thing it is, more than the coins and papers and paychecks we grasp so well, *we stop understanding it*. Our clean equation of 100 cents to a dollar begins to spawn new variables that we cannot readily define. Ironically, when we give money meaning, we begin to lose our grip on what it really *means*.

This is what lay at the heart of the financial crisis that ignited in 2008 with the collapse of the subprime mortgage business and spread around the globe: We lost track of what on earth we were doing with money. Millions of people took out mortgages they couldn't repay for houses they couldn't afford, egged on by a financial industry that convinced itself that its smoke and mirrors was as good as gold.

While speaking before Congress Alan Greenspan, former Chairman of the Federal Reserve, said he was "shocked" his ideas led to the current economic crisis and said, "I still do not understand exactly how it happened."

Well, let me see if I can give it a shot:

Banks bundled mortgages that had been given to people who wouldn't even qualify for jury duty and then sold those along with "credit default swaps," which are basically insurance the seller provides to the buyer in case the purchased entity loses value. However, unlike regular insurance, these swaps weren't regulated, so they failed to meet any standard of responsible business; then, when everything collapsed, it spread like an infection, because when people are making money, they don't ask "how" they just say, "Yay!"

But again, you're the expert.

—Seth Myers, on *Saturday Night Live*, October 25, 2008

What the financial crisis teaches us, more than anything, is that when it comes to money, how we *think* we are behaving and how we actually *are* behaving can be two very different things indeed—and that money can speak in a code so covert, even the experts often seem at just as much a loss as we are to understand its message.

A Money Quiz

To get the most value out of the following quiz, respond to each of these two questions with a single number—and do this *before* reading the explanations that follow.

1. My *current* annual income is $_____.
2. In order to insure happiness and contentment financially, with no more money problems and worries, my annual income would need to be $_____.

I have given this quiz to hundreds of people over the years, and in more than nine out of ten cases, people's answers indicate that their annual income would need to be about *twice its current level* for them to feel happy and free from money worries.

This means that someone who makes $50,000 a year believes it would take roughly $100,000 a year in order to be financially content, and someone who makes $500,000—five times the first person's magic number—believes that the figure would need to be about a million a year.

And that's not all. In discussions with people after they take this little poll, I often find that those who have actually seen their income double over time have, at the same time, doubled their "happy and content" amount. In other words, once those who earn $50,000 achieve their hoped-for $100,000 goal, they then raise the bar and claim that it would now take about $200,000 to be happy.

What this suggests is that the actual numbers (that is, the money itself) have nothing whatsoever to do with it, because even when you change the numbers the story remains the same. In this case, the story is, "I need twice as much as I have to be happy." Double or triple the numbers, and the story still stands. And this is only one example of the most common story threads; there are dozens of others, just as irrational, and just as hypnotically compelling.

"Although there are many self-help books on how to become rich, the fields of psychology and financial planning have been slow to link money and emotion," reported *The New York Times* in a story on money disorders. "And money is still a great cultural taboo that is rarely discussed openly in this country, experts say. . . . The financial storm thundering from Wall Street is likely to force many people to examine their relationships with money well beyond their portfolios and bank accounts, some psychologists say. Even before this month's dire news, an online survey by the American Psychological Association in June [2008] found that 75 percent of the more than 2,500 adults said money was the No. 1 source of stress in their lives."[2]

Money talks, all right, now in shouts and now in whispers. It coaxes and promises, inspires and motivates, threatens and persuades. Yet unless we train ourselves to understand this secret language of money, we hear and understand only a fraction of what it has to say. And so we do the oddest things with our money, and are shocked and dismayed at the results. Intelligent people spend money they don't have. Sophisticated people get scammed. Rational people trade in their leisure time for money—in hopes of eventually buying back some of the very time they just forfeited. We use money to try to buy love, happiness, power, prestige, approval, or self-worth, and often find ourselves ending up in the opposite state from the one we sought.

It sometimes seems as if some other force is directing our actions. We know we shouldn't panic and sell our stock, or buy the watch we can't afford, yet we do just that. We speak out loud, "I can't afford a new television," then find ourselves seated in front of it later the same day. It's as if someone *else* bought the television, and left us staring at the bill thinking, "You know, maybe I *should* call ghostbusters!"

But there are no ghosts involved. Who decides what mysterious things money is saying? You do. It's just that what you think you've said it means is often not the same thing as what you've actually decided it is saying. If that sounds complicated, it is—because money is something that we tend to complicate. The reason the language of money is secret for most of us is that we keep it a secret *from ourselves*.

Not all of us are wealthy heirs like Robert, struggling single parents like Barbara, or baseball fanatics like Popov, Hayashi, and MacFarlane. Still, we all share one thing in common: Each of us has developed our own unique way of understanding what money *means* and the story it keeps telling.

Fortunately, we can learn to decipher that secret money story, and when we do, it allows us to achieve greater wealth and experience more happiness and fulfillment from the wealth we have. In this book, we're going to find out what your money story is, and if that's not the story you want to be living, then we'll find out how you can write a new one.

Notes

1. *The Washington Post*, Tuesday, Feb. 9, 1999.
2. "How to Treat a 'Money Disorder'," by Sarah Kershaw, *The New York Times*, September 25, 2008.

two

WHAT MONEY MEANS

Money is power: so said one.
Money is a cushion: so said another.
Money is the root of evil: so said still another.
Money means freedom: so runs an old saying.
And money is all of these—and more.
Money pays for whatever you want—if you have the money.
Money buys everything except love, personality, freedom,
  immortality, silence, peace.

— "The People, Yes" (1936) by Carl Sandburg

In 2001, the National Household Travel Survey revealed that there was an average of 1.9 personal vehicles owned or available to each U.S. household. That's about two cars per home. For a country in which barely one household in five owned two vehicles in 1960, we've made some impressive strides.

But here's the really interesting statistic: The same survey showed that we have only 1.8 *drivers* per household—fewer than the number of available cars. If every driver in America got into his or her car and started driving at the same time, we'd have something like 10 million cars left over. In other words, it's right now technically impossible for us to drive all the vehicles we own. And since it costs nearly $10,000 a year to own and operate a vehicle, we as a nation are now spending in the neighborhood of $100 billion each year for cars we cannot drive.[1]

When you've got more cars than you can possibly drive, you've moved beyond the realm of utility; you've crossed over into the financial Twilight Zone.

We don't *need* those extra vehicles, and can't use them. So why are we paying $100 billion for them just to sit there, inert, in our garages and driveways? The answer is that, sometimes, a car is not a car. We're not spending that $100 billion for a ride to work, a trip to the mall, or a lift to the ball park. We're spending it on something else entirely.

This reminds me of Brittany. One of the very first compulsive shoppers I'd ever met, Brittany showed up at my practice many years ago. Her experiences were among the first that prompted me to take a close look at the secret language of money.

Brittany described her impulsive use of money as an attempt to possess something tangible, to make herself feel better. "I jump up and run to the mall when I have a powerful urge to buy clothes," she told me. "The urge is like emptiness. I feel frantic, depleted, frenzied."

What originally precipitated Brittany's urge to shop was her feeling of abandonment. Her parents divorced when she was four years old, and she alternated living with each parent, eventually splitting time with an aunt and several grandparents as well.

Brittany was able to adapt surprisingly well to this relationship pattern, and soon found she could use money as the medium of its emotional exchange. Whenever she wanted something, Brittany could intuitively find the soft spot in whichever one of her many parental figures she happened to be with at the time. Her mother would buy her clothes whenever Brittany felt unhappy. She learned how to approach her father for money, and how to tap her grandparents for occasional incidentals.

To Brittany, money was not money: It was the glue she felt she needed to hold together precarious relationships.

A Money Quiz

If we think Brittany's behavior is irrational, we ought to take another peek into our nation's garages. Like Brittany's trips to the mall, the 10 million cars we buy but will never drive are a classic example of the secret language of money at work. For reasons that far outstrip necessity or practical utility, we're spending an extra hundred billion on cars each year. There is a fundamental force at work here, and it has a profound impact on how we earn, how *much* we earn, and how we use our money.

To better understand that force, let's make it personal. Start by answering the following question using a single word only. Don't think long about this; you'll have the opportunity to rethink your answer later in this chapter. But for now, fill in the blank with the single word that first comes to mind:

To me, money means _____.

Your answer suggests a *money equation*—a primary meaning that you attribute to money. Your money equation is a filter or window through which you see people, possessions, and events, a portal through which you make decisions both great and small.

For the soccer mom who equates money with "security," that extra car in the family may be a higher priced but statistically safer Volvo. For her husband, for whom money means "freedom," his vehicle of choice may be an SUV capable of driving through the worst Alaskan blizzard, even though it's parked in his garage in Arizona.

We each have our own unique secret language of money, each based on our own unique money equations. Yet there are a handful of common meanings, a sort of core cultural vocabulary of money, from which many of us unconsciously draw the principal money themes in the lives we create for ourselves.

Money Means Freedom

Since having money typically increases our range of choice, it's no surprise that for many of us, money comes to mean freedom itself. Limitless wealth, we figure, can free us from pretty much any shackles that threaten and open up our lives to horizons without measure. No more boredom, no more sense of emptiness or feelings of deprivation left over from childhood; no more frustrations or failures: Money is the truth, and the truth shall set us free! *Just one lottery win,* we think, *and I'll be free at last!*

However, Jack Whittaker would disagree with us. Jack woke up Christmas morning in 2002 to discover that he had won the Powerball lottery to the tune of $314 million. Jack was wealthy beyond imagination.

Over the next few years, Jack's seemingly unlimited wealth and the boundless freedom it brought led to his being drugged and robbed; hounded relentlessly for requests for money; divorced and vigorously sued; and alienated from his friends and family. His granddaughter, whom he delighted in spoiling with a generous allowance, became a drug addict and was found dead of an overdose, wrapped in a tarp and stashed behind a junked van, just two years after Jack's big win.

Money Means Captivity

For the millions of lottery-playing hopefuls who dream of the freedom wealth could bring them, there are others who avoid money for fear it will trap and enslave them.

Ralph had a degree in accounting, yet never worked consistently at any one position—he felt constrained working for someone else. Ralph valued personal autonomy and sought to avoid any situation where someone else would be telling him what to do. Because of this, soon after starting a new job he would quit, in order to be free to pursue his own interests.

Ralph actually avoided making more money, as he felt it would encroach on his freedom.

When his father died, Ralph was in charge of the arrangements. His father had wished to have his ashes sprinkled on the lake where they spent summer vacations as a young family. Strapped for cash, Ralph was aghast to realize that he could not afford the plane fare to fly to the lake to fulfill his father's request. As he handed his father's ashes over to his sister so she could transport them to the chosen lake, Ralph had an epiphany: In his effort to avoid having his freedom limited, he had created exactly what he strove to avoid. It was not money that had restricted him, but *not having* money.

Money Means Security

Financial security is a measurable and attainable goal. It requires a game plan with specific goals, reasonable strategies for its pursuit, a map to gauge the progress, and measurable results to monitor its arrival. Given those elements, it's entirely doable.

The equation of money with *emotional* security, on the other hand, is a formula without a solution. Recall the exercise in Chapter 1: When we seek to put a dollar figure on that point where we reach "enough," it often seems to recede forever into the distance. Like *pi*, it can be calculated forever without reaching a final answer. (We'll revisit the question of "enough" in Chapter 11.)

When money represents the fulfillment of an emotional need, such as security, love, or power, then you can never have quite enough. There is not enough money in the world for you to spend yourself into who you want to be.

Money Means Love

"I don't care too much for money, money can't buy me love," sang John Lennon and Paul McCartney. Millions of fans sang the words right along with them—and then went on with their lives, earnestly using money in an effort to buy love.

Love and money, perhaps the two areas where we most readily deceive ourselves, become merged when we use one to represent the other. The results are rarely positive.

A parent may substitute money (or the gifts it buys) in lieu of physical presence, say, in a divorce situation like Brittany's, or in the context of a workaholic lifestyle. To satisfy a craving for warmth, we may spend cold cash (or even colder credit) to the point of extreme debt and addiction.

Not all money-love connections are obvious. It can seem far easier to create and manipulate money than it is to find and nurture a loving relationship, and we may thus choose the path of least resistance. Working or running a business is something we can control more readily than a relationship, and so we throw ourselves into these pursuits at any cost.

We may also spend money as a way to prove or demonstrate our love for another, including children, a spouse, parents, or friends—or they may expect us to. We can even demonstrate our love for community, God, and country through our monetary contributions.

Money may not buy us love, but it sure can *seem* like it does.

Money Means Happiness

The idea that more money will bring more happiness is one of the most pervasive and persistent money themes in modern culture. Is there any truth to it?

Research suggests that money, like Prozac, doesn't make you happy. Both, however, can prevent certain forms of unhappiness. Money, for example, allows us to afford better medical care, safety, neighborhoods, gadgets, and at times, a better mood.

Dr. Daniel Gilbert, a Harvard psychologist, has demonstrated that both greater wealth and actual purchases have little permanent impact on happiness. His research shows those events we expect to make us happy often prove less exciting than we anticipated. The increased happiness and pleasure that we predict might come from a raise in salary, for example, or a new gadget, typically fall short of our expectations. And even in those cases where financial gain does bring about a better mood, the good news doesn't last long. University of Illinois psychologist Dr. David Myers found that after an initial excitement with a burst of good fortune, such as inheritance, lottery, or job advance, people revert to their initial *set point* of happiness or gloom.

In another study, Yale political scientist Robert Lane found that income actually did have a measurable effect on happiness, albeit a relatively weak one; however, this positive correlation was significantly (and not surprisingly) more noticeable among the poor. Evidently, money *can* buy happiness within a certain limited context: That is, a certain amount of money can provide enough essentials of living so that we are no longer preoccupied with our survival. Beyond that, the notion that increased wealth will correlate with increased happiness appears to be an equation more imaginary than real.

Money Means Power

The equation of money and power starts in childhood. Infants have a remarkable level of control over their environment: Their cries swiftly bring food, clean diapers, comfort, and cuddling. Healthy, beloved infants are the rulers of their world.

As we grow, however, our power fades. While still relatively helpless, we soon find we no longer wield the unlimited power we once did. We instead come to believe in the omnipotence of grown-ups (especially our parents) and try to reestablish our own power by identifying with the adults around us.

The common fantasy of immense wealth—and thus of unlimited power—is the result of that childhood desire to restore the effectiveness and mastery into which we were born. Almost everyone equates wealth with power, and to at least some degree aims for both. As a yardstick of achievement, money indicates the degree to which we've attained power and respect. Our money thus becomes a yardstick for our power, status, and clout in society, perhaps even our value *to* society.

Yet this is also a double-edged sword. When money comes to mean power, it can also become an autonomous power that wields itself over us, like the sorcerer's apprentice's enchanted broom. Recall the woman we mentioned in Chapter 1, who used to retreat to her study to contemplate how much power she had created for herself through her acquisition of money:

Now, the only thing I can enjoy is getting away on vacations. But even then, I can't relax. Chasing money has taken over. I make all this money so I won't ever again feel helpless or controlled by someone else . . . but then I avoid the money so it doesn't have control over me. I neglect it. I don't even know how much money I have.

Money Means Time

The measurement of money and the measurement of time have developed side by side for thousands of years, changing as our cultures evolved. Just as money grew beyond the confines of simple barter exchange to embrace symbols of value, time outgrew the simpler division of daylight/dark and growing versus nongrowing seasons and took on the attributes of hours, minutes, and seconds.

Modern science and business produced the modern concept of linear time, and with industrialization and a thriving merchant class, time began to acquire a commodity value. Time came to be measured in terms of money. As hours turned into wages, time could now be not only experienced but also *spent, saved,* and *wasted.*

This relationship permeates our lives. "How long does it take?" determines what we do. "How far away from work and school?" determines where we live.

Today, every purchase is a dual transaction: You spend your time and energy to earn money, and then you spend that money to earn the goods and services that are the expression of someone else's time and energy. This time-money relationship can become quite like a dog chasing its tail: We give up our time to purchase the money with which we hope to buy back some of the time we forfeited in order to earn it.

Money Means Autonomy

Like the baby's first steps, our first major purchases—our first car, our starter home, paying for movie and dinner on a first date—often stand out as statements of having arrived as independent, autonomous persons. Conversely, inheriting money at an early age can have the effect of compromising one's sense of autonomy and ambition.[2]

This was the case with my client John, who rose to a top managerial level in a multinational corporation founded by his father. John's division had done extremely well under his guidance, but he felt vaguely dissatisfied. One day he talked with me about his decision to join the family business rather than strike out on his own. "There are advantages in so many ways, it would have been stupid for me not to have gone into the family business," he said. "But could I have made it in some corporation other than my family's? I'll never really know."

John had inherited a position that led to wealth, but also led to him questioning his own value.

For children with trust funds, whose route to wealth is even shorter than John's, the impact is similar. They often inherit their money from trusts at an age when they have not developed their own identity and their lives are irrevocably influenced by the knowledge of a guaranteed financial future. For those who begin life without a silver spoon, their forced autonomy creates a different kind of relationship with money. People who generate new wealth sometimes try to make up, both to themselves and their children, for what they did not have earlier.

One study of the personality traits of successful maverick entrepreneurs concluded that their independent urges have early roots. Many of these self-made success stories had an emotionally charged relationship with a parent who constantly criticized or competed with them, and they developed an attitude of defiance and a compelling need for independence and success. Disinclined to submit to any authority (such as a boss), they were fired frequently. The group studied thrived during economic downturns or when the odds were most strongly against them.

Most of these successful entrepreneurs were motivated not by money but by the desire to build a successful and esteemed organization. The passion to achieve propels these individuals to pursue a goal to its successful conclusion.

Money Means Dependency

While for some, money speaks of autonomy, for others it can represent the opposite, a *lack* of independence.

Nina wanted to open a music store but felt paralyzed by her fear of the risk. She left the house of her controlling mother only to follow her high school sweetheart to his choice of college. After they married, Nina's new husband made all the household decisions. Although she felt quietly angry about the arrangement, she did not object, and his authority ruled with her support and collaboration.

Nina's husband gave her money, but dissuaded her from starting her own business, saying it was too risky and would take more money than they had available. In fact, Nina had a small inheritance that was sufficient to fund her business venture, but she listened and succumbed to her husband's objections. Just as her parents had earlier, Nina's husband fostered dependency.

Nina never tested her own abilities enough to support a belief that she could succeed without the guidance of her mother (earlier) or her husband (now). She lived with the assumption that some all-knowing authority would need to tell her what to do, step by step.

Money speaks the language of its author—as a declaration of independence or a manifesto of dependence.

Money Means Self-Worth

"When I was growing up," recalls Becky, "no one believed in me. My folks never believed I could even graduate from college. Money became the way I could compare, the only way someone would believe in me. It's undeniable proof—evidence. The only way my parents believed in me as a child was when they saw concrete evidence that I could run faster than any other girls my age, or make better grades."

Today, at the age of thirty-four, Becky is an accomplished business-woman who owns an insurance company. By any reasonable yardstick, Becky has indeed proven herself.

"I've spent a lot of time and energy showing them that I've made it," she says, "that I'm worth their love."

Has it worked?

"I wanted more than anything for them to be proud of me," she says, adding, "I still do." She pauses for a moment, then sighs. "Now, I feel the same struggle with my husband."

Becky's money-equals-worth equation continued to lead her from one measurable financial outcome to another in her attempt to put a dollar value on something immeasurable.

Like Becky, many of us have done all the right things and achieved significant rewards, but are still vaguely dissatisfied. We bargain internally and decide that another achievement or more wealth will be the answer, or that a life change such as a career move might fix what is broken or supply what is missing—only to find that the next step again falls short.

Personal worth is quite independent of the price we command in the marketplace or the net worth on our balance sheet, but it's seductively easy to confuse one with the other.

Money Means Fear

The feelings surrounding money frequently spill over into areas of our lives that have nothing whatsoever to do with finances. For example, requesting a bank loan may evoke the fear of personal rejection, rather than being an objective business transaction. Borrowers are often so relieved to have their loan request granted that they accept any condition the bank dictates, rather than taking the time and care to negotiate more favorable terms. The relief of personal acceptance and the allayed fear of rejection create a rush of feelings that obscures the content of the actual transaction.

The fear of lack and scarcity can cut deep and leave lasting scars. One woman spoke to me of the anxiety she feels each time she has to eat from paper plates. As a child, her family was forced from their homeland, losing their family fortune in the process. Paper plates evoke in her the powerlessness of that time decades past. Today she owns 10 sets of dishes. For her, it is not money but the looming specter of *lack of money* that dominates her secret vocabulary.

Money Means Altruism

Money can be used as a conduit to express ideals. Used to express values, money is a commitment, an emblem of our highest and best good. Money carries the imprimatur of our intention for social benefit and charitable causes, helping build visions consistent with ideals.

The nineteenth-century industrialist Andrew Carnegie, in his lifetime considered the richest man in the world, once referred to accumulation of wealth as "the worst species of idolatry," and used his massive fortune in his later years to become the most prolific philanthropist of his century.

"There is no class so pitiably wretched as that which possesses money and nothing else," wrote Carnegie. "Money can only be the useful drudge of things immeasurably higher than itself. Exalted beyond this, as it sometimes is, it remains Caliban still and still plays the beast."

Money Means Greed

For some, money holds the hypnotic meaning of *more*. Money is a promissory note for the acquisition of still more money.

Ivan Boesky, explaining his desire for money after being arrested for insider trading, said, "It's a sickness I have in the face of which I am helpless."

"Lately in a wreck of a Californian ship," wrote the social critic John Ruskin in 1860, "one of the passengers fastened a belt about him with two hundred pounds of gold in it, with which he was found afterwards at the bottom. Now, as he was sinking—had he the gold? or had the gold him?"[3]

Money Means Envy

An advertisement for Visa asks, "Why is the American Express Card green?" The answer: "Envy." The association could not be more apt: The credit card industry thrives on its products' apparent ability to satisfy that green emotion.

Envy made the top seven of Dante's list of deadly sins, and for good reason. All of us have felt the uncomfortable desire, sometimes infused with resentment, for what someone else possesses.

Low self-esteem may manifest as envy, and vice versa. Media and social images press toward appearance, wealth, and prestige. True role models are often replaced with emulated persons, such as film stars. Advertising fuels yearning by touting coveted items and desirable destinations.

Envy results from a simple relationship that happens in an instant without our conscious thought: the comparison of our inside to someone else's *outside*. But this is not an apples-to-apples measure, and thus the deck is always impossibly stacked against us in such a comparison.

Unlike equating money with happiness, for example, in which we hope to replace a sense of lack through money, the driving force with envy is to stop *feeling* it, and become the *source* of it by appearing wealthy and enviable.

Excessive wealth has become a spectator sport. Our fascination with the wealthy is perhaps a not-so-veiled statement of desire. "Who wants to be a millionaire?" asks the popular ABC-TV show, and it's obviously meant as a rhetorical question: Who *doesn't*?

Yet our money envy is a strangely ambivalent obsession, and its obverse face is a kind of *schadenfreude*: our compelling fascination with the fall from grace of the once-rich-and-famous. We are fascinated both by extreme wealth and by its self-destruction.

Money Means Shame

Shame, the result of failing to live up to an internal ideal, can create a serious obstacle to dealing objectively with money. For example, paying bills and taxes late may be accompanied by a sense of shame. Neglecting to address a loan that can't be repaid generalizes to avoidance of any money-related mail or calls. Omitting or disregarding something, like balancing a checkbook periodically, results in a snowballing, cumulative impact of unfinished business.

Shame has a curious way of attaching itself to financial topics of all sorts. This is another curious ambivalence we tend to have around money: In most social settings, such matters as salaries, debt, mortgage payments, and other financial specifics are taboo. For all the importance and even primacy money often has in our lives, discussion of it is often treated as a profanity, something the polite simply do not do.

This is often an aspect of the secret language of money that is learned from a very early age, as family members collude to perpetuate a ban on certain necessary discussions of money, such as income, net worth, important debts, or inheritance.

Novelist and essayist Daphne Merkin describes her shame of violating this taboo of secrecy to discuss money with her mother.

> "I feel irremediably grubby introducing the issue at all—like one of Lear's daughters, the rapacious and hideously-named Goneril or Regan rather than the purehearted Cordelia—but then again, my mother has never warmed (as my father, likewise, didn't when he was alive) to an aboveboard discussion of financial matters, firmly declaring it "none of my business."
>
> "In fact, although these days she would have trouble calling up the strength to bat away a mosquito, my mother becomes so irate at the very unspeakableness of this subject—especially since, as she asserts, the particulars of my family's net worth shouldn't be of interest to someone with my ethereal writerly concerns—that she threatens to throw me out of her room.[4]

Money Means Opportunity

To some, having money simply means we can pay the bills we need to pay to keep our financial house in order. In other words, money provides the ability to continue living the life we're already living. To others, however, money represents the potential to transcend the status quo and substantially alter present circumstance.

"As a member of the middle class, I buy things," said commentator Paul Ford on NPR. "But the rich *do* things with their money. I've watched wealthy men and women turn a million dollars into respect, a partnership, a new business. They convert their funds into opportunities, relationships that translate cash into power, amplify their ideas into businesses, summer cottages, tax shelters.

"I've tried to understand how they work," Ford continues. "I've tried to fathom the stock market, the derivatives, the mergers, and all the voodoo accounting. … [They] think of money as light, money as signal, and know how to listen for opportunity …"

This reflection reveals the speaker's efforts to learn this particular language of money, self-confessing his "middle-class accent" as a nonnative speaker.

Those to whom money means opportunity often seem to attract money like a magnet, while for those who see money as a never-ending trap, a zero-sum scarcity game, it's almost the opposite: They seem almost to repel money.

Money Means Validation

Remember Brittany, who learned to counter her sense of emotional poverty by her spending binges at the mall? For her, spending money as if there were no limit reinforced her sense illusion that she could have anything and everything she always wanted. Even though she logically knew this was not the case, she could not shake it. Why? Because her money was whispering to her in its secret language.

Brittany's purchasing rampages had their roots in her being shuffled from parent to parent as a child. As an adult, Brittany perpetuated that pattern by getting into trouble periodically with her credit cards, at which point she would appeal to one parent or another to help her. The need for a money rescue from the crisis would reestablish the connection.

For someone like Brittany, spending money imparts the validation of our existence. Money was something tangible that the people who were important in her life gave her to affirm their connection to her, and she learned to speak that language like a native.

Money Means Control

Much has been written over the centuries about the use of money by one segment of society as a lever, prison, or bludgeon with which to control another segment. But it isn't only kings, armies, and wealthy landowners who do this: We do it to each other, too.

Money—the granting and the withholding of it—is perhaps the most common instrument through which we exercise control over others, especially our loved ones. Aren't even the best of parents guilty of at least some degree of using money as a means to manipulate and control their children?

I recognized how blatantly obvious this was each time one of my children left for college. After working out a reasonable budget, I would stipulate that two things were not on the budget and were unlimited: the amount they spent for long-distance calls home and the amount for travel home. Of course, any other calls or any travel other than to come home *were* part of the budget. After all, there had to be limits, right?

Money Means Alibi

As much as we use money to exercise control over those to whom we are closest, we also use it to excuse ourselves from direct participation in those same relationships. Money is the ultimate out: "I couldn't make it home for the party, so I sent [read: bought] a card."

A parent may spend money on children to compensate for emotional or physical absence. The stereotype is the divorced "Disneyland dad" who mitigates guilt by money, presents, and (hopefully) memorable vacations. Churches, charities, and florists frequently benefit from guilt payments.

We use money as an alibi not only for our actual absence, but also for not being *as present* as we might have wished to be, hoped to be, or been expected to be. Thus the expensive gift is offered in order to make up for the deficiencies in our participation in the relationship—as if this were a matter of mathematics that could be solved by borrowing from one column to add to another.

Yet as we saw in Chapter 1 with Robert, whose father left him $20 million to make up for lost time (and lost dad)—and who managed to "piss it all away" through gambling and poor investments—money can be a really poor cover story.

Money Means Living

Mike told me that he "felt most alive" when he was involved in business deals. He felt valued when he faced immediate challenges and risks. Whenever he completed a major business project, he would immediately start working on his next—because if he didn't, the void it left made him uncomfortable.

"As soon as I achieve something, I lose interest, like I don't need it anymore," Mike explained. "Whenever I make a deal, afterward I feel empty, sometimes inadequate—like I need to blow part of it. So I constantly create new challenges.

"Whenever something good happens, I wonder when something bad will happen. I'll make half a million on a deal, but focus completely on the thousand dollars that I didn't make. That keeps me from enjoying what I do. Making money is fairly easy; learning to enjoy it is what's hard."

Although wealthy and respected in his field, Mike felt unfulfilled. He was unable to relax, and needed to immerse himself in the activity of deal-making and generating money to *feel alive*.

"The thrill is in the chase," he said, "not the accomplishment. If I relax and enjoy the present, I'll lose my ambition."

Money Means Keeping Score

For many people, money represents a way of keeping track of how well we're doing at . . . well, at whatever it is that we feel compelled to keep track of. Which is what, exactly? Pressed to explain, we might not know the answer.

Does life itself actually require a scorecard? Is there some universal scale of personhood upon which we are rated for performance? If I'm Dave Krueger, for example, is there a proper slide rule, yardstick, or tape measure with which I can check, from day to day or month to month, how well I'm doing at being Dave Krueger?

Evidently, we think so, or at least a vast number of us do. And while weight, physical "attractiveness" (however it is we measure *that*), or job title are immensely popular ways of seeking to accomplish that measuring, there's no universal keeping-score yardstick like good old *do-re-mi*.

Money and the things we buy with it are the most common way we have of answering that perniciously peripatetic self-inquiry, "How'm I doing?"

In *The Art of the Deal*, Donald Trump recounts a visit to billionaire Adnan Khashoggi's apartment, where he was impressed by the size of the rooms. The living room, in fact, was the largest he had seen.

Trump immediately acquired the apartment adjacent to his own penthouse in Trump Tower and knocked out the walls in between the two, so he could expand his living room to huge proportions—even huger than Khashoggi's.

"While I can't honestly say I need an eighty-foot living room," the Donald admitted, "I do get a big kick out of having one."

Money Means Anything and Everything

A wanderer who had gotten lost in the woods was welcomed into the cave of a family of satyrs. After watching him first blow upon his hands to warm them and then upon his soup to cool it, the satyrs became fearful and asked him to leave. There was no trusting a man, they reasoned, who could blow both hot and cold.

—Aesop's Fables

The very trait that makes money useful—that is, its virtually limitless versatility—is precisely what gives it such unbridled power to hypnotize by reflecting back whatever meaning we give it. For example, we may regard the same dollar quite differently, depending on how it was obtained: "Found" money can be consumed frivolously, *gifted* money spent without debate, *salary* money used only after serious consideration, and *savings* money relinquished only in the face of dire need or emergency.

Money is like the man's breath: It can blow both hot and cold. In fact, it can blow any way you want it to. Money is such a powerful and versatile medium of symbolism that it can easily spark emotional reactions of virtually any shade. It can set off ambition, insecurity, envy, fear, jealousy, competition, or guilt virtually instantaneously. If one is competitive, insecure, or prone to fantasize and worry, money offers a reliable and tangible all-purpose focus.

And because we often make decisions on an emotional basis, the feelings evoked by money's secret whisperings become enormously significant. The most unlikely, absurd, or potentially self-destructive of schemes are willingly mounted when financial necessity is invoked, and even the best of ideas can be readily stopped in its tracks by declaring it "too expensive," or "impossible" because there are insufficient funds to carry it out—even when these declarations are irrelevant or blatantly untrue.

Emotional and relationship issues of every stripe and hue can manifest vividly in the financial arena, pulling money into focus as the answer, the problem, the cause, or the result. Money may be the common language of fears of success or failure, impulsivity or inertia. Fear of autonomy and a wish to be taken care of speak the same voice when creating a financial crisis from which to be rescued. We use money to regulate how we feel, affirm accomplishment, assuage guilt, or create attachments.

Money can make any statement, carry any message, and represent any notion. Money is like any object in a dream: It can mean anything we ask it to mean.

Your Money Equation

Learning the secret language of money starts by becoming clearly and consciously aware of the assumptions and beliefs you hold about money. The following exercise can help illuminate the invisible motives and meanings behind the financial decisions you make.

1. What were your most recent three purchases of more than $100?

    a. _____

    b. _____

    c. _____

2. What does that purchase mean to you? That is, how does it make you feel?

    a. _____

    b. _____

    c. _____

3. If it didn't give you that feeling, would you still make that
   purchase, at that price?

   a. _____

   b. _____

   c. _____

4. If you answered "no" to any of question 3, then how much *would*
   you spend on each purchase if it gave you only what you actually
   bought, and not the feeling that came with it?

   a. _____

   b. _____

   c. _____

After you complete these, take a moment to go over your answers and
see if they provide you with any new insights into your own secret language of money. Were you aware, when you made these purchases, of
exactly why you were making them—both the practical reasons and the
emotional reasons?

Now, consider once more the exercise we did at the beginning of this
chapter and see if, given everything we've explored, your answer is any
different.

Again, fill in the blank with a single word:

To me, money means _____.

Notes

1. *Your Driving Costs*, American Automobile Association and Runzheimer International, 2005 Edition. http://www.apta.com/research/stats/fares/drivcost.cfm.
2. In *The Republic*, Plato wrote that those who inherit wealth are often less interested than others in making money and can pursue more important matters.
3. *Unto This Last* (1860), John Ruskin 17.86.
4. "Mother of All Surrogates," *The New York Times*, May 14, 2006.

three

THE COST OF MONEY

*Mugger: "Don't make a move, this is a stickup. Now, come on—
your money or your life. [long pause] Look, Bud, I said, **your
money or your life**!"*
Jack Benny: "Give me a minute—I'm thinking it over!"

The joke, of course, was that Mr. Benny was such a skinflint, he placed a higher value on his money than on his very life. This routine got one of the biggest laughs of Benny's long and illustrious career, and became the prototypical Jack Benny gag.

Of course, no one in real life would say such a thing. Or would they?

An Expensive Hobby

When I met Denise she had been a collector all her life. One of her earliest memories was of collecting china dolls. The essence of her passion for collecting was the sense it provided her of being in control. In the act of acquiring, arranging, and rearranging her small family of dolls, Denise had absolute command over her little universe.

By her thirties her passion for collecting had grown, and she began purchasing through catalogs so as not to be distracted by having to interact with anyone. By age 40 she had switched to the Internet, spending many hours a day perusing online auctions, trolling for more china dolls. She was building a valuable collection, she told herself.

On many occasions Denise attempted unsuccessfully to curtail her Internet spending. She set a weekly limit of time and money, but promptly defied her own authority, rationalizing that the pursuit helped compensate for feeling lonely, empty, or depressed. Yet despite her belief that her continued collecting would make her feel better, the momentary excitement she would feel when the newest acquisitions actually arrived at her home would quickly fade. She soon reached the point where the only thing that would put a halt to her online activity was either exhaustion or when she would run out of money from her monthly trust allotment.

At 43, by the time I met her, Denise had developed considerable expertise and a collection of significant value to go with it. In addition to the hours she spent every day arranging and cataloging her collections, she was spending $8,000 to $10,000 *per month* from her trust fund on additions to her collection. Her preoccupation now absorbed most of her days and was draining away her inheritance. In a very real sense, it was draining away her *life*.

If Jack Benny's mugger had burst in upon Denise and demanded, "Your doll collection or your life!" what would she have said?

The Cost of Money

I first entered the workforce at the worldly-wise age of eight, as a paid farm hand. On hot summer days I would chop cotton for my dad, earning a whopping ten cents a row. The work was hot, hard, and dirty. That summer, I earned every cent I made.

After work I would meet up with my classmates, many of whom were also experiencing their first forays into the world of autonomous economics. Topped up with change from their paper routes and chores, they would hit the nearest store, where they would trade in their fresh assets for sodas and candy. Naturally, I joined them. My treats were quickly gone, and my hard-won pay with them. I was left standing, tired and dirty, wondering, "Was that candy worth a half a row of work?"

It was one of my earliest lessons in the *cost* of money. Not its *value*—I knew exactly how much candy a dime could buy—but the price I had to pay to get it. I learned that you don't just buy things with money; you have to buy the *money* with something, too. It wasn't long before I learned to ask myself, "Will I get enough from this soft drink to justify one row of cotton chopping?" The answer was *no*.

Yet as simple as this lesson would seem to be, it is one that we hide from ourselves again and again.

Money Quiz

List five things in your life that you value.

1. _____

2. _____

3. _____

4. _____

5. _____

Now: Which of these five things would you willingly trade for money?

Chances are good that if you listed five things that you truly value, your answer was something like, "None of them!" After all, if it's something you value highly, why would you trade it for mere money?

On the other hand, depending on what you put on your list, you may have thought about answering the question with another question, such as, "Just how *much* money are we talking about here?"

That is the question David and Diana Murphy wrestle with in the novel and film *Indecent Proposal*. Desperate for money during an economic reversal that threatens to take away everything they have, they hit Vegas in hopes of winning big. The stakes are raised when David is approached by a wealthy man who offers to give him one million dollars—in exchange for one night with his wife.

Even as children we are fascinated with endless variations of this lurid dilemma. How many of us remember playing the game that goes, "Would you [fill in the blank with a despicable or repellent act] for a million dollars?" As grown-ups, we get to watch the fantasy play itself out—and reality TV shows are only the latest in a long tradition of "Can you believe they did *that* for money?" spectacles.

Hardly a season goes by without yet another sensational story in the press about a politician, sports star, or high-profile businessperson who gambled his or her entire career playing some version of this game and acting out the answer. We shake our heads with disbelief, because *we* would never do that.

Would we? Perhaps not, at least not in such a dramatic, high-stakes way as with Denise, or David Murphy, or whomever sits at the eye of the latest media-scandal storm. But are there smaller or more subtle ways in which we do exactly that?

Here are some of the most common compromises we make, often without fully realizing we're doing it, in our struggles to sort out the most important layers of meaning in our lives.

Trading Time for Money

Of all the precious things we trade for money, by far the most common is time.

Time is the basic unit of exchange for most of the working world. If we want more money, most of us need to spend more time to get it, and the trend has been for us to want more and more of it.

Yet we also insist that it's time we *want*, and not the money itself. A survey by the Pew Social & Demographic Trends Project found that 67 percent of respondents ranked free time as their most important priority, compared with only 13 percent who valued wealth the most.

At least, that's what we *say*. How we act tells a different story altogether. Collectively, American workers give a whopping 1.6 million years' worth of unused vacation time back to their employers every year.[1] That's leisure time which we choose to trade for more money, more accolades, or the hope of climbing one rung higher on the ladder.

The irony of our time-money exchange is that we keep trading time for money in order to buy back more *time*. And time is running out.

Trading Freedom for Money

Lamar founded a thriving personal service business. His company and its growth were his creation, an expression of the creativity he had not experienced working for others, or earlier working for his father in a similar business. Although he had given much of his personal time and energy to the long hours in the dozen years to grow his company, he enjoyed being his own boss.

Lamar used money to represent the freedom that he had created—to do whatever he wanted, whenever he wanted. He felt good about his accomplishment, and the money he had amassed.

Then he decided to cash in on his hard work, and sell his company to a large, multinational corporation. The deal promised a massive profit, a windfall Lamar simply couldn't pass up. He stayed on as a consultant, but his narrow role in the new system felt confining to him. He was now wealthier by an order of magnitude, but no longer CEO of his own company. Lamar finally realized that he had paid the currency of freedom to acquire its symbol, the wealth of money.

Trading Health for Money

In 1969, a young worker at a large Japanese newspaper corporation died of a stroke. His death would become the first official case of *karoshi*, or "death by overwork," a phenomenon that *The Economist* would later call the corporate equivalent of *hari-kari*. By the 1980s, *karoshi* was legally recognized as a cause of death in Japan, with court judgments for the families of victims rising as high as a million dollars.[2]

While *karoshi* remains an extreme example of the impact of the time-money exchange, overwork is taking its toll on our health in other ways. The American Institute of Health estimates that stress has a $300 billion cost, exacted in the form of turnover, compensation, insurance, medical expenses, and reduced productivity. Increased incidences of mental health conditions, particularly anxiety and depression, are being linked to work and money-related stress.

We're suffering mentally and physically, and the problem seems to be worsening.

Trading Family and Relationships for Money

If there ever was a time when the stereotypical image of the father and son playing catch on the weekends was true, it's behind us. Americans spend about 40 minutes each *week* playing with their kids. That's less time than we spend shopping and watching television by a *very* wide margin.[3]

It's not only our children who feel our inability to understand the language of money. Money is the most common relationship conflict for couples. A survey by the Financial Planning Association found that 40 percent of financial advisors cited money as a "key factor" in a couple's decision to split up. And while many of these relationship issues really are about money, many use money as a language to express relationship conflict or the dynamics of power. Who controls finances? Who makes big money decisions? How are money disagreements resolved?

The same money equation that uses money as a currency for power can destroy the very relationships that might provide love and happiness.

Trading Happiness for Money

In their book *Being: The Foundations of Hedonic Psychology*, a group of scholars examined the connection between money and happiness and found that money correlates weakly with happiness (about equally with good looks and intelligence).

And the strongest correlation with happiness? Marriage. The very thing that too often suffers most in the quest for financial gain turns out to be the single most likely predictor of happiness. After marriage, the next strongest happiness predictors were other relationships, including family and friends, and immersion in life, exercise, and spirituality — all things that we frequently sacrifice in the pursuit of wealth.

Our pursuit of happiness through wealth would seem to push joy only farther away and replace it with fear, envy, greed, and shame.

Trading Wealth for Money

Is it possible we're sacrificing *wealth* in the pursuit of money? As paradoxical as that sounds, there is compelling evidence that we are doing exactly that.

In April, 2005, the United States officially became a nation of spenders.[4] That month, we spent more than our after-tax incomes, creating a negative savings rate. The trend continued into the following year, and 2006 marked the first full year since the Great Depression that we spent more than we earned. A look at the balance sheet of the average American citizen in 2006 and 2007 would reveal that *they were worse than broke.*

The middle of the first decade of the twenty-first century, however, was anything but the Great Depression. Incomes had been increasing for decades — there had never been a better time to save a few extra pennies — but climbing along with our income (and eventually surpassing it) was our spending. And that spending was driven by our money story.

Money Quiz, Revisited

Before going on, let's ask that question we asked earlier, but in a slightly different way, and see if it brings up any self-insight:

What in your life right now *are* you compromising for money?

Money, Money, on the Wall...

Asked if we would trade our families, health, or happiness for money, our response is almost always an automatic, "No." Yet most of us find ourselves in positions where we are doing just that, over and over again. Why?

Why do we do these things? Why would we trade away the things that matter to us most? The answer has to do with the fact that money speaks in two languages. The first is the language of simple mathematics: addition and subtraction. You have it, you spend it; you earn it, you save it. It's black and white: numbers on a ledger sheet. Simple, right? Sure it is. But then there is the other language money speaks—the *secret* language.

We do strange things with money because we have all developed patterns and habits of using money for all sorts of nonfinancial purposes— from regulation of mood and esteem to a tool for control and competition. As we interact with money it comes to be layered with meanings that often contradict each other.

In Chapter 2 we looked at some of these more deeply layered money meanings and how they color our view of our world. But that's only the beginning. Often these meanings have to do not only with how we see the world, but also with how we see *ourselves*. There is what money means *to* us—and then there is what we say money means *about* us. We've looked at money's hidden meaning by reducing it to single words: a secret-language-of-money vocabulary. What we're after in this chapter is more like a secret-language-of-money *phrasebook*.

Money is a lens through which we see the world around us, a prism that reflects our hopes and fears. Yet as we draw closer to the glass, money becomes a mirror reflecting a desired or disavowed self. Money's secret language speaks *self-statements*.

A self-statement is a unique, personal communication of your experience and point of view. What you do and say are unavoidable self-statements of your beliefs and personal reality. Self-statements equate money with worth, esteem, opportunity, obstacle, desire, or competition. When we talk about money, our experiences and ideas regarding money, we are talking about ourselves.

For example, *conspicuous consumption* is when you buy a red convertible and drive it in the middle of a busy street. *Contemptuous consumption* is when you buy a red convertible in the middle of a mid-life crisis and drive it by your ex-wife's house. Both speak volumes about *you*.

We shape money into a mirror in which we see the selves we hope to become — or fear we might have already become. Money becomes a stunt double both for those attributes we idealize and desire, and for those we fear and lack. Depending on how we like or don't like what we see in our money mirror, we may covet it, crave it, spurn it, or despise it . . . or all of the above.

Money is like a Rorschach image: It is only an inkblot, yet when we are offered the chance to imbue the design with meaning, our interpretations will be as wishful and varied as the fantasies of the individual.

Where Does Money's Secret Language Come From?

Money is primal. Even before we are born, the vocabulary and syntax of our money language is starting to form in the words, actions, and attitudes of our parents.

We learn the language of money the same way we learn the English, Spanish, Japanese, or other linguistic tongue of our family of origin. Beginning at birth (and even, to some extent, beforehand during gestation), we hear words and phrases. Little by little, day by day, we learn to connect meaning to what we have heard. Beyond the language of mere words, we pick up rich layers of meaning from gestures, inflection, body language, and tone.

By the end of our first year of life, we have begun to mimic and master the gestures, facial expressions, tonalities, and phrases of those around us.

While as infants we have no connection with money, we discover it quickly upon leaving toddlerhood. Helpless, unskilled, two feet tall, and unemployed in an overwhelming world, we first begin our fantasies of unlimited wealth to counter our feelings of powerlessness.

As a young child, we become interested in the acquisitive power of money—enough to plan purchases. That future planning, however, ends when we've saved enough cash for a videogame, or other desire. At times, relationships enter our money picture, too—after all, an aunt and uncle from Baltimore might be good for a new iPod at Christmas.

As adolescents we're driven to join and be accepted by a peer group. What we often fail to notice is how often money is the entry requirement. Our group demands the same manner of dress and music, which, along with Friday night movies, require cash.

For the post-adolescent, money buys *future* money in the form of a college education (along with plenty of pizza and beer while we're there). In young adulthood, money speaks of relative worth and value as we establish a career and begin building relationships, family, and security.

Throughout this time our parents provide a money model, which serves as our default approach to decoding financial matters. However, this money syntax is almost always unconscious, both in its teaching and in its learning. Slumped shoulders, deep sighs, and furrowed brows when the topic turns to allowances, tuition, or soccer cleats . . . these all become nonverbal cues in the unspoken language of money.

As we form relationships with friends, colleagues, a spouse or significant other, we also interact with their unconscious and unacknowledged money languages. To some extent, we may pick up their dialect; in others, we may resist the foreign perspective and engage in money-language battles, aware of it or not. With those to whom we grow close, we develop a shared secret money language, both similar to our own and in some ways new and different.

As we become parents, we pass on our own secret language to our kids. What they see in your behavior and hear in your choice of words, tone of voice, and inflection, will be the model they incorporate as their own.

And in the overwhelming majority of cases, we do this all without being consciously aware of it.

An Expensive Hobby, Revisited

Remember Denise and her seemingly irrational obsession with her ever-growing doll collection? That obsession starts to make more sense when we realize that her actions are speaking in the specific phrases of her own private money language.

For Denise, as for all of us, the basic vocabulary of that language established itself in childhood. Denise grew up in a wealthy family. Her parents gave her much, at least in a material sense. They surrounded Denise with the best of everything, always bringing nice gifts from their extensive travels and vacations. But both parents were involved in business ventures and traveled a great deal, leaving Denise and her older sister in the care of a nanny and housekeeper. Denise recalls times when she would go into her mother's closet and cuddle into one of her mother's fur coats, loving the smell and feeling secure inside, as if the coat were her mother giving her a hug.

At an early age Denise was learning her parents' secret language of money, a not uncommon idiom in which material objects (and especially *expensive* material objects) become a sort of I.O.U. substitute for such values as affection, intimacy, approval, and acknowledgment. These inflections are familiar to many. But in Denise's case, her parents' distance and frequent absence was not the worst of it. For three years, starting when Denise was three years old, her older sister was sexually abused repeatedly by their nanny. And during those same years Denise was sexually abused in turn by her sister.

When the nanny's abuse was discovered, the nanny was fired and the sister began therapy. This put a halt to the pattern of abuse—but the sister's abuse of Denise was *not* discovered or acknowledged in any way, and neither of them talked about what Denise had experienced. It was not until she was 14 and began a pattern of promiscuous sexuality that Denise began her own treatment and finally recalled the abuse she had suffered at her sister's hands.

For Denise in adulthood, to spend was to be in control: She could acquire whatever she wanted. Arranging the collection furthered her sense of mastery—the antithesis of that traumatic *lack* of control of her own body she had endured during the childhood abuse. Layered onto money along with affection and approval were the values of control, self-defense, and autonomy.

When she was not with another person, Denise felt lonely and empty. Her shopping would calm her anxiety. Collecting was the consistent arena of her life in which she seemed to be effective.

Denise reported that buying something, especially over the Internet and using a credit card, was like "getting it for free." It was as if, for that moment, she felt satisfied, without any thought of future accounting or consequence. She indicated that during a shopping binge, she had recognized her lack of judgment, but at that time her all-consuming focus was on whatever she wanted; she was "inside an impulse."

Denise described her state of mind after she was online as an extended dissociation—"zoned out" in front of her computer. This was a way she survived when she could not escape trauma at her sister's hands—she could escape internally by dissociating.

Recall that when her doll-buying began to threaten her health and financial stability, Denise sought to curtail her own activities—in vain. That sense, of being unable to behave in alignment with one's rational intention, is a common experience with money. This is because we are often saying two different things with our money—or even many more than two.

In the conscious, out-in-the-open language of money, Denise's actions seemed to say, "I'm building a valuable collection of art objects." If that were all she was saying, it would be a simple matter to put on the brakes. But in the secret language of money, she was speaking a myriad of other messages.

With her money, she was saying, "I am worthy. I am something. I'm an expert!"

With her money, she was saying, "I'm not alone."

With her money, she was saying, "I'm at nobody's mercy—I am in control!"

With her money, she was saying, "I am master, and *nobody's* victim."

With her money, she was saying, "I am surrounded by beauty and innocence."

With her money, she was probably saying dozens of other things as well—and all of them pitched at a level below her own conscious hearing.

Beyond Language to Narrative

I've used Denise as an example here because of the especially dramatic nature of her spending, and the traumatic childhood circumstance at the root of it, but you and I are really no different. We've all had childhoods laced with imperfection, surrounded by similarly imperfect human beings, and we have all, each and every one of us, developed a richly elaborate—and marvelously clandestine—repertoire of what it is we say with money.

When we begin to take into account the full spectrum of all that we say with money, we soon realize that we are dealing with more than money's secret language. There is also what that secret language has created: its own secret *story*—which is what we'll explore in Chapter 4.

Notes

1. http://money.cnn.com/2006/08/03/technology/fbvacations0803.biz2/
index.htm.
2. http://www.economist.com/world/asia/displaystory.cfm?story_id=10329261.
3. *Affluenza: The All-Consuming Epidemic*, De Graffe, J., D. Wann and
T.H. Naylor, Berrett-Koehler Publisher, Inc., 2001.
4. http://money.cnn.com/2006/12/21/news/economy/savings_rate/index.htm.

four

YOUR LIFE IS A STORY

*Ilsa, I'm no good at being noble, but it doesn't take much to see
that the problems of three little people don't amount to a hill of
beans in this crazy world. Someday you'll understand that.*

—Rick, in *Casablanca* (1941)

In 1940, four French teenagers and a dog named Robot set out in
search of treasure. Legend held that a long-lost underground passage
filled with riches led from a nearby castle beneath the neighboring
estates. While they found no gold or silver, the group discovered considerable riches of another type. Beyond a narrow entrance, they found
a cave containing hundreds of magnificent rock paintings. Eventually,
researchers would catalog more than 2,000 images in the Lascaux
Caves, dating back to the Paleolithic period some 17,000 years ago.

What is truly remarkable about these images—and there is much to
consider remarkable, including the use of such advanced artistic tech-
niques as perspective—was that the images were *sequential*. From left
to right, a group of images might show a band of hunters chasing an
ancient herd, making a kill, and returning home victorious. Like the
frames of one of Todd MacFarlane's comic books, the ancient images
showed a series of events unfolding in time. In short, they told a *story*.

The paintings in the Lascaux Caves are now considered the earliest
examples of human storytelling. They are powerful proof of the existence

and importance of stories in the lives of *homo sapiens,* a tradition that lives on as powerfully as ever today.

In the beginning was the word—and the word told a *story.* The need for stories is perhaps our single most widely shared human trait, and certainly one of the most ancient. From the Lascaux Caves and Sumerian clay tablets to podcasts and blogs, human existence is consistently chronicled and illuminated by story.

Because of its intuitive structure that uses the passage of time—with beginning, middle, and end—as its foundation, storytelling is hardwired into humans. The earliest humans used stories to make sense of such incomprehensible events as birth and death, thunder and lightning, stars and seasons, and eclipses. While we've grown far more sophisticated in our grasp of the mechanics of reproduction, weather, and astronomy, we still use stories to explain other uncharted areas of our lives, including our emotions, desires, hopes, and dreams.

For example, one parent chooses to take a pay cut in order to have more time at home with her young children. Another decides she'll return to work as soon as possible in order to provide her family with a better standard of living. What do they have in common? They're both acting out an internal belief system, a *parenting story* that they tell themselves, most likely unconsciously.

The first parent's outward expression is "stay-at-home mom," but the hidden parenting story is, *I'm a good parent because I stay home with my children and offer them my time. If I didn't, it would mean I loved them less.*

The second parent's outward expression is "working mom," but the hidden parenting story is, *I'm a good parent because I provide the best for my children so they can get ahead in life. If I didn't, it would mean I loved them less.*

These two people are both attentive, devoted parents who clearly want the same thing: the best for their kids and validation that they're doing the best they can. They may be alike in myriad other ways as well.

Yet they behave in opposite ways, because of only one thing: They have different internal stories.

Stories make sense of things. More than mere narratives that string together ideas or events over time, stories show relationship and causality: They describe the links between things that define what causes what and what means what.

Our identities and assumptions about the world around us are shaped and established by stories. We understand the world—and ourselves—through stories. This is not a matter of entertainment or diversion: This is the stuff of sanity and survival.

We sort information into recognizable categories and patterns, seeing and remembering those details and inflections that fit coherently into the plot we are crafting. That plot, fashioned from our unique, individual set of beliefs and assumptions, determines how we create and understand the experiences along our life's storyline. The plot informs how we choose from an infinite sea of possibilities, what experiences we look for, and how we process them.

When we see someone sitting in first class in an airplane, do we see it as the fruits of greed or of accomplishment? As a reward for hard work or the windfall of undeserved good fortune? The answer depends on our storyline.

We seek the data that validates our beliefs and fits the plot of the story we are telling ourselves. We register information and experiences that fit our existing belief patterns and ignore or disbelieve what doesn't fit into those patterns. We write the script of our lives and remain loyal to it, even at times when certain beliefs may be limiting. Through the stories we weave of our circumstances, we create who we are.

This is the key point about stories: They don't exist in and of themselves, like the rocks, trees, and sunsets of our environment. They are not preexisting entities upon which we happen to stumble. They exist only because *we make them up*. Stories, in other words, are the product of the choices we make, consciously or not.

Two Stories

When I met Roberta, she was struggling to make it through business school. Her first two years of graduate training had gone poorly; the past six months her problems had grown worse, and she was now facing a suspension from school.

Roberta described to me the unfair treatment she had received, particularly by one woman professor in her current business law class, and several other instances of victimhood that had resulted in various relationships being compromised. She had become involved with a man she felt was emotionally unavailable and married to his work. When she became pregnant, he abandoned her without offering any sort of monetary support, which only reinforced her sense of victimhood. Roberta seemed a collector of injustices.

Interestingly, Roberta was a person with exceedingly high expectations for herself, professionally and financially, far higher than those of anyone else in her family. She was quite ambitious—but in her mind, that ambition was linked with the overcoming of major obstacles. That was the story Roberta was living, and as a result, she had developed an astonishing inclination to snatch defeat from the jaws of victory.

Then there's the story of one W. Mitchell. Years ago, the robust ex-Marine was working as a street-car tour guide on the hills of San Francisco when a freak motorcycle accident left him with disfiguring burns on 65 percent of his body, burning off his fingers and face. After a seemingly interminable series of skin grafts and operations, Mitchell picked himself up, moved to Colorado, where he became a successful businessman and eventually mayor of his town.

Then one day while flying a small plane, Mitchell was in a second accident. Ice on the wings took his plane down, and he wound up in a wheelchair. Now burned beyond recognition *and* paralyzed and wheelchair-bound, what did Mitchell do? He picked himself up again, got active in politics, became a renowned conservationist, and now gives speeches all over the world.

"Before I was paralyzed," says Mitchell, "there were 10,000 things I could do. Now there are 9,000. I could dwell on the 1,000 I've lost, or on the 9,000 I have left."

When you look at Roberta's life and Mitchell's life, do you see the difference? They are living out two different stories. That's really the only difference: All the rest is just the details of how the stories play out.

Our Story Influences Our Reality...

Two anthropologists were chosen to enter separate, essentially identical ape colonies to live and observe for a year. The two men were matched for similarities of personality, philosophy, and education, in order to be as alike as possible.

When they emerged a year later to compare notes, they naturally expected that they would have had quite similar experiences. Instead, they found remarkable discrepancies.

After an initial period of transition, the first anthropologist had been accepted by the apes as one of their own and integrated into the colony. During his year, he had experienced an extraordinary level of unity and comfort within the ape community.

The other anthropologist, by contrast, never managed to move beyond his initial position as an outsider on the periphery of the colony. Continually careful and vigilant throughout the year, he never came close to feeling accepted by the apes and always felt he was on the cusp of a conflict.

The men puzzled over this for months, trying to discern what could have made this dramatic difference. Finally they realized what single factor had been different between them. When the two men entered the two ape colonies, the second anthropologist brought a gun with him.

The gun never showed; he never used it, and the apes never even knew he had it. But *he* knew he had it: He knew that if things got tough, he had an "out." The anthropologist who had no gun had a commitment:

He knew from the beginning that he would either make it or not make it on his own.

The two men went into identical situations with two different stories, and it was the stories they brought with them, not the situation itself, that created their completely different realities.

Note that it was not the gun itself that created such drastically different outcomes. It was the fact that the man knew he had the gun.

Each of us enters every situation in our lives, day after day and year after year, with a hidden gun, just like the second anthropologist. That hidden gun is *our story*. Like the anthropologist, we are often unaware of the stories we are living—even though we have written them ourselves. The plotlines of our own stories are often hidden from view, even from our *own* view. Yet just because a story is hidden doesn't mean it doesn't have a profound impact on our lives.

...In Fact, Our Story *Creates* Our Reality

As they were wheeled through the University of Kansas Medical Center with rows of stitches smarting down the center of their chests, the patients were uncomfortable but happy. The heart surgery they had just undergone, *internal mammary artery ligation*, may have left them with some mild and temporary discomfort, but that certainly beat the ongoing discomfort and danger of *angina*, the coronary artery obstruction that had brought them to the hospital in the first place.

And in fact, they did feel a lot better. Not that this came as a big surprise: After all, that was the whole point of the surgery. If they had known the truth, though, it *would* have come as quite a surprise indeed—because in fact, they had not had any surgery at all.

The patients were participants in a UKMC study in the 1950s, in which only *some* of the patients underwent the real operation. The rest had an incision, but no actual procedure. Where doctors normally would have tied off two arteries in an attempt to increase blood flow to the heart, the no-surgery patients received a simple incision and were then promptly stitched up again.

Still, a full 100 percent of the patients who received the "surgery" felt better—so much better that many considered themselves "cured" and returned to physically demanding work.[1]

The plot thickens further. Internal mammary ligation—that is, the actual surgical procedure—was in later years determined to have no beneficial effect whatsoever. But that only made the results more astounding. The "real" surgery recipients still clocked in at a 70 percent "feel better" rate. Though technically pointless, even the real process of tying knots in the arteries of patients' hearts—an ineffective operation that, if anything, should have made things worse—made patients feel *better*.

The UKMC study was just one more in a long line of dramatic research demonstrating the *placebo effect*: a dummy medication or treatment that creates medical benefits.

The placebo effect is an especially powerful example of the power of thought to change reality. We find examples of the placebo effect in everything from headache relief to asthma treatment, and it's a staple of good medical research, helping to separate the effect of an actual treatment from the effect of how we *think* about that treatment. It has even spawned the term *nocebo*, which describes the *ill* effects that can be produced in patients simply by warning them of drug side effects or their susceptibility to diseases and other health risks, even when those risks are completely fictional.

What scientists have gone to such trouble to document is something that mothers have always known about banishing closet monsters: A placebo generates the effect of the story that accompanies it. Along with the inert pill, the patient is prescribed some expectations—in other words, is told *what's going to happen*—and in the majority of cases, they manifest. By anticipating an experience, one can create it.

The placebo doesn't create the medical effect; it creates the expectations that go with the story. The story generates a truth so powerful that it can even *reverse* the pharmacological effect of a real medicine. The placebo is a white lie, a fiction that becomes a truth.

To a far greater extent than most of us realize, the fabric of our lives is woven of threads spun of placebo and nocebo. We don't just live the stories we tell; we literally become them. Your life story isn't a story *about* your life: It *is* your life.

What's Your Story?

In the 2006 film *Stranger Than Fiction*, the hapless IRS auditor Harold Crick (played by Will Ferrell) makes a disconcerting discovery: The life he thinks he is living is actually a story being written by a bestselling novelist. The worst part of it is, he isn't sure whether it is a comedy or a tragedy—and neither is the novelist.

What about your life? What kind of story is it?

To help you answer that question, take a moment to observe your own life story. Imagine your life 10 years from today. What do you see? Are your life circumstances substantially different from how they are today, and if so, how?

Now look for a moment at the time between now and then: What kind of events will have unfolded over the course of that decade? And by the way, it's cheating to say, "I have no idea, how can I possibly know?" You don't have to know, you just have to imagine. When you think about the next 10 years, what do you expect to see happening?

Now ask yourself this: Did you see difficulties and challenges on the road ahead? Or did you see primarily new vistas, achievements, and accomplishments?

"A pessimist is one who makes difficulties of his opportunities and an optimist is one who makes opportunities of his difficulties," according to Harry Truman. That nicely sums up the difference between the classic ideas of tragedy and comedy.

Of course, life is not black and white, happy ending or unhappy ending.

In his classic text *Poetics*, Aristotle describes four types of storyline: tragedy, comedy, epic, and lampoon. The stories we sample in today's movie theaters offer considerably wider range and variety, including (but not limited to) comedy, tragedy, drama, adventure, war picture, space epic, Western, soap opera, documentary, adventure, police procedural, detective story, horror flick, fantasy, satire, and farce.

If you had to describe your life story with a single word, what would it be?

*My life story is a(n)*_____.

What Part Do You Play in Your Story?

Every story has its cast of characters. It may have its hero, its villain, and its innocent bystander who, tragically in the wrong place at the wrong time, happens to get gunned down in the first reel. The main characters, the supporting cast of costars, and hundreds or thousands of extras all play a part of the story.

Who is the hero in *your* life story? Who is the victim? The colorful sidekick? The main character's love interest? And which one of these characters is you?

In my life story, I play the _____.

Perhaps, like Harold Crick, you aren't sure what kind of story you're in and aren't sure what character you're playing in it. Like Roberta, you may sometimes feel you've been cast as the victim. At other times you may seek to be like W. Mitchell, the irrepressible hero who rises above every difficulty. There may even be times, when you're not proud of something you've done, when you wonder if you are really the villain of your own story.

But these are all only temporary roles. The truth is, *you* are not any of these characters. You do have a role, but it is not to be found anywhere in the previous paragraph. And if you have any wish to change the way money works in your life, the only way you can effectively accomplish that goal must start with recognizing the one role you actually *do* play in your own story.

To see what that role is, let's pay a brief visit to the immortal world of Warner Bros. cartoons.

In the classic Chuck Jones cartoon *Duck Amuck*, Daffy Duck starts the action as a swashbuckling swordsman in a renaissance court.[2] "Thtand back, Muthketeerth," he declaims, "and they shalt thample my blade!" A dazzling flash of his swordplay ensues, but as he brandishes his saber the scenery suddenly disappears.

"Hey," says Daffy, "whoever's in charge here—where's the scenery?" The scenery dutifully reappears—only now he's on a farm. Okay, he reasons, change of plans: He'll go along with it. He starts sauntering along while singing, "Daffy Duck he had a farm, ee-aie ee-aie ohhh…" but the cartoonist swaps scenery on him yet again, and suddenly he's standing by an igloo.

Things go from bad to worse. Finding himself guitar in hand, he tries to play, but the noises that emerge range from machine-gun to donkey. He tries to talk: It comes out all ape and rooster. His entire body is erased and replaced with a sort of extraterrestrial flower-bug. When he parachutes out of a plane, the parachute is erased and replaced with (of course) an anvil. Still trying to get along by going along, he starts hitting the anvil with a hammer. The anvil turns into—what else?—a bomb that explodes in his face.

Finally exasperated beyond control, Daffy glares at the camera and screams, "All right, enough is enough! This is the last straw. Who's responsible for this? I demand that you show yourself! Who are you?! Huh?!"

But the frantic duck's demands are stifled as the cartoonist's pencil draws a door and gently pushes it closed with its eraser end. The camera pulls back to reveal a cartoonist's drafting table and the animator who has been drawing all this bedlam: Bugs Bunny. Bugs turns to grin at us and delivers the cartoon's famous closing line: "Ain't I a stinker?"

He is a stinker indeed. And this is just what our lives can often feel like. Events keep getting out of control. The landscape keeps changing on us. Just as we are about to achieve some victory or other, the farm turns into an igloo. We parachute out of a tight situation—and the parachute turns into an anvil. Sometimes it seems no matter what we do, circumstances always seem to take a left turn and, to switch metaphors, get the upper hand.

We may even become as exasperated as Daffy Duck, and shout, "Enough is enough. Who's responsible for this?!" But when we pull back for a longer view, we discover that the cartoonist's hand that's drawing all these bizarre scenarios belongs not to Bugs Bunny, but to . . . *us*.

You may feel at times like hero or antihero, plotter or dupe, best friend or nemesis, the victorious or the vanquished—but the one role in your story that you play consistently, every day and throughout your life, is *author*.

A Work in Progress

The single most important thing to understand about your story is that it is a work in progress. Your life story may at times feel predetermined, as if the events in your life were being blown by the winds of fate or determined by a pattern of stars set down before your birth. But the world is full of people who have transformed the course of their own futures after less than auspicious beginnings. Elvis Presley, Oprah Winfrey, Bill Clinton, Michelle Obama . . . these are just some of the better-known names among the millions of people who have been born into one story, only to create a new one.

Forbes magazine estimates that almost two-thirds of the world's billionaires made their fortunes from scratch. They did not inherit their wealth, or win the lottery, but did the opposite—they started off at the bottom of the heap and worked their way up. *Harry Potter* creator J.K. Rowling was a mother on welfare when she began writing the first book of the series. Within a few years, she was named by *Forbes* as the first person to become a billionaire by writing books.

Nothing about your future is ordained. Its direction is yours to shape. As the author of your story, you can rewrite, edit, or create a new chapter. Like a movie director, you can change the script, call *Action!* or *Cut!* whenever you choose. And just as this is true of your life in general, it is true of that uniquely versatile, mysterious, and powerful plot thread called your *money story*.

Notes

1. http://www.theatlantic.com/issues/2000/10/fisher.htm.
2. *Duck Amuck* (1953) by Chuck Jones, story by Richard Maltese.

five

YOUR MONEY STORY

What's Christmas time to you but a time for paying bills without money; a time for finding yourself a year older, but not an hour richer; a time for balancing your books and having every item in 'em through a round dozen of months presented dead against you? If I could work my will, every idiot who goes about with "Merry Christmas" on his lips should be boiled with his own pudding, and buried with a stake of holly through his heart. He should!

—Ebenezer Scrooge, A *Christmas Carol* (1843) by Charles Dickens

Jerri was an accomplished professional in her late fifties when she first arrived at my office. She had written a book about Chinese porcelains, was married to a very successful architect, and was on the board of a prominent nonprofit organization in a major city. On the surface, her life story spoke of accomplishment, excellence, and success. Yet her actual behavior with money told a very different story.

Despite her affluence, Jerri would not buy anything for herself unless she found it at a bargain. Although she could afford significantly better, her house was furnished almost entirely with items she bought for pennies on the dollar at estate sales and discount houses. Her closets were filled with clothes purchased at fire-sale prices. She felt undeserving of the best, or even of the next to best. In fact, she didn't even feel she deserved the *fairly good*.

She felt cheap.

It was Jerri's mother who had passed on the story of inadequacy to her daughter through the secret language of money. Jerri was shamed by her mother for wanting full-price clothes and a nice home. She was chastised for spending on herself. Abandoned by her mother emotionally as a child, the adult Jerri still felt she did not deserve what she could obviously afford.

Though the outward circumstances of her life had changed significantly over the years, Jerri's money story remained true to her roots. Every action and conversation from her mother contained the message that *she was not worthy*, and she had remained steadfastly loyal to that basic tenet. With all the force of placebo power, her money story was and remained that she was not worth spending money on.

Your Money Story

Your money story is the subconscious tale you continuously tell yourself about who you are, what money means *to* you, and what it says *about* you. It's a running dialogue about how much you deserve, how much you're worth, and how much you're capable of, what would happen if you had more, or if you lost it all.

When we see a new car and "want" it, what we're really doing is acting out our money story. Just below the level of our conscious awareness, we're adding a new plotline to our money story that says, *this car will prove that I'm worth something. This will erase my struggles. This will make people respect me. This will validate me.*

For example, suppose in your life story, the role money plays is one of poverty and lack; let's say the plotline goes something like this: "Things aren't great, but I manage to get by."

In this story, even if you create a stated goal of financial freedom or prosperity, that implacable internal narrator's voice will keep whispering, "But I will *never* get out of credit card debt." And if that's the story you tell yourself, whether or not you hear it consciously, that's the storyline your life will follow.

If a doctor can tell you you'll feel better, and as a result, you do, then what happens when the people in your life tell you that you're worthless? What happens if your parents, friends, or spouse tell you that you can't become wealthy—or when you repeatedly tell yourself that?

And what happens if they tell you, or you tell yourself, that you *can*?

Our money story isn't only about money: It's about *everything*. It permeates everything we do and ghostwrites every aspect of our lives. What we eat, drink, read, fear, plan, and buy are all affected by our money story. Our health, our jobs, our families, our dreams—they're all unerringly guided to their preplotted destinations by our money story. Day by day, thought by thought, dollar by dollar, our money story becomes our *life* story.

This was exactly the case with Jack Whitaker. The outward circumstances of his lottery winnings didn't change his personal poverty and conflict-fraught life story one iota. Instead, his life story transformed his winnings, from a potential blessing to a series of curses. And Jack's story, while especially dramatic, is on the whole fairly typical for lottery winners: The majority wind up back in a struggling and debt-ridden lifestyle before long. The money story is a powerful force indeed.

And it works the other way as well. Remember that the majority of billionaires were not born rich. Why did they end up that way? Because that was the story they told themselves.

Money Quiz

Let's look at an example of how you author your own money story. In Chapter 1 we asked the question, "How much money do I need to be happy and content?" Now let's look at a related question: What is the greatest annual income you can reasonably *expect to earn*?

This isn't meant to be theoretical, as in, what *anyone* can expect to earn. The question is about *you*, personally and individually. And not, say, if you suddenly won the lottery, or quit your job and in a fit of inspiration created the next Google, but what you can *reasonably* expect.

To get the most out of this exercise, answer the following question with a specific dollar amount *before* you continue reading the rest of the chapter:

What is the greatest annual income I can reasonably expect to earn?

$ _____.

Now, let's take a close look at that answer. Why is that the number you chose?

Do you know of anyone who earns more than that? Who earns twice as much? What about 10 times as much? Are there people who earn 20 times, a hundred times more than the number you wrote? Sure there are, thousands of them. Of course, some are amazing athletes, and you know you are no Tiger Woods. You also know you are no Garth Brooks, or Julia Roberts, or Bill Gates. But there are hundreds of thousands of people in the world who are not famous film stars or tournament golfers, and who are no more intelligent, gifted, or born to advantage than you are, who have created large fortunes.

The question, then, is this: Where did that "reasonable expectation" come from? From your story. In fact, this might be a more accurate way to ask that question:

What is the greatest annual income my money story will allow me to have?

$ _____.

Like the two anthropologists who joined the ape colonies, you will be right about your assumption, whatever it is, because you live your life according to the script. You will let yourself make and keep only the money you think you're worth.

Your belief system contains what is inevitable. Without awareness and ownership of your money story, the only way to exert any mastery over a limiting assumption is to determine how and when the inevitable will happen, and then bring it about by your own hand.

For example, when people doubt their ability to set and collect top dollar for their services, they end up underpaid. If they are afraid that their request for a raise will be rejected, not asking for it will bring about what they most fear—by their own hands.

If you believe you will be short-changed, there are three likely scenarios: You will find and interact with someone who will bring that about; you will act in a way yourself to bring that about; or you will perceive things in such a way to validate the assumption, regardless of how things actually turn out.

And by the way, such self-limiting money stories do not necessarily always revolve around lack and poverty. It's just as easy to become enslaved by an unconscious storyline that revolves around an overabundance of money as by one that centers on the chronic deficiency of it.

A former secretary from Texas who had come into some significant wealth dreamed for 10 years about the house she wanted to build. Eventually she and her husband, the son of a grocer, built this dream house, a 48,000-square-foot fantasy chateau.

It is one of the biggest houses in the world, valued at some $48 million. The front door is a good city block from the massive driveway gate. The home contains, among other things, a tea room patterned after the Tavern on the Green restaurant in New York City, two elevators, indoor and outdoor pools, a theater, ballroom, bowling alley, racket ball court, and a 15-car garage. The couple, whose name was Goldfield, called their mansion *Champ d'Or*, meaning "house of gold." And they lived in that storybook palace happily ever after, right?

Not quite. Mrs. Goldfield lived in her dream house for two months before deciding to put it on the market. "Some dreams are best left unexpressed and unexplored," she quietly reflected.

The Secret We Keep from Ourselves

Most of us are not as fortunate as Mrs. Goldfield, not because we don't get to live in $48 million homes but because we never glimpse the truth about the money stories we are living or take steps to change them into new stories that would make us happier.

For most of us, the greater part of our money story lies hidden. The problem this creates is that if we don't see it, we cannot examine it and won't change it. Socrates may have been harsh in his assertion that "the unexamined life is not worth living," but it's safe to say that the unexamined life is virtually impossible to change for the better.

I know a financial advisor in southern California who has been in practice for a quarter of a century. Over the course of his practice, he has asked hundreds of clients to prepare a simple income/expense statement. He asked me to guess approximately what percentage of those clients, over all those years, have come back with a statement that accurately and honestly reflected their true numbers. Half? I thought. Maybe a quarter? The answer was zero percent. Not one.

This is a testament to the hypnotic power of story: intelligent, educated, and sophisticated though we may be, we keep our own stories hidden from ourselves. Here are a few of the more common examples of how we do this.

Denial

We conveniently forget how much we charge on credit, keeping each purchase separate and independent in our mind so we aren't quite able to keep track of the total spent. "It *is* expensive, but this *one time* isn't so bad," we tell ourselves—putting out of mind how many other similar instances have occurred in the recent past and will again in the near future.

Categorization

When money comes unexpectedly, such as a bonus or tax refund, we spend it differently than money from savings. "We weren't expecting it anyway, so it doesn't really count, right?"

Rationalization

We justify a large purchase by amortizing its cost over a long period of time. "This seems like a lot of money to spend on a stereo, but if I spread it out over the next three years, it comes to only six cents a day."

Avoidance

We hold onto a stagnant, loser stock, ignoring the evidence of our eyes and hoping for a rebound we rationally know will probably never come. Or, knowing we can't afford a purchase, we make it anyway, but on a credit card, so it "isn't really there." Or, knowing a bill is coming that will be a stretch to pay, we let the due date pass in silence and inaction. (Perhaps, if we say and do nothing, it will go away!)

Bargaining

We give ourselves permission to proceed with an indulgent purchase in exchange for the promise we make to ourselves that we'll start a rigorous savings plan . . . *next* month.

Disloyalty to Yourself

After establishing goals, initiatives, and a specific strategy, such as a planned contribution to savings, we allow diversions to distract us and disregard the structure we'd created.

Defiance

Having established a budget that we know is in our own best interest, we are confronted with something we really want to spend money on that exceeds that budget limitation, so we stand tall in our saddle and follow the popular bumper sticker: *Question Authority*, thus adding a flavor of heroic nonconformity to our defiant purchase—even though the only authority we're challenging is our own.

The Anatomy of a Secret

To understand why we typically don't know our own money stories, it's helpful to understand how we put them together in the first place. There are four distinct layers to a money story, each quite different from the others.

1. *Feelings*: our gut reactions connected with the strivings, emotional attributions, beliefs about and representations of money in our lives and the world around us.
2. *Behaviors*: the things we do for and with money.
3. *Thoughts*: how and what we think about money and its symbolism.
4. *Experiences*: our overall reactions and responses to money, its significance, and symptoms in our lives.

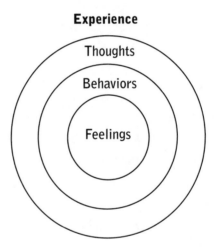

Feelings

We make money decisions based on underlying feelings, which give money its emotional meaning to us; over time these money meanings crystallize into our beliefs about money.

In Chapter 2 we explored more than a dozen different emotional "meanings" we often associate with money, but there are dozens and dozens more. Money can stir deep feelings of anger, resentment, admiration, compassion, lust, hostility . . . really, the entire spectrum of human emotion is open season for the magnetically symbolic potency of money.

Of the four layers of story, feelings are the deepest; they form the core of our money story.

Behaviors

Our behaviors are the clearest windows to our true beliefs about money. Unlike the hidden, internal world of our feelings, our actions are clearly visible. Our behaviors represent the secret language of money at its most readable and *least* secretive. What we *say* we believe is one thing; what we *think* we believe may be yet another. What we *actually do* is the clearest expression of what we really do believe.

When Todd MacFarlane paid millions for a $5 baseball, his behavior spoke volumes about his true beliefs about money and what he could accomplish through its use. When we choose to cancel a vacation, quit a job without provocation or obvious reason, or shop beyond our means, our behaviors offer lucid glimpses of the truth about what, to us, money actually "means."

Thoughts

We don't often think logically or even consciously about our true money beliefs, but we do think about our money behaviors—at least, sometimes. However, our thoughts are not usually central to the process (even when we think otherwise!). We tend to buy emotionally and *then* justify rationally, not the other way around. In other words, thoughts follow after the fact.

Thoughts are what we tell ourselves the story means, not necessarily what it really means. Like any "official" history of events made up after the fact, the story we tell ourselves is often a whitewashed version of what really happened. And this logical explanation often drives the real story underground.

The result is a curious paradox. Otherwise balanced individuals spend extravagantly or hoard compulsively. Reliable people ignore financial matters until they snowball. Gifted people can't seem to exchange their talent for a proportionate income. People with integrity write their own exceptions to rules about money, compromising their values and even breaking the law in the process.

Experience

The various elements of our encounters with money all combine together to create an overall experience, which becomes what, to us, money *means*.

When we look at a photograph of a loved one, such as a child, we see more than the flat image of an instant in time. We look *through* that moment to our entire experience of the person. It's only a photograph— but to us, it evokes an entire chapter within our life.

The experience surrounding money, in all its dimension, including our money behaviors, the feelings and beliefs that drive them, and the thoughts, opinions, and rationalizations that we have about them, all comprise what in time becomes the substance of our money story.

Peeling Back the Layers

In order to see our own money story for what it is, to lay it out in the open so that we can examine it and potentially change it for the better, we need to see it in *all* its layers.

Typically we simply live within our experience of money, without standing back and examining to see what elements, if any, we want to change. And if we do decide to take a closer look, the tendency is to go only as deep as our thoughts. For example, we may ask ourselves "what we really think" about the situation in which we find ourselves.

Q: Hmm, it seems I'm $30,000 in debt. What do I think about that?
A: Well, I'm not really sure how this happened, because I think that normally I am very responsible with money. But now that I think about it, circumstances have been difficult lately, haven't they? . . . Yeah, the economy's really taken a downturn. No wonder I'm in debt. And as I think about it further, I imagine that by putting a

little extra aside [or fill in whatever other strategy or rationale of choice], I'll probably get out of debt again, sooner or later.

But that's only what we *think*. For a surprising number of us, we don't look beyond our logical thoughts to truthfully answer the question, *Yes, but what have I done? What am I doing? Never mind my words—what are my actual behaviors?* No wonder our predictions about what we're *going to do* are often no more accurate than educated guesses!

Putting our actual money behaviors on the table can require quite an act of courage, not unlike facing the fact of an addiction. Yet even this does not take it far enough. To genuinely see our money story for what it is, we need to go even deeper than the simple behaviors themselves, and explore the root feelings that lie behind the things we do with money. We need to examine the default assumptions and beliefs that are carried in our story. The only way we'll be able to get to work on the parts of our money story that need to change is to draw it out into the open, take a good look at it, and understand the hidden reasons why we do the things we do.

As with Jerri, the enduring themes of our money stories typically have their roots in childhood. Here are just a few common money story themes we might have learned at our parents' knees:

- Money doesn't grow on trees, you know.
- Hey, you think we're made of money?
- If it was good enough for your father and me, it's good enough for you.
- We deserve to have enough for the basic necessities; anything beyond that is greedy.
- You have to work really, really hard to make big money—and if you do, it will probably be taken away from you.
- Money is the measure of what really counts; people can talk all they want, but until there's real money on the table, it's all hot air.

- Money and genuine value are mutually exclusive: There are people who chase money, and people who do good in the world, and never the twain shall meet.
- Money *does* grow on trees: It's called credit, and if you're clever enough to know how to work it, there's an unlimited supply.

Do any of these ring a bell for you? Can you think of others that resonate with your own childhood?

As you review your own story, both past and present, here are three steps that can be helpful in directing your inquiry:

1. What are the beliefs that form the premise of your money story?

In the previous chapters you've already done a good amount of exploration into your feelings *about* and the meanings you ascribe *to* money and its role in your life. These feelings and meanings crystallize as the beliefs you hold.

Although appearing as facts, beliefs (like actions) are personal creations. Fed by feelings, each belief emerged from an original adaptive decision at some point in your life, and exists today as a decision that you continue to make. Remember that you are always free to change your mind.

2. Can you track when in time you made the original decision that led to each view or belief?

For example, an original decision often follows a grievous disappointment or painful episode. A child knowing about his parents' worries about money or the sudden loss of a job can lead to a decision to be anxious or cautious about finances. This guardedness may have beneficial results; for example, it may create a healthy motivation to save and prepare for the future, or to carefully examine financial risks. But it can also result in irrational and unhealthy money behaviors, such as a vague sense of shame that inhibits any honest discussion of money; or avoiding even the reasonable risks necessary to growth; or difficulty charging a fair fee for your services as a way of not valuing your full worth.

Your genes do not carry monetary problems; however, an assumption such as victimhood or being chronically underpaid can become a powerfully organizing storyline, even an aspect of identity.

3. **Look for the connection between the original decision and the view or perspective you now hold.**

Acknowledge the impact your assumption has on your current life, the emotional and financial costs, and the exchanges that you make in its services. Examine each belief in turn, asking, regardless of its origin, is it serving you now?

For example, if your parents were secretive about money and uneasy talking about it, for you it was adaptive to restrain discussion about it. In other words, the decision may have served you at the time, but you may have now outgrown its usefulness. Is it still worth the cost that you pay? Are you exchanging energy for your current restraint, as well as missing out on valuable information or feedback?

Realize that you decide what to perceive. You also decide what meaning to attach—and you decide what behavior you'll associate with that meaning.

A Money Story Quiz

Don't think long or hard about the question below that follows: Just read it and answer with the first three things that come to mind:

What have been the three most significant experiences with money in your life?

a. _____

b. _____

c. _____

Now let's take a closer look at your answers.

Examining each in turn, were these experiences that had to do with earning or receiving a large amount of money? Or of being in a large amount of debt? Of buying something for an especially large sum? Or of doing something for the first time, such as buying your first car or first house, or receiving your first paycheck or bonus? Or finally paying off a debt?

Now think back on each of these experiences, and ask yourself, what are the feelings you associate with each? What is it that made each one so significant to you?

a. _____

_____

b. _____

_____

c. _____

_____

Now think back on each experience once more, and see if you can discern what is the story that experience "proves." If you were to describe what happened and conclude your telling with, "And the moral of this story is . . ."—how would you end that sentence?

How well you understand yourself and what you do with that understanding determine the success of your money story. Money will not buy happiness, but how you create and live your money story determines a good deal about what your life experience will be.

Every important relationship has its own history, develops its own story, and evolves its own language. The longest-running relationship in our life is our relationship with money. Our parents discussed money before we arrived; our heirs will deliberate it after we leave. We might get 10 years out of a car, perhaps 50 with a spouse—but money you can't break up with, divorce, run away from, or coax into loving you more. That means we better get it right.

And here is the real power of your money story: Because it infiltrates and penetrates so many aspects of your life story, it is a fantastic access point. If you can change your money story, then you will have created powerful changes in your life story.

A Visit from Three Spirits

In Charles Dickens' *A Christmas Carol*, Ebenezer Scrooge was visited by three spirits who helped pull back the curtain and reveal the true nature of his life. Thus Ebenezer, a man who had thought about little but money throughout his career, came face to face with his own money story for the first time—and it sparked one of the most dramatic and beloved life-story transformations in the history of literature.

You may think of the following questions as another version of Dickens' three spirits. Perhaps their contemplation may lead to unexpected insights, if not as dramatic as Scrooge's, then certainly more meaningful: After all, they're about *you*.

The Ghost of Money Past

- What childhood experiences, attitudes, and ideas about money can you remember?

- When you were growing up, what ideas and attitudes were you presented with regarding money, its use, and its importance?
- How did your parents feel about and behave with money?
- How did they feel, talk about, and behave toward those who had more money than they did?
- How did they feel, talk about, and behave toward those who had less money than they did?
- What did your parents tell you about money?
- Was this consistent with how you saw them behave about money?

The Ghost of Money Present

- What do you now believe about money? For example:
  - *People who have a lot of money are lucky.*
  - *People get money when and if they deserve it.*
  - *Wealth and spirituality are mutually exclusive: You're either rich or good, but not both.*
  - *Wealthy people are different than other people.*
  - *It's hard to make good money in this economy.*
- What do you use money to express or do:
  - for yourself?
  - for or to others?
  - as reward for obedience or performance?
  - to enhance growth?
  - to create opportunity?
  - for control (such as buying for your family what you really want yourself)?
  - for punishment (for example, by withholding)?
  - to manipulate behaviors or attachments?
- If we consider how you treat money as being the most direct expression of your deepest sense of self, then what statements do your money behaviors make about your sense of who you are?

- Does your money and/or its pursuit connect you to others and the wholeness of your life, or separate you from others?

The Ghost of Money Future

- Do you use money to advance your sense of freedom? Creativity? Power? Authority? Self-worth?
- How fully and honestly do you speak with your spouse or partner about money, finances, spending, goals, savings, and debt?
- How open with your children are you about money details?
- What do you tell your children about money?
- How consistent is this with how they see you behave about money?

Part II

PLOT TWISTS

six

YOUR BRAIN ON MONEY

*First of all, let me assert my firm belief that the only thing we have
to fear is fear itself—nameless, unreasoning, unjustified terror which
paralyzes needed efforts to convert retreat into advance.*

—Franklin Delano Roosevelt, first inaugural
address, March 4, 1933

At Harvard University, researcher Joshua Greene is asking groups of
volunteers to run people over with trains and learning a lot about
the brain in the process. Let's join Professor Greene for a moment and
get a sense of what he's driving at.

Read the question following and answer, out loud, with an immediate *yes* or *no* before reading on:

An onrushing locomotive will kill five unsuspecting people on the track
unless you push a sixth man in front of the train. Will you do it?

Yes, you will push the man, or *no*, you won't? Say your answer out
loud before continuing.

Again, the point is not to spend any time weighing the moral issues
or pondering the circumstances—it's to give an immediate answer.

Have you answered the question? If so, then let's go on to consider a
second question. Again, just read it through and give your immediate
answer, out loud, with a simple *yes* or *no*:

Five people stand on the left fork of a railroad track. One stands on the right. A runaway train will kill the five people on the left unless you throw the switch, diverting the train to the right-hand track so that it kills the one man standing there. Will you do it?

Yes, you will throw the switch, or *no*, you won't? Again, say your answer out loud before continuing.

Greene's research uses the *moral dilemma,* a classic philosopher's tool in which participants are asked to make a decision between two options, both of which breach their ethical codes. It makes for an awfully uncomfortable choice, but it also delivers great insight into how the human mind operates.

So what do Greene's volunteers say? Nearly all answer the first question with a "no," that is, they choose *not* to push the man into the train's path. However, the majority of volunteers also answer the second question with a *yes.* In other words, while they *would not* push a man into the train's path to save five others, they *would* throw a switch that would divert the train and cause it to hit that one man instead of the other five.

Logically speaking, both decisions should have the exact same outcome: Both *yes* answers would result in one person dying instead of five. Yet the majority of us will make a different decision depending on the scenario.

Such dilemmas have for centuries fascinated philosophers and psychologists who study the human mind. But Greene doesn't just guess or deduce what is going on in the brain as these life-or-death decisions are being made. He actually *watches it happen,* in real time, through the use of functional magnetic resonance imaging (fMRI) equipment. When Greene poses his ethical dilemmas, the fMRI lets him view what is actually going on in his subjects' brains while they make their decisions.

What the fMRI reveals is fascinating indeed: In the process of imagining the two different train scenarios, different regions of the brain become active.

The scenario of shoving a man into the locomotive's path activates the same brain regions, in the frontal and parietal lobes, that are stimulated by fear or grief. The internal resistance to actively pushing the man to his death lights up the brain region of emotional processing, the posterior singulate gyrus. But when the test subject considers whether or not to flip a switch, this emotional region of the brain is not activated.

In their reasoning *minds*, the subjects understand that both actions have the same outcome; nevertheless, their *brains* respond to each differently. This points to a critical distinction that makes all the difference when it comes to making emotional decisions: The mind and brain each have a say—and sometimes they speak different languages.

From the very opening pages of this book, as you've read about so many ways in which we defeat ourselves, outsmart ourselves, and deceive ourselves with money, you may have been asking yourself some pretty hard questions. Questions such as, *How can we be so stupid? What's wrong with us?!* If so, take heart: It's not that we're stupid. It's more that we're a little, well . . . complicated. We may think we're logical consumers who look rationally at our purchases and investments to get the greatest benefit. The truth is far less rational. Our buying decisions are based on a complex soup of thoughts and emotions, including memories and past associations, response patterns surviving from childhood, herd mentality, and a host of others. And underlying it all is a brain that has evolved to be at times anything *but* logical.

In fact, advances in neuroscience reveal this strange truth: Under certain conditions—especially in emotionally charged situations—we humans are hard-wired to make downright poor financial decisions.

Many Brains in One

We tend to regard it as one big mass of gray matter, but the human brain is actually composed of a variety of separate structures that are specialized for different activities, ranging from complex roles, such as speech and memory, to basic autonomic body functions, such as regulating temperature and keeping our hearts beating. Scientists have cataloged hundreds, even thousands of different areas within the brain, but there's one structural distinction that is particularly important when it comes to wealth and your money story, and that is the three distinct layers that reflect the brain's three stages of evolution: the reptilian (inner), mammalian (middle), and neocortical (outer) brains.

Deep inside, our innermost brain area is often referred to as the *reptilian* brain. This is our oldest and most primitive brain structure, and one we share with all animals possessing a backbone. The reptilian brain, which has remained virtually unchanged by later evolution, controls our most basic functions, such as breathing and temperature regulation. Because the reptilian area of the brain is most concerned with survival, it is also decidedly instinctive. Its actions are automatic—and they're *fast*.

As we evolved from reptiles to mammals, our *mammalian* brain developed. The mammalian brain took over some of the temperature regulation functions and also developed an enhanced function of memory, and therefore the ability to react based on the experience of past events rather than on pure instinct alone. The mammalian brain also brought with it our first conscious feelings about events. For the first time, we could feel fear and act on it.

The largest leap in brain evolution came with the development of the *neocortex*, the outermost layer that we generally consider the truly *human* brain. This is the true "gray matter," the grooved lump of pudding-like substance that we typically imagine when we think of the brain. The neocortex makes up about 85 percent of the mass of the brain, and for good reason. It is involved with abstract logic, imagination, complex emotion, and the high-level functions of speaking, reading, and writing—activities that require a lot of brain hardware.

The distinction of these different brain layers is not the only significant structural division here. The human brain is also divided into left and right hemispheres, connected by a thick bundle of nerve fibers called the *corpus callosum.*

Left and Right Brain Hemispheres and Their Characteristics

Left Brain	*Right Brain*
systematic	intuitive
logical	spatial
reason	feelings and emotions
process-driven	image-driven

Over the last few decades, we have learned that as the cortical or "human" brain developed, there has been a great deal of specialization in how the right and left hemispheres each function differently. The left hemisphere is highly verbal; it is systematic, logical, and process-driven. The right hemisphere is image-driven, spatial, intuitive, and concerned with feelings and emotions. Depending on what activity we're involved in at the moment, either side of the brain may be more or less active.

Rational Money and Emotional Money

Not surprisingly, all this brain complexity has a significant impact on how we deal with our finances.

On the surface, money appears as if it should be a very logical operation. After all, it's just *math*—simple operations like the sum of our next two paychecks, the rate of return on our investments, or the discount on a new pair of shoes. Analysis by the left brain, it seems, should yield the right decision almost every time.

Such a logical approach to money is what economists call *rational.* It assumes that humans are logical creatures who always strive to maximize what they get from any situation. This assumption of rationality has dominated the field of economics since its inception. But the reality is not that simple. Advances in neuroeconomics show clearly that we're *not* logical creatures—at least not all the time. We're often driven by emotions, and research like Joshua Greene's train-track dilemma shows that emotional processing resides at a different neural address than logical reasoning.

> You are driving along, calm and peaceful, when suddenly you see an oncoming car swerve into your lane, headed directly for you. Your life could be over in a matter of seconds. In an instant, you react. Everything slows down. Without thinking, you reflexively hit the brake pedal and horn while sharply banking the steering wheel to the right.
>
> In a flash, your physiology has changed radically, triggering the release of chemicals that course through your system, instantly shifting your state of mind from reflection and thought to survival and drastic action. The transformation will last for less than a minute, but its repercussions will echo through your nerves and blood vessels for hours.
>
> You pull over to the side of the road to recoup for a moment, and as you do you realize you are short of breath and your pulse is racing. Later that day, you wonder why you are so exhausted.

This is a dramatic example, but the truth is that *every* thought or feeling has a chemical consequence, and the changing flow of chemicals alters both body and brain.

The brain's *limbic system*, a neural network that drives the instantaneous functions of instinct and basic emotions, is in charge of such fight-or-flight reactions. Strong emotions—such as the desire evoked by the prospect of food or sex, the fear upon seeing an approaching pedestrian who just might be a mugger, or the panic sparked by the swerving car heading toward us—light up the limbic system, activating the more primitive areas of reptilian and mammalian brain and overriding the more rational neocortex.

In the process, we temporarily lose access to exactly that brain software we need to perform the kinds of long-term analysis and reasoned decision making that smart money actions require.

The chemicals of our emotional state hijack the rational brain, causing us to process information as though we were in a mortal crisis. This automatic alarm system, essential for survival in the wild, instead leads to mistaken perception and judgment. A hot stock tip, a business deal gone sour, a family tragedy . . . any one of these or a thousand other situations may touch off an emotional state of mind and alarm response geared for survival at any cost, rather than the more measured responses that are probably more appropriate to the situation. As revealed by Professor Greene's train scenario experiments, such primitive, survival-focused brain activity can even influence ethical decisions.

Or take our neurological response to the emotionally charged situation of an auction in full swing. Recall Max Bazerman's $100 bill auction scenario we encountered in Chapter 1, where we wondered, "How could reasonable, intelligent people pay over four times more for something than it's worth?" Here, finally, is our answer: The reason those intelligent, financially informed people in Bazerman's experiment act like they're not using their heads is that *they're not.* Or more accurately, they are using only a specific *part* of their heads: the reptilian part.

This takes on an almost eerie significance when we realize that the stock market does not function like a store or a catalog: *It's an auction.* Only instead of a simple auction where bidders drive the price up, up, up, and then the highest bidder wins, it is an auction where bidders drive the price up, up, up, and then down, down, down, and then up again, and then down again, and up, and down.... No wonder we can get so readily caught up in the prevailing market mood of exuberance or depression. Extreme emotions, such as fear or greed, may easily derail us from our normal neocortical brain tracks and shift our state of mind. Decisions made in a fearful state of mind follow the survival mode, and involve quite different principles than those of long-term investing. Present fear renders the past and the future as inaccessible as logic and reason.

In the film *Fear and Loathing in Las Vegas*, based on the real-life experiences of "gonzo" journalist Hunter Thompson, there is a scene in a Vegas lounge where Thompson (played by Johnny Depp), under the influence of massive amounts of hallucinogens, sees all the bar's "lounge lizard" patrons as having transformed into actual, human-sized lizards. As surreal as Thompson's drug-induced vision seems, the neurophysiological insights of the fMRI tell us that during a bad day on Wall Street, this is more or less what is actually happening: Thousands of reptilian brains are reacting to the day's financial news, their lizards' responses draped in a disguise of human language.

As the stock market came crashing down in the fall of 2008, the U.S. government rushed to pump $700 billion into the nation's credit system. Why? As frightening as the looming economic crisis was, the majority of Americans still had their jobs, their homes, and food on the table. The toppling of such Wall Street icons as Lehman Brothers, Merrill Lynch, and AIG, and the specter of others possibly following in their wake, did not represent so much a genuine fiscal hardship for most of the public as much as a crisis of confidence. When FDR famously said in his 1933 inauguration, "The only thing we have to fear is fear itself," he was illustrating the same point: The crisis was one of our *state of mind.*

The $700 billion bailout's principal goal was *to restore public confidence.* A quarter of a trillion dollars is quite a price tag for a PR campaign aimed at changing an emotion, but that only underscores the truth about money and the human brain: It is a fragile combination. Physiologically speaking, the $700 billion package was really a massive public-works program designed to shift the population's focus the two-inch distance from midbrain to forebrain.

Marooned in the Right Brain

It is not only our primitive brains that can hold us hostage in times of stress and high-stakes decisions. Even when we are functioning fully in our forebrains, we can become thrown off balance and lurch into one hemisphere at the expense of the other, often with disastrous effects.

The study of trauma's effect on neurophysiology provides revealing insights into how emotions can override logic and short-circuit all our "reasonable" game plans when it comes to making decisions about money.

Normally when we process information in our forebrain, we use both the left and right frontal hemispheres, the left representing the more rational, logical executive function, and the right evoking more the emotional feeling function.

Dr. Bessel van der Kolk, founder and medical director of the Trauma Center at the Justice Resource Institute in Brookline, Massachusetts, has demonstrated that for most people, during a time of emotional stimulus, both right cortex and left cortex light up on a PET scan, and EEG activity also increases on both sides of the brain. However, people who have suffered significant trauma in their histories respond differently to that same emotional stimulus: On the PET scan, only the right cortex (emotional) activity increases, and EEG readings reveal that the left cortex (logical) does not respond *at all*.

For these trauma-sensitized individuals, emotional responses predominate without the mediating balance of reason or logic. In other words, these people are put in the unfortunate position of having to process difficult information with the side of their brains that has the least ability to sort and analyze it rationally. They become marooned on the emotional desert island of the right brain, their left brains powerless to anchor them in any sort of logical or sequential reasoning.

To complicate matters still further, the right hemisphere is also wired to the mammalian brain, which in turn is connected to the reptilian brain, making it all the more likely for such "unthinking" reactions to bypass altogether the process of rational analysis.

Now, we could simply chalk up all this as one more aspect of post-traumatic stress—except that van der Kolk's findings don't stop there. Here's where it all becomes especially significant: Further study reveals that during moments of especially strong emotional stimulation, *even those of us who have absolutely no history of trauma* make this same shift to emotional right-brain processing, effectively shutting off access to the logic and reason of the left brain.

This is why, when we are faced with very good or very bad news, we may suddenly abandon our best strategies and most carefully thought-out game plans. In extreme situations, such as when the stock market is robustly rallying or precipitously falling, it is most difficult to stay with investment strategies and planned principles. Greed or fear shift us to right-brain predominance. Thus, in times of very good news (a large and unexpected bonus check) or very bad news (a stock market crash), we may suddenly abandon our best-laid financial plans. Emotional override creates a myopia with regard to future consequences. Hyperfocused on the present moment, as if our very survival demanded it, we become absorbed exclusively in the question, "What will make me feel better *right now?*" The surprisingly large bonus check is turned into a new car or television instead of paying off our credit card or going into our 401(k), and the stock market crash triggers a complete abandonment of our carefully crafted "buy and hold" strategy. What might happen *later* is out of sight, out of mind, along with the reflection, "What is actually in my best interest?"

Money, Brain, and Gratification

When Lynnae McCoy, who runs the blog beingfrugal.net, popped her credit cards in a Tupperware container full of water and froze them into a block of solid ice which she then stored in her freezer, she knew from experience what neurologists know from fMRI scans: We are wired for *instant gratification*, the compelling urge to spend what we don't have to get what we can't wait for.

It's not that our rational brain can't grasp the long-term implications of our actions in the moment, because it can. In fact, that's essentially the problem. Our prefrontal cortex, the home of logic and reason in the brain, activates for longer-term thinking—but not for immediate thinking. For example, consider the following question: "Would you rather have $15 in two weeks or $20 in four weeks?"

Because this involves projection into the future and a relatively long timeframe, your prefrontal cortex lights up as you ponder the question. However, now consider a question with more immediate consequences: "Would you rather have $15 *now* or $20 in two days?"

They seem like very similar questions—but the brain treats them quite differently. This time, as the fMRI reveals, the prefrontal cortex appears to ignore the question and it is instead the more primitive midbrain that lights up. And that reptilian structure stands a very good chance of making a knee-jerk decision—and acting on it—before your cortex has fully grasped what's happening. As Peter Whybrow, head of the Semel Institute for Neuroscience and Behavior at UCLA, said in an interview with *Wired* magazine, "The instinctive brain is well ahead of the intellectual brain. Credit cards promise us that you can have what you want now, and postpone payment until later."[1]

It may be this same sort of brain reaction that keeps people from saving for retirement, even when they know they should. As many as 40 percent of those eligible for retirement plans with their company still aren't saving for their future. Putting money into a 401(k), an IRA, or other retirement plan creates a conflict between the emotional and rational brain. The prefrontal cortex says, "I am saving for my future," while the limbic system snarls, "I want the money now!" And you know which system often wins out.

Money, Brain, and Risk

It's hard to find a significant money decision that doesn't involve some risk. Choosing a new career, starting a business, buying stocks, selling your home—they're all big-ticket decisions that come with an element of the unknown.

Risk is subjective. Even "rational" risk management decisions such as asset allocation and portfolio diversification are made in the context of how we feel about risk, and that's a unique sensation for each of us.

The whole gray area of risk is complicated further by our gray matter. Deep in a component of the limbic system called the *hippocampus*, events are assigned meanings, creating a type of emotional memory that has a powerful and long-lasting effect. Being burned in the stock market makes us less likely to participate in the market for a significant time afterward, because the emotional coals of defeat are still burning in our limbic system, ready to be fanned into flames at the slightest hint of risk.

Conversely, the high stimulation of success can sensitize our *amygdalae* so that we tolerate increasingly higher levels of risk, a phenomenon revealed in the brains of investors during the surging tech market of the late 1990s.

So, if we could just keep our emotions out of it, we'd make much better financial decisions . . . right? Not so fast. In studies at the University of Iowa, the famed Portuguese neurologist Antonio Damasio found that people with no emotions are also bad at making decisions. By studying people who had sustained significant damage to the amygdalae, Damasio discovered that the utter lack of any fear of risk led people to lose money in situations where a more balanced and cautious investor would more likely have declined to act.

The Chemistry of Winning and Losing

The brain's communication network depends on two chemicals that activate synapses: *dopamine* and *serotonin*.

Dopamine is the pleasure chemical: It produces an excited state or "natural high" in response to unexpected rewards. Serotonin is more responsible for our mood over time and helps maintain a sense of safety, security, and confidence.

Neurophysiologist Wolfram Schultz at the University of Cambridge, England, has demonstrated that the rush from dopamine motivates us to take risks. That euphoric feeling of a winning blackjack hand, a risky stock investment score, or a surprise lottery win is spurred on by dopamine production.

To further complicate things, the less predictable a reward is, the longer and stronger our dopamine neurons fire, giving us more of that natural high. If a laboratory mouse is given regular, predictable rewards for pushing a lever, the behavior stops quickly when the food pellet rewards stop. However, if the food pellets are infrequent and unpredictable, the mouse will keep pushing the lever almost indefinitely. This behavior is not confined to laboratory mice, either: Spend a few minutes watching a bank of slot machines in Vegas and you'll see the same scenario, complete with reward pellets and lever pulling.

The moral: People easily fall into the unconscious pursuit of dopamine and its accompanying pleasure despite the obvious logical downside.

One reason this happens is that the brain doesn't actually require a tangible reward to produce dopamine: The mere anticipation of a reward will do just as well. When a day trader sits down at his home computer, the sheer possibility of a big win (however unlikely) causes a release of dopamine and the slight euphoria that goes with it, before he even begins to trade. In fact, research shows that the anticipation of a reward can be even *more satisfying* than actually receiving it, because attaining the goal shuts down the chemical engine of anticipation and the high that goes with it.

In other words, looking forward to the big win can be even more thrilling than actually getting it.

While winning is closely connected to dopamine, losing has a profound impact on serotonin, the brain's other messenger chemical. Reduced serotonin levels are found in chronically depressed individuals (many antidepressants act to raise serotonin levels). The same effect has been observed in people who have experienced repeated investment losses. The experience of loss causes a far more significant drop in serotonin levels than the rise in levels caused by experiencing euphoria. This is why short-term investing can be so inherently self-destructive. Richard Peterson, M.D., concluded that to avoid this outcome investors needed to, "profit on more than two-thirds of their trades and not grow accustomed to expecting success—not a likely scenario."

With decreased serotonin in the brain, our concentration and energy decrease, our sleep is disrupted, and our biology slows down. Cocaine, amphetamines, and high-risk investments with the expectation of a big reward are all ways to self-medicate for low serotonin. None of them have good statistical outcomes.

Managing Your State of Mind

Evolved over eons to cope with the hunt-or-be-hunted conditions of the wild, our brains respond to this civilized world of money in ways that often work at cross-purposes to our actual well-being. Gaining mastery over your money requires gaining some degree of conscious control over your psychophysiological state of mind.

Each of us lives within a continuum of different states of mind, such as calm relaxation, reflective thinking, focused alertness, worried anticipation, and emotional stimulation. *Spaced out, freaked out, in a fog, in a panic*, are all expressions that describe distinct states of mind that bring with them different degrees and types of compromised decision-making capacity. When we are *in the zone*, our critical faculties are honed to a razor's edge; when we are *zoned out*, the opposite is true.

We all enter and exit different states of mind fluidly and invisibly, like the precision baton passage between relay team members, intuitively seeking whichever state is most conducive to the task at hand, from the alertness of business endeavors to relaxation for sleep. More sharply focused pinpoint attention is useful when giving a speech, while relaxation moving into somnolence works best for bed time. In fact, often difficulties of performance in various arenas have more to do with mood regulation than actual competency.

Throughout history, artists and writers have learned how to fine-tune this process and enter a creative state of mind to fit their intended work:

- Dr. Samuel Johnson and W.H. Auden kept themselves in a stimulated state with continuous consumption of tea when they wrote. Coleridge used opium before each writing session.
- Willa Cather read the Bible to set the right tone prior to her writing. Dame Edith Sitwell's preference was to lie in the stale solitude of an open coffin as a prelude to working on her more macabre mode of writing.
- The French novelist Baroness Dudevant, *aka* George Sands, went immediately from lovemaking to the pen. A century earlier her compatriot Voltaire wasted even less time: He simply used his lover's back for a writing desk.
- William Turner liked to be lashed to the mast of a ship and taken out to sea during fierce storms, so he could later recreate this experience on canvas. Benjamin Franklin took to the water in a more subdued fashion, focusing his thoughts by writing while soaking in the tub.

Many authors will play a particular piece of music over and over during the course of writing a given work, to create a specific emotional framework to house their evolving story. Like these creative artists, we can learn to consciously manage our states of mind for the outcomes we want. Mastering the regulation of state change can determine how effective you become at any task, including the task of making effective money decisions.

Mastering your money requires having principles, consistency, and a game plan. It also requires that you are in an optimum state of mind when you make your money decisions. The majority of money loss in investing is the result of emotional decisions that trump otherwise good information, advice, and strategy. Mastering your state by learning how to ground yourself will help you gain access to your full range of brain capacity, including both rational and intuitive, big-picture thinking and accurate in-the-moment observation, and focus your best judgment on the decision at hand.

A Brief Grounding Routine

Grounding yourself in your body allows you to center inside your experience and attain a fully present state of mind. This grounding and centering creates a sense of being relaxed yet alert, focused but not tense. The present state of mind allows full access to all aspects of experience, especially self-awareness.

If you feel detached or ungrounded in your body or present experience, it helps to focus your awareness on specific details of your body and your immediate environment. Specific focus on present experience and attunement to state of mind also fosters stronger connection of mind and body.

The following principles are derived from my work with athletes and artistic performers whose physical performance must be aligned with a present, concentrated state of mind.

- Focus your attention on being aware of your body, here and now.
- Balance your posture, so your weight is evenly distributed.

- Relax your arms, legs, and shoulders, then your jaw, tongue, and face.
- Breathe evenly and deeply, from your diaphragm and stomach.
- With your eyes looking straight forward, become aware of your entire field of vision, including the periphery.
- If possible, jump lightly up and down a few times to feel fully present in your body.

Six Guidelines for Making Grounded Money Decisions

A safety deposit box requires two keys being placed and turned to open the box: one by the bank and one by the owner. Financial decisions need the same thing: the keys of the left and right brain operating simultaneously. Here are six guidelines that will help you keep your limbic system and your money separate, so that the lizard in you doesn't get to make your money decisions.

1. **Avoid making important money decisions when you are emotional.** Heightened emotion—good or bad—narrows your perspective, cuts you off from your sense of the big picture, and makes it more difficult to logically see the long-term consequences of your choices.

   Paradoxically, attempting to use reason and logic with someone who is in a heightened emotional state only deepens the automatic alarm pattern, and will usually lead the person to dig in his heels and spiral into more extreme and less considered impulses. Empathic listening and communication of understanding are far more effective at deescalating things.

2. **Avoid making important money decisions under tension or fatigue.** Increased tension produces emotional regression. With increased tension and advanced conflict, the stress response

reaction can move someone into a more emotional pattern characteristic of a much earlier age. The same holds true for fatigue. Make important decisions after tension has calmed and you are rested.

"Never go to bed angry" is an age-old maxim for healthy relationships, and with good reason. It's easier to fly off the handle when fatigued and say things we might later regret. Or to *buy* things we might later regret. A good maxim for healthy financial life might be, "Never make important decisions after 9 p.m."

3. **Be willing to sleep on it.** There are few true emergencies in life. Investing isn't one of them, and neither is buying that plasma television. If it is a good decision today, it will be a good decision tomorrow, after you have had the state change and perspective of sleeping on it.

   Be clear on the distinction between being passive and making an informed decision not to act right now. "I'll sleep on it" *is* a decision.

   Especially in times of traumatic or crisis situations, sleeping on it can revert a "hot state" to one of cooler reason. Recognize if you are vulnerable to emotional news or gyrations in order to devise a strategy to not react in the financial arena. Limit exposure to emotional triggers, such as checking a stock ticker each day.

4. **Have a well-informed and fully structured plan.** Look at the big picture and your long-term objectives, and create a strategy and game plan based on facts rather than on emotions or instinctive reactions. Seek out whatever assistance you need to become fully informed on the issues involved. Periodically review your plan to make sure it is in alignment with objective expert advice by a money or investment specialist.

5. **Stick to your plan.** Especially in times of doing extremely well and feeling euphoric, stick to the plan. Get your excitement and take your risks in areas other than finance.

6. **Worry about the right things.** Decide what you can control (your plan, your actions, your decisions) and what you can't (market conditions, external events), and put all your effort, energy, and focus into those things you can affect. When things happen that are beyond your control and that you cannot determine, stick to the plan.

Notes

1. http://blog.wired.com/wiredscience/2008/10/american-dream.html.

seven

BUBBLES AND
BUBBLE BATHS

A billion dollars isn't what it used to be.

—Nelson Bunker Hunt, former Texas oil billionaire,
upon declaring bankruptcy in September 1988

In late 1593, a botanist named Carolus Clusius brought to his native Holland a new type of flower he had discovered in Vienna and planted the bulb in the Leiden botanical gardens. By the following spring, Clusius's horticultural efforts had succeeded in bringing to bloom the Netherlands' very first tulip.

The beautiful coloring and unique shape of the tulip quickly gained people's attention. Growing and crossbreeding began in earnest, and some of the most spectacular varieties became status symbols. "It was deemed a proof of bad taste in any man of fortune to be without a collection of them," wrote Scottish journalist Charles MacKay in *Extraordinary Popular Delusions and the Madness of Crowds*. Before long, prices on the burgeoning tulip market began a stratospheric rise as the elite rushed to join the new craze. The simple flower's new elevated status drove incredible demand. What came to be known as "tulip mania" soon migrated from the wealthy elite to the middle class, until people at every level of the economic scale were converting their property into cash in order to have more money to invest into flowers. At the peak of tulip mania, bulbs were traded on exchanges, and had their own tulip futures for speculators. Frenzied buying drove prices ever higher, to a point where certain varieties sold for as much as 5,000 florins, then the equivalent of more than 30 years' pay for a skilled craftsman.

"Everyone imagined that the passion for tulips would last forever," reported MacKay, "and that the wealthy from every part of the world would send to Holland, and pay whatever prices were asked for them."

But everyone imagined wrong. The tulip frenzy didn't last; by 1637 prices were starting to unravel. When traders could no longer find buyers for the insanely inflated bulbs the market collapsed, sending the tulip industry into a shambles and bankrupting many. Today, the United States imports billions of tulip bulbs each year at a cost of pennies apiece.

Does this scenario sound familiar? It should. All you have to do is change the word "tulip" to "Tickle Me Elmo," "Beanie Babies," or "dot-com IPO." Or for that matter, "credit-default swap." The tulip mania of sixteenth-century Holland is often referred to as the "original speculative bubble," a phenomenon that has been echoed innumerable times over the years. The unsubstantiated confidence, the prices that inflate well beyond reasonable value, the headlong rush of the middle class into the market, and the eventual collapse . . . these are the classic attributes of this ever-cycling collective money soap opera that seems to run in perpetual reruns.

Oh, how we love those bubbles. So why are we surprised when we discover we have just taken a bath?

"You would think people would have learned about bubbles by now," says Yale economics professor Robert J. Shiller, author of *Irrational Exuberance* and *The Sub-Prime Solution*, "but they're hard to see as they are happening." Professor Shiller had no trouble identifying the recent housing market effervescence for what it was, even as it was happening. In a 2005 interview on NPR, he called the U.S. real estate boom a bubble, explaining that the term meant that "prices are out of touch with economic reality," and predicted that it would soon burst. "The only question," he added, "is when." Three years later, the world had the answer.

In retrospect, this now seems obvious. But in a bubble, people believe that there is something fundamentally different about now than before. It seems, feels, and appears to be real—so it must not be a bubble. Emotions seize and hold hostage the rational investment mind. What everyone else is doing becomes the point of reference.

Dr. Vernon Smith won a Nobel prize in economics by demonstrating how market bubbles are created. Unifying psychology and economics, he demonstrated how a new bubble danger is inherent when a new generation of investors joins the market. He found that investors behave in particular ways, such as "once burned, twice shy." Educated and sophisticated investors abort cerebral theories in emotional decisions.

Dr. Smith ran a series of trading experiments in which economics graduate students were informed the fair value of a security was three dollars. These traders *knew the actual worth* of the security—a significant advantage over the normal Wall Street trader's situation—but they still ran the price up significantly past the three-dollar mark. When other traders in the experiment stopped paying a premium, the laboratory market crashed.

In a second experiment, the same group formed another, smaller bubble. It was not until the third time around that the investors wised up enough to stay with the security's actual value—even though they had *known* this from the very start. When Dr. Smith repeated the experiment with finance professors and other economic specialists, the same bubbles formed, followed by the same crashes.

Apparently, there is some seemingly irrational force that overrides our logic and knowledge and causes us to believe that rising prices will continue to rise indefinitely—or at least as long as we're betting on them. That force, of course, is *human behavior*. Supply and demand is driven by suppliers and demanders, each with a reptilian limbic system as well as a forebrain and with both left *and* right hemispheres. The flaw in the economic system is that it is run by buyers and sellers—in other words, by *us*. And we all operate from the perspective of our own money stories, complete with their complicated stew of feelings, personal histories, money meanings, limbic responses, and right-brain maroonings.

The mind is a powerful thing. From turning a placebo sugar pill into medicine, to paying millions for a fifty-cent baseball, its capacity to interpret events, drive our actions, and determine our futures is staggering. Howard Hughes, who spent hours sorting his peas with a specially designed fork, is famous for his unique mix of fabulous wealth and eccentric behavior. But it takes neither storied riches nor a psychiatric disorder to behave irrationally around money.

Over time, research has revealed a number of money fallacies, common mental biases that cause us to behave financially in ways that are illogical, irrational, or at times downright crazy. In this chapter, we'll examine 18 of the most common of these patterns, along with some simple prescriptions for avoiding these neural traps. Some of these are decision-making biases identified by behavioral economists or other writers; some are established concepts that are here newly applied to financial decision making; and some are original with this writing.[1]

Framing Effect

Imagine you're suffering from a serious disease, one that threatens your life, and your doctors tell you they have come up with two viable options for you to choose from: (1) Procedure A, which gives you a 32 percent chance of dying within a year, or (2) Procedure B, which gives you a 68 percent chance of living for more than a year.

Which path would you pick? If you're like most patients, you'd choose option B—and according to one study, so would 75 percent of doctors, which is rather remarkable, considering that both statements describe the *same procedure*.

This thought experiment illustrates what is known as the *framing effect*, and it describes how the way in which a question or situation is presented can cause us to think in an irrational way.

The framing effect is just as applicable to financial scenarios. Consider the case of my client, Beth, who drove 10 miles across town to save $5 on a $20 electric mixer and was thrilled with her 25 percent savings. A few days later, she noticed that a $200 coat she was about to purchase was offered at a store 15 blocks farther away for $190, but decided it was not worth the hassle of the extra drive to save a mere 5 percent.

Logically, of course, this makes no sense: Beth drove 10 miles to save $5, but would not drive a fraction of that distance to save $10. Thinking in terms of percentages, rather than in actual dollars, skewed her decision.

The framing effect also causes us to treat identical amounts of money in different ways, depending on the context we create for them. Rationally speaking, in other words, a dollar is a dollar, but we assign a different value to it depending on how we earn it, receive it, and perceive it. "Found money," for example, such as a gambling win, an unexpected bonus, or a tax refund, is framed differently and thus spent differently than a regular salary or savings.

Rx for the Framing Effect

Consider each spending or investing decision as an independent choice, separate from the source of the money used. Ask yourself, "Would I make this purchase if I had to take it from my salary? From my savings?"

Reframe the purchase in a larger context of time. "Is this a choice I will be proud of tomorrow? And have no regrets later?"

Loss Aversion

Research shows that we typically experience the negative feelings associated with loss about twice as acutely as the pleasurable feelings from gain. For example, a $100 loss generates double the pain as the pleasure from a $100 gain. Not surprisingly, the impulse to avoid loss tends to be far stronger than the urge to pursue pleasure, a preference that is termed *loss aversion*.

We encountered an example of loss aversion back in Chapter 1, when we looked in on Max Bazerman's auction experiment: The bidder in second place felt compelled to up the ante in order not to lose what he'd already bid—even though it clearly upped the odds that he would have to pay even more.

This preference for pain avoidance has particularly strong implications for investors. Because we're rarely aware of our loss aversion, we tend to hold onto losing investments longer than we should, hoping for a rebound, rather than selling and "locking in" the loss—as if the loss so far were not real until we confirm it by selling.

Loss aversion can also cause us to abandon profitable investments too soon. Terrance Odean at the University of California, Davis, studied 10,000 accounts at a brokerage firm over a seven-year period, and found evidence that individual investors tend to sell winning investments too quickly and keep losing ones too long. For example, investors were more likely to sell stocks that had *gained* value than those that had *fallen* by the same amount! And sure enough, the stocks that the investors dumped performed better by an average of 3.4 percentage points over the next 12 months than the ones they held onto.

Rx for Loss Aversion

Predetermine criteria to balance emotional reactivity. Loss aversion is an emotional decision: panic selling in a rapidly declining market or, more commonly, the inertia of holding on to a losing investment to avoid making the loss seem "more real" by selling. What's needed is a better choice architecture: to move from the emotional position to a logical, objective assessment of present value, not letting feelings or the inertia of a comfort zone blind you to making an objective assessment and decision.

Extrapolation Error

We are neurally wired to predict patterns and forecast events. The brain instinctually recognizes patterns, what Emory University's neuropsychiatrist Gregory Burns calls a "learning without awareness."

Researchers led by neuroscientist Scott Huettel of Duke University have demonstrated that the brain anticipates a repetition after a stimulus occurs twice in a row. Thus, if a stock has two years of positive growth, we automatically expect a third. This is *extrapolation error,* a poor decision based on an attempt to predict the future based on data from the past.

This tendency to predict the future from the past makes it very difficult for us to make wise decisions, and it is one of the prime reasons we repeat financial mistakes. In fact, the single most common mistake investors make is to let the experience of the previous period dominate their thinking. Peter Bernstein, whom *Money* magazine says "knows more about investing than anyone alive," calls extrapolation errors investors' most common error. The riskiest moment, says Bernstein, is when you are right about investment. "That's when you're in the most trouble, because you tend to overstate good decisions."

The emotional component of investing accounts for why, despite all the growing sophistication of knowledge about how the stock market behaves, the public has not gotten any smarter in its investment decisions—and probably never will.

Rx for Extrapolation Error

Resist the temptation to assume that the future will be a replica of the past. Remember that (1) your brain will automatically impose predictive patterns onto any given set of events in an effort to know the future; however (2) nobody knows the future.

To balance the possibility of extrapolation error, look at a range of possible outcomes, including both best-case and worst-case scenarios, and make sure you are comfortable with the worst-case outcome if it should come to pass.

Invincibility Bias

Like so many of his fellow physicians, Paul had a very busy practice. Despite a heavy overhead, he still netted over $200,000 a year, almost all of which was committed to Paul's lifestyle expenses, led by a huge mortgage and country club dues. And why not? Every year since graduating medical school a decade and a half earlier, Paul had seen an increase in his net earnings. There was no reason to think this wouldn't continue, just as it had for his colleagues. And so his plans and expenses gradually escalated—until the mid-nineties.

Suddenly, things changed: Managed care had arrived on the scene. Physician fees were reduced, often by half, and administrative work increased. Soon all Paul's colleagues were joining the new networks out of fear of being left behind. Within a year, Paul had to reduce his staff, sell his home, and move to a smaller house and office.

Paul made the mistake of *invincibility bias*, first cousin to extrapolation error and one of the most common predictive fallacies. Invincibility bias says, "Yeah, I know that happens a lot—but it won't happen *to me*."

Rx for Invincibility Bias

Again, set limits prior to an activity. For example, gamblers can set a predetermined daily amount of maximum money exposure.

Research variations of outcome, taking the time and care to actually list them, thus focusing your brain on the genuine possibilities rather than the illusion of the favored outcome.

Anchoring

A roomful of students are directed to write down the last two digits of their Social Security numbers. They are then asked to bid in a mock auction on a series of items such as chocolate and bottles of wine. When the bids are examined, an odd pattern emerges: Those students with higher two-digit numbers have bid 60 to 120 percent higher for the items than those who had written down lower two-digit numbers. Somehow, the simple, seemingly unconnected two-digit number was enough to significantly change spending patterns.

This experiment, as reported by MIT professor Dan Ariely in his book *Predictably Irrational: The Hidden Forces That Shape Our Decisions*, illustrates the phenomenon called *anchoring*: the tendency to make decisions in ambiguous situations based on an arbitrary point of reference.

Anchoring can rear its head in almost any purchasing and investing decision. When the $15,000 price tag on a used car is reduced to $10,000 for a "quick sale," we are elated at the 33 percent price drop; meanwhile, the validity of the original sticker price goes unquestioned. Likewise, the person who buys a stock at $100 is much less likely to sell when it goes to either $90 or $110 than the person who bought it at $40, because the purchase price of $100 serves as an anchor—regardless of the underlying value of the stock itself.

Extrapolation error is a type of anchoring: We base our predictions of the future on the anchor of present conditions and resist the idea that the future could be wholly different.

Rx for Anchoring

Rather than accepting the current price of an equity or the marked price of an item as the anchor, research the true value. Be objective in your comparison and due diligence.

An example of setting your own anchor price is to preview an auction item and establish the maximum price you will pay, regardless of the swirl of bids that unfolds once the auction gets underway.

Confirmation Bias

For five years, from 1984 to 1989, economists Barry Staw and Ha Hoang studied performance trends in new NBA basketball players. They measured distinct skills, such as scoring, quickness (assists and steals), and toughness (rebounds and blocks), as well as injuries and all other significant variables they could think of, to see if they could learn which factors were most significant in determining actual playing time.

Logically, one would think that in deciding who to put into the game, when, and for how long, the coaches and managers would be keenly interested in how well the players actually played. But like Wall Street stockbrokers, doctors, and everyone else, coaches and managers are human beings with reptilian and mammalian brains along with their frontal lobes.

The researchers found that one variable had consistently greater impact than any of the actual performance data: the players' *draft selection order*. In other words, the order in which the players had been chosen *before the season even began* had more impact on how much playing time they were given than any measurement of how well they were actually playing. And that initial draft order continued to be the number 1 correlate with playing time throughout the five years of the study. How the teams' managers *expected* these players to perform was a far more significant factor than how they actually *did* perform—a perfect example of the neurological fallacy known as *confirmation bias*.

Confirmation bias is the distortion of available data to accommodate preexisting beliefs or impressions. In other words, we tend to cherry-pick among the facts at hand to confirm our foregone conclusions. This bias is the reason researchers tend to find data to support their conclusions, and why so many people regard psychics as accurate, even though they get an overwhelmingly large number of predictions wrong. We have a tendency to remember the hits, and forget the misses. We see what we expect to see.

This bias is also prevalent in our financial lives. In everything from real estate to stock picks to buying clothes or a new television, we tend to single out "objective information" that confirms or supports the choices toward which we are already leaning.

Rx for Confirmation Bias

Be aware of the tendency to find the story you want to hear and see only what you already believe. Question your assumptions; probe your reasoning. Practice playing "devil's advocate" with yourself: No matter how good or right a financial decision looks, take the time to try on the opposing viewpoint. Where spending money is concerned, make "just for the sake of argument" a catchphrase. Ask for feedback from others whenever possible, and be open to what you hear.

Perceived Value

Researchers at Caltech ran a wine-tasting experiment to see how different factors influenced people's choices. In blind trials where subjects knew only the price of the wine, the study found that people consistently rated a $90 bottle of wine as better tasting than lower-priced wines. There was a catch, though: The $90 price tag wasn't always attached to the same bottle. When the researchers swapped the pricier selection out for a $10 wine, the subjects still preferred it.[2]

This tendency to assign value to objects based on price tag affects us in a myriad of ways. Researchers Hal Arkes and Catherine Blumer discovered that people who pay more for theater tickets are more likely to attend the shows. Our perception of the value of companies and their stock is dramatically influenced by quarterly reports. And remember the placebo effect? We tend to think that more expensive medications work better, too.[3]

You might be wondering whether this is truly a fallacy, or if there isn't some factual link between a product's price and its quality. *Consumer Reports* wondered, too: In a 2007 survey they looked at the relationship between price and actual value and found very little correlation. In fact, in fully one-third of the cases they surveyed there was actually an *inverse* relationship: The higher-priced product was of *less* value than the lower-priced one.[4]

Perceived value vanishes as quickly as the faith that underlies it. One company, after showing increased profits for 26 quarters in a row, had a projected earnings growth of 24 cents for the current quarter. When they announced an earnings of only 23 cents, they lost $1.5 billion in market value within five minutes.

Rx for Perceived Value

Make sure your plan is informed by expert information and knowledge of basic value. If the basic value does not change, don't change the plan. A company that fails to meet analysts' estimates by one penny per share does not change its underlying value as a company, even if there is a precipitous sell-off on the earnings news; it simply means the analysts missed their prediction.

Sunk Cost Fallacy

When Robert and Jennie began their backyard deck and gazebo project, they estimated it would cost about $5,000. They took a home equity loan and hired a contractor. Before long the contractor had drawn the full $5,000 but was barely halfway through the project. New estimates now showed it would take an additional $6,500 to complete the work — but the finished improvement would add only about $4,500 in total new value to the house. Robert and Jennie didn't have the money, but they borrowed more anyway. "We've already put five grand into it," they reasoned, "now we *have* to complete it."

Robert and Jennie had fallen prey to the *sunk cost fallacy*, more commonly known as "throwing good money after bad." It is easy to be sucked into spending money in an effort to vindicate money we've already spent. This is why gamblers try to bet their way out of a hole, or why we may feel compelled to buy more of a losing stock. "In for a penny, in for a pound," we say, as if there were some sublime folk wisdom inherent in this nonsensical adage.

Rx for Sunk Cost Fallacy

Remember that every decision you make is a present choice, regardless of your previous decisions. The past is the past and is useful only for what learning you can glean from it. Look at each new money decision as one you are making on a blank slate. "Today is the first day of the rest of your life" may be corny as a bumper sticker, but it's an excellent perspective for making sound financial choices.

Spending Justification

Justifying an expenditure means creating a "just cause," usually through a contorted algebra of cost and value comparison: "If A equals B, then it only follows that C equals D"—even when neither A nor B have anything whatsoever to do with C or D.

- "If I can spend $9 on my special coffee beans, surely I can spend twice that on a Reidel glass to drink my wine, because it will be around a long time."
- "If we spent $65 on dinner last night, shouldn't we be able to spend half that amount on these candles?"
- "If we can afford a $200 business dinner, we can certainly afford to spend an extra $200 to fly business class."
- "Hey, it's a vacation—we didn't come all this way to save a hundred dollars on a hotel room."

Through justification, luxuries have a way of evolving into "necessities" over time. The special coffee beans become routine, the better restaurant becomes the assumed standard, and our expenses sneak upward and expand laterally.

The goal of cost justification is nearly always the same: legitimizing an expense that we really know is of questionable legitimacy. Thus, justification by definition is a form of self-deception, making it doubly dangerous: It not only allows us to spend money we can't afford, it also contributes to a progressive estrangement of our spending habits from our financial realities. Each accepted justification lends support by implication to the next, and it becomes easier and easier to snowball into a mountain of debt and overextended lifestyle.

Rx for Spending Justification

If you have to justify a financial decision, it needs to be examined—under bright lights and with at least one witness. Examine each financial decision in terms of the entire system and the principle involved, rather than segmenting the decision as a standalone issue.

Spending Rationalization

Drazen Prelic and Duncan Simester at the Massachusetts Institute of Technology constructed an actual sealed-bid auction for Boston Celtics basketball tickets. Half the participating purchasers of the auction were told that if they won, they would have to pay for the tickets in cash, though they would be given sufficient time to get the funds together. The other half were told that the winning bidder would have to pay by credit card. The average of the bids of those who believed they would be paying in cash was *half* the average bid made by those who believed they would pay with a credit card.

In other words, the value of cash was viewed as twice that of the same dollar amount charged to a credit account. Or to put it differently, when using a credit card, an expense is only half as real as when paying cash. Other studies have shown that spending increases by an average of more than 23 percent when credit cards are used, as opposed to check or cash.

Why do people spend more when charging than paying cash? Because they tell themselves, consciously or not, "It's only a charge; it won't show up right now." This is one of many forms of *rationalization*.

Like justification, rationalization is the articulation of seemingly good reasons for a bad decision. One of the most common forms of rationalization is to minimize the impact of an expense through the slight of hand of amortization: "Sure, this $400 stereo might *seem* expensive, but it will only cost you twenty-two cents a day for the next five years!" Extrapolated over a large enough period of time, *any* purchase can be rationalized. (A million-dollar home? Why, that's less than $100 a day over the next 30 years.)

There may be an anatomical basis for such self-deception. Recall that unlike the neocortex, the more primitive limbic system does not think in terms of future consequences. The more our fight-or-flight, trauma- and-anxiety-response system becomes intertwined with money decisions, the more we will tend to spend "like there's no tomorrow"—because to the part of us that's doing the spending, there *is* no tomorrow.

Rx for Spending Rationalization

As with justification, if you have to rationalize a decision, it needs to be examined under bright lights with at least one witness and scrutinized in terms of your overall plan.

Internal Bargaining

"Lord, give me chastity and continence—but not yet." Nearly two thou- sand years later, St. Augustine's famous prayer still sounds an awfully familiar note. When we say, "Okay, I'll have this cheesecake now, and start my diet Monday," the illusion of future commitment creates a false sense of virtue that somehow compensates for the knowing infraction. It's as if we are borrowing against our future restraint to pay for our pres- ent excesses. But the promise of future dieting has never lost its author a single pound.

This is the fallacy of *internal bargaining*, that fascinating form of self- deception that equates plan with action. In poker, internal bargaining sounds like this: "I just need to win one more big hand, then I'll quit," and it's much the same idea in personal budgeting, investing, and every other area where financial decisions are involved.

Rx for Internal Bargaining

A commitment is a decision you only make once. The challenging, courageous part of change is not the initial decision, but the continu- ing willingness to stay the course. Success is never final. Don't get com- placent.

Nostalgia Bias

Nostalgia bias, also called "rosy retrospection," is the tendency to regard past events as having been better than they really were at the time. Nostalgia recalls the ideal rather than the real—airbrushed memories backlit by idealization. Thus, we attribute the bad real estate deal (when we think of it at all) to market conditions beyond our control. But that lucky stock buy? Pure genius.

The problem with nostalgia bias is that when we inflate our abilities or past successes by retrospection, the distortion can easily inflate our present expectations. Rose-colored glasses can be wonderful, but they make red ink invisible. Thus self-hypnotized to overlook our past mistakes, we think we make better decisions than average, that we exercise more than average, and eat better than average. A survey by *Harpers* found that 19 percent see themselves as being in the top 1 percent of income!

Nostalgia can be a wonderful thing—but not when it comes to making money decisions.

Rx for Nostalgia Bias

Review the negative indications, red flags, and warning signs that you overlooked in any past poor decisions. Search yourself for any tendency to gloss over what you don't want to remember or to minimize your past mistakes. Gazing at the past with a cold, clear eye is the best way to find your best path to a warmer future.

Optimism Bias

In 1990, the stock market pushed shares of AOL to a price that a reasonable earnings model could support only if the Internet giant had 18 billion subscribers—triple the population of the planet. This was a vivid example of *optimism bias* on a massive scale.

Optimism bias is closely related to nostalgia bias: While one inflates the past, the other inflates our expectations of the future and minimizes potential negative outcomes and warning signs. For example, those who have remarkable success in one field, such as physicians, may fall prey to the belief that their expertise in their chosen field will transfer to other fields, such as investing. (It won't.)

One physician invested $25,000 in a silver mine following the sales pitch of a neighbor who'd recently gone into the investment field. The doctor reasoned that the investment had to be sound because the man down the street had to face him daily. Both assumptions were wrong. The silver mine had no glitter, and the investment seller divorced his wife and vanished from the neighborhood.

On the other side of the equation, optimism bias minimizes negative possibilities. Despite knowing the odds of success are always against them, gamblers discount this information and continue to bet, dollar after dwindling dollar, thus financing a guaranteed long-term negative return.

Rx for Optimism Bias

Examine those areas where you are "probability blind." Notice patterns that you are likely to expect that have no basis in reality. For example, if the roulette wheel stops on red four times in a row, you may expect it to do so a fifth time, even though logic tells you that the next spin has no more than a 50 percent chance of landing on red.

Don't listen only for what you want to hear. Look for the shadow side of every story.

Transference Fallacy

In psychoanalysis, the tendency to redirect feelings from a past context to a current one is considered a type of *transference*. Negative childhood feelings toward one's father, for example, might be felt in adulthood toward someone who reminds one of that parent, even if the two have no connection at all.

The effect also appears in the world of money. Investors, for example, tend to draw analogies where none exist. After one bad experience in the stock market, we paint similar companies, sectors, or entire markets with the same brush.

- During the Gulf War, the stock market dropped 14 percent between July and September 1990, partly due to the emotional connection to other war times, such as World War II, when stocks faired poorly.
- In 1990, when Digital Equipment Corporation posted a 13 percent decline in earnings, the value of Hewlett-Packard collapsed half its value that same day, even though its operation was untouched by the troubles that were plaguing DEC.

When transference fallacy is projected forward onto the future, it becomes extrapolation error. When a stock doubles in value, the tendency is to expect it to continue to grow—a self-reinforcing story that under the right circumstances can expand unchecked to become a bubble.

Rx for Transference Fallacy

Isolate your decisions within their own context and in the present time. Is this situation genuinely similar to other past situations? And if so, specifically in what is it—and in what ways is it not? Recognize that the past does not necessarily equal the present nor determine the future.

Affinity Bias

When you lose $20 betting a favorite in the Super Bowl, we call it unlucky. When you lose $2,000 betting that your alma mater will win their college game even though they have the worst record in the conference, that's *affinity bias*.

Affinity bias is the tendency to underestimate the risk and overestimate the value of things we like, such as alcohol, tobacco, a prized possession, or favorite investment. The University of Oregon's Paul Slovic and Carnegie Mellon's Baruch Fishoff have demonstrated that the distortion of affinity bias can explain how even professional investors may overlook the risk of seriously inflated stocks, as happened in the run-up to the tech stock bubble of 2000.

Affinity bias also works in reverse: We tend to underestimate the influence and abilities of what we *don't* like, such as an opposing team or political party, which can also contribute to the relative blindness of overly optimistic projections of those forces we're rooting for.

Rx for Affinity Bias

Be aware of explicit affinity biases, like bets on the stocks of companies you're fond of (or your alma mater's football game). Again, play a version of devil's advocate here: Imagine your research and/or the advice of an advisor you trust had told you that it would be a better decision to put your money on a company (or football team) you don't especially like. How differently would you feel about making the investment?

Pattern Bias

We love patterns. As we have seen, we are neurologically wired to look for them, and for good reason: Recognizing patterns in the world around us has helped us to survive. But our predilection for patterns can get us into trouble.

Studies by Nobel laureate Daniel Kahneman and his late colleague Amos Tversky, for example, have demonstrated that people readily see patterns in data that are actually random. This is *pattern bias*: the perception of patterns that aren't really there. When we get a raise for three consecutive years, pattern bias convinces us that we'll get one next year, too. When that doesn't happen (and we've already pre-spent the expected raise), our lifestyle and reality start to part company.

A related effect, the *gambler's fallacy*, describes how we look for breaks in patterns to even out expected odds. If we toss a coin three times and get three heads, for example, the gambler's fallacy makes us think that the next toss is more likely to be tails, even though in reality the odds are still 50–50 — just as they are on every toss.

Rx for Pattern Bias

Rather than basing decisions on what may appear to be a pattern or trend, seek to base them on solid research, tangible facts, and demonstrably reasonable guesses. Review past performance to recognize what kinds of decisions have worked and which have sabotaged investment returns. Use your awareness of those patterns to help guide your choices in times of panic (such as a sharp market downturn) or greed (in a sharp market upturn).

Availability Bias

When we attempt to predict the likelihood of an event, we scan through our memory of similar experiences to pull data for comparison. What we don't realize is that our memory tends to skew toward more recent and more emotionally charged events; because these are more accessible, they become more credible as evidence for predicting the future. If you recently had a car accident, you are more likely to view driving as dangerous. The recent robbery of a close friend tells you that he lives in a dangerous neighborhood, even if more accurate but less dramatic evidence points to the contrary.

The availability bias makes it hard for us to make accurate financial decisions because it skews our assessment of risk. A painful real estate deal makes real estate "too risky," but a hot streak in Vegas makes gambling odds "better than you'd think."

Rx for Availability Bias

My favorite coach consistently said, "Keep your eye on the ball and your head in the game." Focus on the present moment without distraction (*keep your eye on the ball*) and see the big picture, the purpose, and game plan (*and your head in the game*) so that everything you do moves you forward.

Group Momentum (Herd Mentality)

In 1848, a popular circus clown named Dan Rice raised awareness for presidential candidate Zachary Taylor's appearances using the tools at his disposal: music and a bandwagon. The idea gained momentum; soon "getting on the bandwagon" became popular for politicians hoping to cash in on Taylor's growing popularity, and an expression was born.

Our individual actions are easily swayed by the action of larger groups; this herd mentality has an enormous impact both on the stock market overall and on our own individual behaviors. *Group momentum* tends to keep stocks moving in the direction they're headed, as more people climb on or off the financial bandwagon, creating overinflated or undervalued stock prices, and consistently inaccurate analyst forecasts. When the stock market rises, we reach for our calculators to plan early retirement. When it declines, we worry whether we'll *ever* be able to retire. As more and more of us react to short-term events, our fears and hopes become self-fulfilling prophecies.

Herd mentality overreacts to trends and in so doing *creates* trends.

Wall Street analysts are not immune to this phenomenon. Research consistently indicates that consensus analyst forecasts range too high or too low by an average of 40 percent. Momentum largely occurs because of investors' tendency to sell winners more rapidly than losers, and to hold onto losing stocks longer because of hating to acknowledge mistakes. This momentum effect of buying and selling triggering more buying and selling causes stocks to continue in the direction in which they first moved.

Rx for Group Momentum

Stay open to other people's views and insights, but remember that the stock market is not a democracy: Just because the majority are swinging a certain direction does not mean that's where the results are going to show up. Be willing to take in new information, but distinguish emotional information from fundamental business data.

Remember that even "experts" have limbic systems. No matter what the magazine headlines, television pundits and financial gurus are saying, and how confidently they say it, remember that they are often wrong.

When in doubt, consult a trusted advisor and remember that even your financial planner is your employee, and you are the CEO. Do all that you can to make the best decisions you can— including sleeping on it—and then make your plan and stick to it.

Quiz: What Is Your Investing Mindset?

- Do you seem to consistently lose money on investments?
- Do you feel paralyzed or afraid when it comes to investing money?
- Do you feel overwhelmed by the prospect of learning more about managing and investing your money?
- Do you expect or allow other people to make money decisions for you, even if they are not experts?
- Do you respond to financial gains with depression or feelings of guilt?
- Do you respond to financial losses with self-recrimination or feelings of anger or futility?
- Is it painful for you to admit mistakes or to cut your losses?
- Do you have trouble putting aside thoughts of "what might have been if only" you had purchased investments earlier, or sold them earlier?
- Do you resist seeking suggestions and advice, even differing opinions, to judge a prospective investment or business decision?
- Do you feel you are fully able to make all your own financial decisions by yourself—despite consistent evidence to the contrary?

17 Common Investing Pitfalls and Their Remedies

1. **Not having a master plan informed by expert information and knowledge.**

   Rx: Design your own plan. Be sure you and your system are a comfortable fit. Not having a plan leaves you vulnerable to hot tips and emotional decisions. An objective, structured game plan includes goals, strategy, target points of date or money, regular (in time periods and/or dollar amounts) contribution to a savings and retirement fund.

2. **Not regarding investing as a business.**

   Rx: You are the CEO of your finances. What you do with your money is at least as important as how you obtain it. Investing is a business requiring the expenditure of time and money to yield return.

3. **Not using others' knowledge and expertise.**

   Rx: If you don't already have one, find a financial advisor whom you trust, and review your plan with him or her regularly. Base this review on a predetermined calendar time (once a year, quarterly, etc.) rather than as precipitated by an emotional event. Also consider forming a personal or business board of advisors or mastermind group to help brainstorm your financial plans.

4. **Inconsistently adhering to your plan.**

   Rx: Having a plan is half the battle; sticking to it is the other. When things are going very well or very badly—such as a bull or bear market, or a spectacular rise or fall of your stock—resist the pull to act. It is at times of strong emotional stimulation that your brain and mind have difficulty *not* reacting. In a rocking boat, one effective way to avoid seasickness is to focus on a fixed point on the distant horizon. Your financial plan is that fixed focal point, especially in times of storm. Keep your plan clearly in view, and stick to it, *especially* when you are most tempted to abandon it.

5. **Acting on someone else's formula, methodology, or system.**

   Rx: Set and prioritize your own goals. Clarify the resources you have available and identify the potential obstacles. Develop your own principles and objectively monitor your progress at regular intervals.

6. **Blaming others for your mistakes.**

   Rx: Own your decisions. Don't shoot the messenger, blame the broker, or fault the floor trader. When you admit your mistakes, you recognize the choices as yours, which puts you in charge. With ownership comes the capacity to avoid repeating the same mistakes.

7. **Setting goals to get rich quickly.**

   Rx: Fear and greed, the greatest enemies of any investor, lie within all of us. Patience and persistence are an investor's best friends.

8. **Being overconfident in your ability to pick stocks.**

   Rx: Be willing to admit mistakes, let go of losers, and recognize that success in one business arena may not transfer to success in another (investing).

9. **Failing to diversify.**

   Rx: *Wall Street Journal* personal finance columnist Jason Zweig concludes from his research that diversification "is the single most powerful way to prevent your brain from working against you." Remember Enron. Remember Marsh and McLennan. Spread your savings and investment money around different investments.

10. **Not designating separate portions of your portfolio for calculated risk and for secure, no-risk investment.**

    Rx: Like our perceptions of middle age and old age, our perception of what is risky changes as we approach it. Consider maintaining at least three piles of money: one for long-term retirement, one for value and growth investing, and one for speculative, aggressive growth—your gambling pile. Having a gambling pile insulates serious money from the vagaries of your amygdala and the yearnings of your dopamine receptors.

11. **Acting without full emotional acceptance of the decision.**

    Rx: If any part of you disagrees with what you are about to do, you will not be able to make a full commitment. Delaying a decision is better than acting on a half-hearted commitment.

12. **Becoming paralyzed by the fear of losing money.**

    Rx: Distinguish how much you can emotionally afford to lose, as well as how much financially you can afford to lose. Note the difference.

13. **Hoping that a stock will return to its former level.**

    Rx: Clinging to this continued hope may be a bad business decision. For a stock to return to break even after dropping, say, from $80 a share to $15, it would have to significantly outperform the market by growing at a rate of 15 percent every single year for 12 years straight.

14. **Being unwilling to cut losses short.**

    Rx: We naturally abhor losses and want to disregard them, holding onto the hope of reversal. When you cut a loss short by selling, you acknowledge it and make it real. This may seem painful, but is good: Ignoring reality can be expensive.

15. **Putting energy into things you can't determine.**

    Rx: Focus on what you can determine; accept and let go what you cannot. Focus on facts rather than feelings—a counterintuitive move at a time when feelings run high. Avoid frequent market monitoring to reduce exposure to reaction-producing (positive or negative information). Minimize emotion by having sound principles and a well-thought-out system in place.

16. **Disregarding stress.**

    Rx: Take a self-inventory at regular intervals. At stressful times, refrain from making significant decisions until you are calm and objective. Create a daily relaxation or meditation ritual.

17. **Making decisions on impulse.**

    Rx: Remember that there are few genuine emergencies in life, and investing isn't one of them. An appeal for instant action, a short-fuse deadline, or to get in quickly with a "chosen few" should all be pondered and researched. At the same time, getting stuck in a holding pattern of perpetual research and postponement can turn into avoidance of action, which may be fueled by the wish to avoid anticipated negative consequences. Make your decisions carefully—but make them.

Notes

1. Those previously named by other writers include anchoring, confirmation bias, extrapolation error, group momentum, loss aversion, perceived value, and sunk cost fallacy. Established concepts here newly applied include affinity bias, availability bias, and optimism bias. Those original to this writing include internal bargaining, invincibility bias, nostalgia bias, pattern bias, spending justification, spending rationalization, and transference fallacy.
2. Proceedings of the National Academy of Sciences, January 22, 2008, vol. 105, no. 3, 1050–1054.
3. http://www.usatoday.com/news/health/2008-03-04-placebo-effect_N.htm.
4. http://www.cba.ufl.edu/mkt/docs/mitra/ObjectiveQuality.pdf.

eight

SPEND, BABY, SPEND!

If Imelda Marcos changed her shoes three times a day, and never wore the same pair twice, it would take her more than two years and five months to work through her shoe supply as it existed on the day she fled Manila.

—"The Shoes of Imelda Marcos," **Time**, March 31, 1986

Shannon wanted to break away from her boyfriend in order to be emotionally and financially independent, but was frightened of being alone. When she and Bert finally parted ways she felt an intense urge to "go into a store and get something new—even some little things like a silver bracelet or tee-shirt—just to buy something new."

Shannon ended up charging $600 to buy a shirt, jacket, belt, shoes, and earrings—all of it at a shop where she and Bert had shopped together. She said, "I wanted to believe that I could still go and spend money. At the moment that I was purchasing those items, I felt powerful and confident. A few moments before that, I felt depleted and completely without power."

It wasn't that she really wanted the clothing and jewelry items; what Shannon really wanted was how it felt to buy them. The act of spending itself gave her a feeling of pleasure, power, and self-worth. Unfortunately, those feelings were temporary. In fact, once she was out of the store, she realized that the spending spree had put her in such a financial bind, she would have to call Bert to ask him to help her out.

You may not relate to the specifics of Shannon's story, but it probably still has the ring of familiarity. Most of us have been in situations where we have spent money and afterward found that the expenditure didn't live up to our expectations, or even that it turned out being a wholly different experience than we intended. It's no accident "buyer's remorse" is such a common expression.

The reason we get into trouble with money is that we think we're *thinking* about what we do. Because we are intelligent, self-aware beings, we continue to suffer under the illusion that we rule our actions with our thoughts. But we don't. When it comes to money, typically our *feelings* rule our actions, and thoughts come into the picture only afterward, like the CSI team brought onto the crime scene in its aftermath to sort it all out and come up with an explanation for how and why the heinous deed might have happened. Remember: Feelings come first, followed by actions, with thoughts coming in third—and depending on the state of the brain, often a very distant third indeed.

Spending is emotional. This is the critical point to remember. In fact, if there is nothing else you take from reading this book but these three words, chances are excellent that your financial life will still improve significantly, simply by recognizing this central truth. The act of spending changes how we feel—and feelings rule.

The Compulsive Spending Cycle

We spend for as many reasons as there are stories. We may spend to fill loneliness or emptiness, or to contain anxiety, or to make a statement of power and self-worth. The problem is that the effect doesn't last. Our attempts to spend our way to peace of mind don't address the true cause of our discomfort, and in time only make things worse as the tension release of spending is replaced by the stress of debt—which can trigger a new round of impulsive spending.

Shannon's story follows a typical sequence marked by distinct stages that tend to repeat themselves.

Discomfort → Targeting → Constriction → Justification → Discomfort

Discomfort. A rift in a relationship, a feeling of restlessness, or a sense of emptiness creates an urge for tangibility.

Targeting. We pinpoint that urge, giving it a concrete focus—new clothes, for example.

Constriction. Driven by the intensity of the underlying urge, we narrow that focus, causing us to lose sight of the big picture; issues such as affordability, utility, or need go out the window.

Justification. We reconcile the illogic of our actions by making up a story to fit the circumstances: We tell ourselves, "If I don't get it now, it may not be available again," or "To hell with it—I *deserve* this."

Discomfort. Reality eventually arrives in the form of guilt, shame, and the forced need to deal with the financial consequences: The credit card statement arrives, our spouse learns what we bought, we have to borrow to make up a shortfall, etc.

The actual enjoyment of the purchase is typically short-lived, and when the discomfort returns, perhaps is even amplified. The cycle begins again, often escalating to larger purchases and higher stakes, and in time what began as an occasional impulse unfolds into a full-fledged compulsion: *Impulsive spending* becomes *compulsive shopping*.

Compulsive shopping is an ongoing pattern of behavior characterized by the compelling urge to spend money, typically on things one can't afford, didn't plan to buy, and don't need or perhaps even really want. Like most addictions, compulsive shopping is typically an effort to remedy a depressed or empty feeling, or is driven by an emotional craving for the feeling of connectedness with others.

Quiz: Are You a Compulsive Spender?

Even those of us who are not in the grip of the full-blown compulsive spending cycle may have tendencies that run in that direction. See if any of the following descriptions feel familiar to you.

- Do you go shopping, whether in person or on the Internet, to escape feeling bored, empty, defeated, angry, or scared?
- After a setback or disappointment, does it feel like spending money will help you feel better?
- Do you shop or spend money in a way that creates conflicts for you, or between you and others?
- Do you spend impulsively and later wish you hadn't bought the items?
- Have your spending habits created chaos in your life?
- Do you buy things with your credit cards that you wouldn't buy if you had to pay cash?
- When you shop or make a purchase, does your mood change?
- When you spend money, do you sometimes feel a secret thrill, as if you're doing something taboo, dangerous, or defiant?
- Do you think about money that you don't have, money you wish you had, or money you owe, and then still go out to shop?
- Do you compromise your life or leisure to adjust to your shopping debts?
- Are you unable to fully enjoy what you purchase because you feel bad, guilty, ashamed, or embarrassed about your purchases?
- Do you make purchases to enhance your self-esteem?
- If no one else noticed or observed that you had bought certain items, would you be significantly less likely to buy them?

If you answered *yes* to any of the above questions, you may be using money or shopping as a way to regulate your feelings or esteem. If so, your spending may to some degree be in control of *you*, rather than the other way around.

When spending gets out of control, it is tempting to apply a superficial limitation: Cut up the store credit card; make a promise that you won't do it again; set yourself a "house limit" of X dollars per store. The problem is, these are all efforts to logically control your spending, when the issue isn't your logical mind, it's your feelings—and it is your feelings, not your thoughts, that are dominating here. The only lasting solution is to address the feelings themselves, which means dealing with whatever the underlying issues are that you are seeking or escaping from.

Competitive Spending and Conspicuous Spending

Research reveals a fascinating perspective on the relative value of monetary wealth: In one study, given a choice between earning $100,000 in a social circle where everyone else earns about $150,000, or earning $80,000 in a community where the typical earning is $60,000, we'll take the smaller salary—because although it's smaller, it's still bigger than what those around us are earning. It's not a drive to be rich that we feel so much as a drive to be richer than those around us.

Competitive spending is beautifully captured in the archetypal expression, "keeping up with the Joneses," and has been a staple of ridicule for theater, film, and television comedies and sit-coms in our upwardly mobile culture.

Competitive spenders use the expenditure of money to measure social prestige and to compete with others in their social group. Such competition, of course, can quickly become an endlessly upward spiral—a neighborhood fiscal arms race. Each new benchmark drives the next raising of the bar; the only way to assert your superior position in the escalating pecking order is to spend ever more money on visible markers of wealth—houses, cars, clothing, furniture, and other consumer goods.

Spending becomes an activity engaged in not in order to enjoy the objects of purchase but for the acclaim or admiration of others. An audience is required to witness the lavishness of the purchase. Thus a competitive spender may make a great show of picking up the check at dinner, or may give money to organizations that publicize the monetary gifts they receive, and competitive spending also becomes more and conspicuous.

In Chapter 1 we met Barbara, who had fallen into a pattern of buying herself extravagant jewelry and clothing despite a fixed salary that barely supported her and her two children. Like other conspicuous spenders, Barbara saw money as a measure of social prestige.

For generations, the paunchy, aging, overgenerous "sugar daddy" with a young trophy woman hanging on his arm has been a familiar cartoon figure in society pages and at red carpet events. He is an object of ridicule not because of his irresistible urge to spend in public but because his choice of what (and whom) to spend it on guarantees that he'll be repaid in the false coin of insincere flattery and feigned sexual attraction. He is sadly comical because he is seeking to buy something that is far superior when it's free.

And that is the core tragedy of competitive and conspicuous spending, like all dysfunctional types of spending: The spender's true goal, whether it is affection, intimacy, prestige, esteem, comfort, or connection, is something that *money cannot buy*.

Revenge Spending

Where conspicuous spending is by definition a distinctly public form of consumption, *revenge spending* is often carried out quietly and privately, as a form of secret self-indulgence used to express anger or resentment.

Lisa was a self-confessed "catalog addict" who spent hours browsing the stacks of catalogs she had delivered to her home, not monthly, not weekly, but *daily*. She often couldn't remember what products she'd ordered from which company, so when the packages arrived they seemed to her more like presents than like purchases.

Lisa was most likely to make a purchase immediately after a quarrel with her husband, Jack. The couple argued frequently, and many of their disputes centered on money. Lisa considered Jack tight-fisted and selfish. Jack viewed Lisa's spending as irresponsible.

Lisa could not tolerate arguing as long as her husband could. While he seemed to draw energy from his anger as the argument went on, she would feel more and more drained. When the quarrel had gone on too long for Lisa, she would simply withdraw, not conceding but simply bowing out and postponing the outcome for another day. Going directly from quarrel to defiance, she ordered clothes. It was her way of saying, "My desires count, too." *You ought to send me a dozen roses after that fight*, she'd think, *but since you're not going to, I'll just send myself a new dress instead.*

Women are subtly socialized to engage in revenge spending. The limits on assertiveness that women often learn in childhood can keep them from carrying an argument to its conclusion. That premature withdrawal from conflict often leaves unexpressed issues and residues of anger that can later (or almost immediately, in Lisa's case) be expressed indirectly.

Men, too, engage in revenge spending. A man may buy himself an expensive piece of recreational equipment, or even deliberately blow some of his paycheck at a bar to express anger at his wife—especially if he's angry because she's just bought something for herself. If he experienced deprivation from a withholding mother, his wife's actions may resonate with this experience and spark an outburst of revenge spending. Or he may seek indirect revenge on a withholding or disapproving father when he indulges in some long-desired and not really affordable purchase just after a fight with his male boss.

Pathological *Under*spending

Of course, not all of our spending problems are a result of overspending.

Stephen made enough money as an accountant to maintain a good standard of living, but he was overcome by such a strong inner fear of economic insecurity that his ability to spend money comfortably and reasonably was deeply inhibited. He tried to combat his fear by combining a minimal, subsistence level of spending with a maximum rate of saving. Still, he didn't feel satisfied and continued to worry about his finances beyond any realistic point. This pattern had afflicted him for most of his 34 years.

Stephen's life and pleasures were equally constricted. He was cautious about dating too much and especially too extravagantly. He spent considerable time hunting for bargains, and used much of his free time repairing his own home and car so he wouldn't have to pay someone else to do it.

Although he could well afford them, he deprived himself of many things he needed, and he regretted each dollar he spent, as though it were a departed friend whose loss he actively mourned. In fact, Stephen drew satisfaction from actual contact with money—not only with cash but also with bank books, deposit slips, and other symbols of his security.

Consciously money-hungry and unconsciously love-hungry, Stephen had interpersonal relationships that were equally spartan and isolated. As a child, he had lived a strictly regimented life. His parents made liberal use of directives and punishments to make him feel guilty if he didn't respond exactly as they wanted. They would reward him with money for good deeds, good grades, and other outstanding adherence to family protocol. Money, the reward he learned to elicit quite effectively, came to represent the love, affection, and security he desired.

As an adult, he rewarded himself for outstanding work (such as cleaning his entire house himself) with a bag of chocolate chip cookies, a rare "extravagant" expense. He equated spending money with a fear of losing control. Stephen hoarded his feelings as carefully as his money.

Will's money behavior was similar to Stephen's, but in his case, it not only hurt him personally but also effectively impeded his career.

A perennial bachelor and expert technician with a comfortable income, by age 37 Will was easily able to afford a large house in a good neighborhood. But he could not bear to pay the utility bills for services it took to make his house comfortable. In order to save on utility bills, Will often stayed late after work hours to use the electric lights in his office. At home, he painstakingly sorted all his trash for composting, recycling, and burning—he warmed his house by burning household trash in his fireplace—and paid no garbage bills at all, creating some awkwardness when he had to explain to city sanitation officials why he required no garbage service.

Will found a sort of social life as a Scout leader, teaching young boys his skills at recycling, repairing, and "making do" with almost no resources.

Will also could not bear to spend the money it would take to buy the appropriate clothing he needed for work. He also had increasing difficulty keeping up with the latest developments in his fast-changing field because of his reluctance to pay for the books and equipment he needed to do so.

Healthy spending, like healthy eating, is not a simple matter of "the less the better." A balanced, healthy approach to spending your money means using your money in those ways that best serve your values and your goals in life. The irrational compulsion to *save* can be just as negative an influence in your life as the irrational compulsion to *spend*.

Money as Conflict

Former beauty queen Donna Campbell's suspicions about her husband Amim Ramdass began when he disconnected the phone line and kept abruptly turning off the family television. His excuses sounded thin; to her, it almost seemed as if he was trying to censor the flow of information into their home. But what could be so terrible that he wouldn't want her to see it on TV? And what could that have to do with incoming telephone calls?

Finally Donna did an online search on her husband's name and soon discovered what it was he had been hiding: He had won a share of a $19 million jackpot with some friends at work, and had been trying to keep her from hearing the news of his good fortune.

Donna sued for half the money, but by this time Amim had vanished, making it impossible for the process servers to do their job. After months of trying to locate him, Donna showed up alone at their hearing—where Presiding Circuit judge Jennifer D. Bailey dismissed the suit, suggesting that "a divorce court might be a better venue to resolve the dispute."

Judge Bailey had a point. Sometimes money issues in a marriage are about money; often they are about something else. As we saw in Chapter 2, money can serve as a tangible focus for the expression of a wide range of feelings and meanings. Because money is such a pliable and versatile container for any number of issues, it can also serve as the staging ground for virtually any sort of hidden conflict. Along with sex and food, money is one of the three most common vehicles on which emotional issues hitchhike.

Unspoken assumptions about money, power, and gender often remain silent until crystallized by a specific situation. That situation might be sudden scarcity, such as the loss of a job, or sudden windfall, as in Amim Ramdass's case. It might be the role reversal that takes place when one spouse begins earning more income than the other. Inheritance and divorce can also serve to bring money matters to center stage.

One money dance couples sometimes do is a sort of transference tango through which one partner projects some unwanted or disavowed aspect of self onto the other. The way this typically plays out, one assumes the role of desire, and the other becomes the obstacle. For example, the husband (or wife) wants to buy a new car, and the wife (or husband) wants to save. One wants to have sex, the other is not ready. When eating out, one wants to experiment with a new, pricier restaurant, while the other adopts the conservative stance: "Why not eat where we always eat? We know we like the food there—and it's not so expensive."

The truth, of course, is that this is mostly play-acting. The forces of desire and obstacle, adventurous and cautious, both exist within both parties, but as long as one of the two components is subcontracted to the other, neither has to recognize it.

These roles of *no* and *yes* may shift, such as when the spendthrift is suddenly no longer opposed because the tightwad suddenly says, "Oh, okay, let's go ahead and buy it." The spendthrift must then either own the avoided aspect of him- or herself, which is the relatively more rare result, or make a corresponding shift him- or herself: "Well, wait a minute, maybe you had a point and we shouldn't be so hasty."

Emotional inertia dictates that the implicit contract of each partner taking a role to embody half the ambivalence of the other should remain unbroken. If one dance partner threatens to break the pattern by stepping out of character, the other mirrors the new step, and they continue the dance for a time in their newly reversed roles, until switching back again, which usually occurs fairly soon. Thus the system is maintained and the dysfunctional equilibrium is maintained—and the genuine needs, feelings, viewpoints, and thoughts of both parties are never fully explored.

And it is not simply that we learn to play these roles during the course of a developing relationship: Sometimes we actually bring them to the table and they play a role in sparking the relationship in the first place. Partners are often selected, in other words, whether consciously or unconsciously, for just these purposes.

Actually, it would be an oversimplification to assert that this is an entirely dysfunctional exchange. The hoarder and the spender both have justifiable reasons for their contrasting points of view. It makes sense to have the security of saving. And it makes sense to enjoy present living. Both are reasonable and even noble financial aspirations. The dysfunction lies in the reluctance to communicate openly and honestly about our genuine feelings and values—not a good precedent for a long and fulfilling relationship.

His Money, Her Money

One reason money often plays such a complex role in relationships is that men and women tend to regard money with different eyes. Research has shown that gender informs a significant number of our spending and investing decisions. In the course of my practice, I've often noted that men tend to view money as representing power and identity, while women tend to regard money as security and autonomy.

Here is a sampling of findings on gender and money from various surveys and studies:

- Men tend to invest to grow their principle; women invest to protect their principle.
- Women investors are less aggressive, trade less, and consistently earn higher return than men.
- Women tend to worry more about losing money than about the risk of doing nothing; men see inaction as the greater danger.
- Women tend to feel guilt if investment money is lost; men are less likely to feel personally responsible, and tend instead to deflect blame onto the market, the economy, or the broker.
- Women perceive the role of a financial advisor as a long-term and trusting relationship, with the advisor in control of investment decisions. Men see themselves as being in control of investment decisions, so building a trusting relationship with an advisor is far less important.
- Men orient toward results; women put a higher priority on the relationship than on the results.
- The business conversation for men primarily preserves independence and maintains their position in a group; women focus initially on connection and intimacy and see these qualities as facilitating the business transaction.
- Men view effective money management in terms of long-term strategies, such as planning for taxes, retirement, and choosing

investments. Women view good money management in terms of shorter-range goals, such as finding bargains, balancing the checkbook, and eliminating debts.

Money Deception

One of the most common symptoms of dysfunction in a relationship, as Donna Campbell learned the hard way, is *money deception*. A survey conducted by *Money* magazine found that 40 percent of spouses have lied about the price of a purchase to their partner, and about one out of six had even hidden purchases outright. Women were more likely to have misrepresented the price of the purchase for clothing or gifts, while men understated technological toys and sports tickets. Men more likely spent on themselves and hid higher-ticket items, while women hid items bought for the children and those costing under $100.

Even more revealing was that 44 percent said that in their opinion, it was okay to keep financial secrets from your spouse, at least under certain circumstances. And a stunning 71 percent—nearly three out of four—admitted to one kind of money secret or another.

One might be tempted to assume that, as in Amim Ramdass's case, money deception is most often motivated by greed or the desire to have "more for me and less for you." But nearly half the respondents in this survey said they deceived a spouse *in order to avoid conflict*. Some of the blurred thinking in this deception may also be self-deception, confusing not wanting to be judged with not wanting to be held accountable to it. To avoid a spouse's disapproval, anger, or judgment may eclipse personal accountability. In this same survey, 29 percent misled family and friends about their financial situation. In essence, they faked a lifestyle.[1]

Compounding the plot twist of money deception is that we often hide our deceitfulness not only from others but also from ourselves. Strange as it sounds, when it comes to money, we often come to believe our own lies. For example, a study by the financial services firm Genworth Financial found that many Americans spend more than they can in an effort to keep up with people around them. No surprise there, right? But here it gets interesting: While eight out of ten of the study's subjects could point to this failing in others, only one in ten recognized it in themselves.

The *Money* magazine study cited above found that about one out of three people (36 percent) go to great lengths to avoid facing up to financial reality. One in six avoided seeing financial advisors, and about the same number refused to look at bank balances or financial statements, all for the same reason: to avoid having to think about money. More than one in ten (13 percent) put off paying bills, not necessarily because they didn't have the money, but because it was a way of staving off a reality they didn't want to face.

A Money Exercise for Couples

Experts disagree on exactly how large a factor money issues are in marital discord and divorce, but all available evidence makes it pretty clear that it ranks right up there with sex as one of the major causes in relationship breakdown. And at the heart of both problems—money and sex—lies the same issue: lack of trust and communication.

The following exercise is designed to help build a foundation of trust and communication by exploring your individual money stories, that is, by becoming more aware of how you each uniquely look at money and feel about money.

The first part is done separately. Each of you sit down with pen and paper and write out your answers to the following money questions. Don't write essays here, or even full sentences; keep your written answers as brief as possible. It usually takes just one or several words to identify each answer.

1. What are the three things you have done with money that make you feel the proudest?

   a. _____

   b. _____

   c. _____

2. What are the three things you have done with money that make you feel the most embarrassed or ashamed?

   a. _____

   b. _____

   c. _____

3. What are the three smartest money choices you've ever made?

   a. _____

   b. _____

   c. _____

4. What are the three worst mistakes you have made with or about money?

   a. _____

   b. _____

   c. _____

5. What are the three best money investments you have made?

   a. _____

   b. _____

   c. _____

6. What are the three worst money investments you have made?

    a. _____

    b. _____

    c. _____

7. What are the three things most important to you that you've bought with money?

    a. _____

    b. _____

    c. _____

8. What are the three things most important to you that you've traded for money?

    a. _____

    b. _____

    c. _____

9. What are the three most important things that money will buy for you?

    a. _____

    b. _____

    c. _____

10. What are the three things that money will not buy for you?

    a. _____

    b. _____

    c. _____

11. What are the three things you would agree to give up in your life for more money?

    a. _____

    b. _____

    c. _____

12. What are the three most important things you would do with more money?

    a. _____

    b. _____

    c. _____

Once you've both made your lists, sit together and one at a time, read your list out loud to your partner. As you go down the list, feel free to elaborate a bit on your brief written answers.

Your partner's job is to listen with compassion and acceptance, and without any judging, criticizing, or evaluating of any kind. Before you begin, the partner agrees, out loud, not to comment on any of the content spoken—only on the process and only in positive terms, such as expressing gratitude and respect for the honesty or courage it takes to share any especially difficult material.

When you have fully gone through one list together, then switch, and have the other partner read his or her list.

If, when you are the listening partner, you feel tempted at any point to judge or criticize in any way, resist it. Just take a breath and let it go.

If at any point the listening partner *does* make a critical or judgmental comment, then the rules of the game dictate that you start back at the beginning again, so you can go through the entire list together. It's crucial that you both work through the entire list without any evaluative or interpretive interruption.

Think of it as the still surface of a pond. If either party pitches a rock into the water, you must both sit together on the pond's edge until the ripples have receded again.

Notes

1. "Secrets, Lies and Money," by Scott Medintz; *Money*, April 1, 2005.

nine

INTO THIN AIR: THE SECRET LANGUAGE OF DEBT

Then, the real estate market crashed. I owed billions upon billions of dollars—$9.2 billion, to be exact. I passed a beggar on the street and realized he was worth $9.2 billion more than I was.

—Donald Trump, *How to Get Rich*

During 2008, the once prosperous country of Zimbabwe was in the grips of a massive economic crisis. Faced with hyperinflation so severe that prices doubled every 17 days, Zimbabwe's central bank eventually issued a $100 *billion* note.

A hundred billion dollars: sounds pretty impressive. Sadly for Zimbabweans, a $100 billion bill was worth just one U.S. dollar, an amount that at the time wouldn't quite buy a loaf of bread in that country (although it would get you four oranges). The currency was so inflated that the average Zimbabwean had a weekly budget that ran into the trillions.

One hundred billion is the number one followed by eleven zeroes, a number so huge that counting it would take several hundred lifetimes. Indeed, the figure was so large that most cash registers, calculators, and bank ATMs in the country were unable to handle the number of digits. And it was as unfathomable a sum for the people of Zimbabwe as it was for their machines. Their money had become so large it was an abstraction. Many even stopped using the bills altogether, and turned to gas coupons as a form of currency, while companies began to pay their workers a portion of their wages in food instead of cash. Paper money, the universal standard for trade and value, had begun to lose its purpose.

As if to illustrate just how great the gap between cash and actual value had widened, the Zimbabwean $100 billion note that was worth just one U.S. dollar soon appeared listed for auction on eBay—priced at 80 bucks.

And in January 2009, the Zimbabwe's central bank announced that it would soon be releasing $10 trillion, $20 trillion, $50 trillion, and $100 trillion notes.

The Zimbabwean financial crisis is an example of how intangible money can become, and the weird extremes and convoluted meanings that can result. But you don't have to travel to Africa to find extreme examples of how money can turn from reality into fantasy. Right here in the United States, we managed to crash our own economy and trigger the first genuine global financial crisis in history, all by playing a game of "let's pretend."

The game itself was pretty simple: We decided that living in nice houses was such a neat idea, we would all just pretend that we could afford them, even if we couldn't. Banks and mortgage companies started lending us money based not on how much we could reasonably expect to pay back, but on how much we all *pretended* we could pay back.

That, in a nutshell, is the essence of the secret language of debt, and the subprime soap opera offers a classic object lesson in how extraordinarily compelling and seductive that language can be. Spending money generates the perception (read: the *illusion*) that we actually have that money to spend. This illusion is fostered by advertising (there are a few things in life that are priceless, "and for everything else, there's Mastercard"), and we willingly collude with Madison Avenue through rationalization ("Don't worry, we have a year to pay it off"), optimism bias ("By the time the bill comes due, that raise should have come through"), and all the other tricks of the mind we discussed in Chapter 8.

In today's highly leveraged culture, choices abound to wink at limits and blur boundaries. Overdraft checks and lines of credit allow the spending of money we don't have based on promises of repayment we can't make. Home equity loans and margin accounts allow using a house and a stock as if they were fully owned and paid for. Deferred payment schedules delay reality's timeline. Debt wears many costumes of modern credit instruments. We may not know exactly what the term "credit default swap" means in detail, but we are all profoundly familiar with its essence, because it represents an activity we have engaged in enthusiastically from the days of our childhood: *Let's play pretend.*

Cash Cows and Shell Games

In a sense, the game of *let's play pretend* lies at the core of the entire notion of a monetary system: A dollar is only worth a dollar's worth of stuff because we all agree that that's what it's worth.

It didn't start out that way. The oldest form of human economy is the system of exchange known as *barter,* in which items of equivalent value are traded for each other. Livestock and grain, needed by all and readily traded for other items of more particular value, are considered some of the earliest forms of money. The modern words *salt* and *salary* both derive from the Roman word *salarium.* This is no coincidence: Roman soldiers were paid in salt. There was no pretending involved here: Cattle, wheat, and salt were very real essentials of life.

Bartering was an effective economic system, but it relied on both parties wanting what the other person had at that moment in time. Swapping a cow for a sack of grain and a few spears was not always practical and was complicated by the fact that there was no clear standard of value to determine what a cow, a sack of grain, or a spear was really worth. Thus developed over time the idea of *commodities*: tangible, tradable materials that possessed an inherent usefulness—metal, for example, which could be reliably fashioned into tools, weapons, and other essential objects—and therefore could be easily accepted as trade, because they could be reliably traded again in the future.

Representative money, the idea that something with little or no practical value could serve as a *symbol* of value, was the historic first step in the abstraction of money. Cowrie shells, stones, and other objects were assigned value, becoming the world's first true currencies. In the Micronesian island of Yap, twenty-first-century tourists can view the giant round stones that are still in use today as a form of payment.

For centuries, metal coins bridged the gap between usable commodities and purely representative symbols, because they still held some inherent "real" function as valuable objects that could be melted, reshaped, and repurposed if necessary. The abstraction of money took another leap forward in seventh-century China, when the first paper notes appeared; by the ninth century, the Chinese government had moved the nation's economy from iron coins to the new paper money.

An original plot twist occurred in the early eighteenth century when the Scottish economist John Law introduced the idea that an institution could offer more notes than it had gold to back them, by securing the notes at a future value with government land rather than gold. Forerunner of the modern bank system, this novel concept catapulted France from a struggling nation to a solvent one and created so much new wealth for so many that the French coined the new word *millionaire*. Unfortunately, Law's pioneering concept of virtual wealth was a two-edged coin, and his massive land-speculation project in Louisiana, now known as the "Mississippi Bubble," led to the utter collapse of the French stock market and ruination of the French economy (along with the bankrupting of many of those new millionaires). It would be 80 years before the country reintroduced a paper currency.

Abstract though it was, paper was still generally tied to something physical of value, such as gold, but even that tenuous level of tangibility vanished in the United States in 1971 when the federal government took our economy off the "gold standard" by ending the convertibility of dollars to gold. Paper money was now truly independent of material reality. From gold as currency, to a piece of paper backed by gold, to the piece of paper all by itself, the abstraction of money had reached escape velocity.

In the decades since, credit cards, debit cards, online banking, electronic cash, and other digitizations of the dollar have pushed the boundaries of money reality even further. It is now possible to spend money using cell phones, retinal scans, and fingerprints. We can pay by typing, swiping, speaking, or scanning. As money transforms into something entirely ethereal that exists only as digital information, we'll see it embedded in everything from our clothing to our physical bodies. According to *The Economist*, frequent flyer miles are now the world's second largest form of currency.

In 2004, electronic payments surpassed cash for the first time in U.S. history. AC Nielsen research predicts that by the year 2020, a mere 10 percent of U.S. transactions will be in cash. Cash may still be king, but it is perched on a shaky throne.

The Abstraction of Money

In 2002, a company named Black Snow Interactive opened an office in Tijuana, Mexico. Running 24 hours a day, the company maintained three shifts of low-wage workers whose sole occupation was to continuously play the online game Dark Age of Camelot. The workers would gradually increase the value of the game's virtual characters and their possessions—then auction them off online for real-world dollars.

In 2005, Edward Castronova, associate professor of economics at California State University at Fullerton, studied the virtual economy of another online game, Everquest. He found that the game's online economy theoretically made it the seventy-seventh richest country on earth (ranking somewhere between Russia and Bulgaria), and made its currency more valuable than the Japanese Yen.

When Sony, the game's creator, prohibited the sale of virtual Everquest goods in the real world, the result was a thriving real-world black market for the virtual-world goods.

Researchers are not the only ones aware of our vulnerability to the abstraction of money. Casino owners have long recognized that having their patrons gamble with plastic chips generates a far bigger profit to the casinos than letting them gamble with stacks of actual cash. This idea has spread from the pit to the casino floor, where a nickel slot machine that takes an actual nickel instead of a plastic card or a token has become a rarity.

Credit card companies have worked out their own version of the casino's highly profitable *let's play pretend* strategy: They now mail "checkbooks" to their customers that allow them to write a check at any time. Of course, the money to back purchases made with these "checks" does not come from an actual checking account, but is simply added to the balance on the card—but the sales letters don't emphasize that. Rather, they point out the convenience of being able to buy whatever you want with a scrap of paper you just received in your mailbox.

An estimated 25 percent of the world's actual paper currency is used for illegal purposes. Drugs, terrorism, and illegal weapons all rely heavily on cash. In the eyes of government and enforcement agencies, that's a compelling case for continuing the abstraction of money—digital money, so the argument goes, would be easier to track and control (and, by the way, to tax). In fact, that's exactly the tack Sony attempted to take: In an effort to stem the black market transactions for Everquest, the company launched its own currency exchange. However, while the new exchange did cut down on black market transactions, it immediately also opened the door for money-launderers to use the system.

The Great Illusion

Whether or not it helps authorities crack down on crime or feeds the hand that steals it, the abstraction of money certainly makes our everyday life more convenient in many ways. It makes money easier to carry, access, account for, and leverage. The problem, of course, is that it also makes it easier to *spend*.

With accelerating ease and temptation to spend virtual money, debt accumulation has become an enormous and growing national problem. Offers of low-interest credit cards regularly arrive in the mail, appealing both to need and desire. As of the end of 2008, Americans owed about $2.5 trillion in consumer debt,[1] nearly three times the value of the nation's total circulating currency.[2] In 2003, the total consumer debts assigned to America's collection agencies, resulting primarily from credit cards, healthcare, and student loans, totaled $135 billion. In the years since this figure has more than doubled.

According to the public advocacy organization Demos, the average U.S. family now has six credit cards with a combined limit of $21,000. The average American household, according to Carddebt.com, owes more than $9,000 in unpaid credit card balances.[3]

Steve, a market consultant, carries a credit card balance that has not gone up or down significantly in two years. He regularly admonishes himself to devise a system to pay it off, to charge no more, even to just take the money from savings to pay it off. Instead, he transfers balances from one credit card to another. Like 50 million other Americans, Steve is what card companies call a *revolver*. Marketing studies profile the revolver as someone relatively young, recently relocated, earning less than his or her peers, and bargaining internally to use credit cards as a way to supplement income, perhaps for a brief period. Revolvers have a greater number of cards than nonrevolvers. (The affluent, with fewer cards, are least likely to revolve.) Two out of three cardholders (and 40 percent of all Americans) are revolvers; altogether they pay in excess of $18 billion a year in finance penalty fees alone.[4]

That's $18 billion to accomplish nothing other than moving debt from one place to another. Talk about paper-pushers.

Now kids can get in on the act, too. In 2004 a company named Legend Credit Inc. launched a "Hello Kitty" branded debit MasterCard designed for children. The card's stated goal was to "help kids learn to manage their finances." The Kitty card is prepaid: The parents activate an account and put money into it before children start spending. Hello Kitty enables parents to bypass the age restriction of 18 in order to open a credit card account. Currently the Kitty Card has a $15 annual activation fee, a $3 monthly maintenance fee, a $1.50 ATM user fee, and a $1-per-minute fee for the privilege of talking to a customer service agent.

Credit card companies make the most money when the cardholder falls behind. According to Cardweb.com, Americans pay an average of only 14 to 16 percent of their credit card balances each month. Many simply make the minimum payment without thinking twice. For a credit card debt of $2,500, making the minimum payment each month at 17 percent interest will take over 30 years to pay off, at a the total cost of $7,733. A debt of $5,000 would take 40 years to retire. Total cost: $16,305.

As Scarlett O'Hara said in the closing moments of *Gone with the Wind*, "Home. I'll go home. And I'll think of some way to get him back. After all . . . tomorrow is another day."

Anatomy of an Addiction

For those who suffer with eating disorders, food is anything but simple nutrition. Presented with a plate of pasta, an anorexic is faced not with mere caloric fuel but with a host of symbolic meanings, from nurturing and comfort long denied to control, protest, and power. For many of us, money is exactly like that.

Perhaps the greatest negative impact of money's abstraction is that the more intangible it becomes, the more we try to do intangible things with it. We shop for a new home or car, but we're really seeking self-esteem, peace of mind, or happiness. We buy video games and clothing, but we're really trying to buy the love of our children and our peers. Like the anorexic faced with a plate of powerful symbolism, our wallets are filled with plastic cards that stand for anything and everything. And like the anorexic attempting to fill a need with something that cannot fill it, the compelling yet ultimately unfulfilling rush of spending can become gravely addicting.

Remember Denise, the avid China-doll collector whom we met in Chapter 3? At the height of her obsession, Denise was pulling $8,000 to $10,000 from her dwindling trust fund every month to finance her purchases.

Denise had made strenuous efforts to curtail her Internet spending, but when one is addicted to something, the hardest thing to do is nothing. Collecting was the one arena of Denise's life where she consistently seemed to be effective, and whenever she would attempt to stem the tide of her continuous buying spree, she would feel worthless.

For Denise, the story of shopping is the promise of supplying what is missing, of feeling better. She described the urge to shop as a desperate, driven yearning for something or someone; an emptiness so vague and formless that she felt baffled about its meaning. She simply felt a compelling urge to "hold onto something" specific, concrete, palpable. If she didn't, she said, she would feel she "would burst."

Denise described her state of mind after she was online as an extended dissociation—"zoned out" in front of her computer. As a child, Denise had learned this as a means of surviving trauma: When she could not physically escape being sexually abused by her sister, she could escape *internally* by dissociating. As an adult, she extended and elaborated the salvific effect by escaping into the Internet.

Even though she knew, logically, that she was depleting her trust fund with her compulsive purchasing, that knowledge did not prevent her from continuing. Denise explained that buying something with a credit card, especially over the Internet, was "like getting it free." It was as if, for that moment, she felt satisfied, without any thought of future accounting or consequence. The reality of her pain, already one step removed by transference onto the act of buying dolls, was further removed by using her credit card on the Internet—a symbol of a symbol of a symbol.

The Debt Cycle

Debt problems don't appear overnight. They sneak up on us, starting with our first student credit card or a small home equity line of credit, and snowball to become something beyond our ability to repay. That gradual creep is no accident. It doesn't "just happen." It is the direct result of a sequence of behaviors driven by our money story.

As with the scenario of compulsive spending we looked at in Chapter 8, the process of accumulating debt happens through the ongoing repetition of a self-reinforcing cycle.

Compulsion → Shame → Disavowal → Compulsion

We will examine the stages in the debt cycle one by one.

Compulsion

The debt cycle begins with an urge to buy something that we cannot right now afford to buy—and that we *know* we cannot afford to buy. Even though we know we cannot afford it, we feel compelled to buy it anyway, because of how we believe it will make us feel.

Again, the core truth that underlies the entire mechanism of debt is these three simple words: *spending is emotional.* Motivated by such driving forces as conspicuous consumption, revenge spending, a sense of emptiness, or craving for connection—or any one of a thousand other emotional impulses—that compelling urge to spend creates a need that drowns out the internal call for logic, reason, and common sense.

How do you meet that need when you don't *have* the money to spend? By using credit: the illusion of money. Credit creates spending power, and we equate spending power with *financial* power. Card in hand, we head for the mall or home computer.

Shame

If all we did was spend more than we had, there would be no cycle. We'd return from the store, say, "Ohmigosh, what have I done?!" and then budget the rest of the week, month, or year to make up for the shortfall created in our moment of lapsed judgment.

But things are not that simple. We don't return home and say, "Ohmigosh, what have I done?!" and then make a payment plan. We say, "What have I done?"—and then, after looking over our shoulder to see if anyone is watching, we set about wiping down the crime scene to remove our fingerprints and erase all evidence of culpability.

These two responses form the next two stages of the cycle.

First, that "Ohmigosh, what have I done?" For those caught in the debt cycle, this is more than a realization or a quick recovery of perspective. Instead, when reality catches up with us it brings with it a punitive message. *How could you be so stupid?* we tell ourselves. *You knew you couldn't afford that! What's wrong with you?* That mental glance over our shoulder to see if anyone has seen us walk into our home with the smoking gun in our shopping bag is quite telling: We hope nobody else sees what we've done.

But even if nobody else sees it, *we* see it. Not understanding how readily the prefrontal cortex can be sidestepped by the emotional drives of the limbic system, we cannot grasp how or why we could have acted in such an irresponsible way—and our self-castigation blankets us with a sense of *shame*.

Disavowal

Research has shown that credit card users tend to underestimate significantly how much they owe on credit cards. Lawrence Ausubel, an economist at the University of Maryland, found that cardholders admit to only four of every ten dollars they owe.

Why would intelligent people willfully disavow 60 percent of their debt? For the same reason that many alcoholics underreport the number of their arrests for drunk driving, and even lie about how many drinks they have had that very day. The same reason people suffering with eating disorders may hide food in their dresser drawers. The common denominator is shame, which leads us to bottle up the shameful actions as a closely guarded secret.

This is where our mental wiping off of fingerprints comes into play: We wish we hadn't done what we did and so decide to pretend that we actually *didn't*. Common disavowal tactics include: not opening bills when they come and putting them away where we won't see the envelop; paying the minimum on credit card statements while carefully avoiding seeing the actual balance due; hiding bills or statements from a spouse or other family member; lying about bills owed or balances due, or about a purchase price; and shunting balances from one credit card to another.

One of my clients noticed that each time she tried to openly discuss the state of her finances, her throat would literally close up as if in an allergic reaction, making any honest discussion about money nearly impossible. She was deep in the third stage of the debt cycle: Ashamed of her debt, she was physiologically determined to keeping it a secret, even from anyone who might be able to help.

This is precisely the tragedy of the debt cycle. Because once we enter the stage of disavowal and engage the fantasy that the debt isn't really there, to our emotional brain it is as if the debt does not in fact exist—and it's a short trip to the mall, computer, or car lot to start the next round of the cycle.

A Debt Quiz

Answer each of the following questions with a *yes* or *no*, circling the scoring number in the corresponding column. For the first 10 questions, each *no* scores 5 points, and each *yes* scores *minus* 5. The next two questions are each worth 15 points, and the last is worth 20. When you've answered all the questions and circled all your points, add up your total score.

Question	Yes	No
1. Do you routinely make minimum payments on credit card balances?	−5	+5
2. Are the balances on your credit card statements gradually increasing every month?	−5	+5
3. Do you have a balance on one or more cards of more than 50 percent of the credit limit for that card?	−5	+5
4. Do you often use cash advances on your credit cards to pay other bills?	−5	+5
5. Do you routinely "play the float" on cards (juggle payments between cards) in order to pay bills?	−5	+5
6. Do you regularly have past due bills, rent, or mortgage payments?	−5	+5
7. Do you have little or no savings?	−5	+5
8. Have you been denied credit or had a credit card purchase declined during the last quarter?	−5	+5
9. Have you had one or more checks bounce during the last quarter?	−5	+5
10. Have you had one or more notices or phone calls from a collection agency during the last quarter?	−5	+5
11. Do you ever hide, misrepresent, or neglect to mention a debt to your spouse or other family member?	−15	+15

(Continued)

Question	Yes	No
12. Do you ever hide a bill or credit card statement from your spouse or other family member?	–15	+15
13. Are you unable to state, offhand and without sitting down to go through your records, the exact total amount of money you presently owe?	–20	+20

Total Score

Possible scores range from 100, a perfect score, suggesting you have no significant problem with debt, to *minus* 100. Obviously, the lower your score, the more likely you are to some extent caught in the debt cycle. Truthfully, though, if you answer *any* of these questions with an immediate *yes*, then there is probably at least some material in this chapter that has special meaning for you.

What is the solution? How does one escape from this vicious cycle? Because the entire sequence depends on playing "let's play pretend," relief starts by saying "no more games" and coming clean with the truth.

The Power of Coming Clean

As children, we used secrets as our way to create a private space within; the secret became the silent older sibling of our earlier and quite vocal "No!" That more primitive expression, the archetypal hallmark of the "terrible twos," is sometimes misread as an expression of negativity, but this is not its true meaning. Far from simply being ornery or contrary, it was our way of making the statement, "This is where you end and I begin. I am not an extension of you. I am me." Now, as we grow older, having a secret continues the process of securing an aspect of ourselves as distinct from our parents, yet it also assures that this separateness itself will remain hidden. The assumption of the need for the secret is part of the secret.

As adults, we continue with the strategy—only now we often use secrets to keep things hidden not only from others, but also from ourselves.

Having a secret is a way to continue to hold onto something and freeze it in a time capsule. The possibility of telling a secret threatens unleashing the feelings packaging it, especially shame, as well as dissolving the illusion that is part of the secret. Often the hardest part of telling a secret to yourself is facing the illusion—the promise never kept and no longer possible—that is part of the secret.

Telling a secret is the most intimate thing you can do with yourself. It can be both frightening and exhilarating at the same time. It can mean facing fear, embarrassment, and shame, yet can also produce the thrill of new freedom.

The only way you can truly know all your secrets is to tell them out loud to someone else. Keeping a secret preserves its power, but it is in its breaking open that the secret's true power is finally released, as if through a mysterious sort of emotional fission.

Recognition of a secret's existence is what begins its telling. Sometimes that recognition starts out as denial, as if the only way we can bear to engage the thing for the first time is to deny its existence. But once identified, even if by refutation, the matter of the secret is on the table.

Tapping the Thrill of Repayment

For Denise, the journey back to balance began by recognizing that she was using her flights of Internet shopping to effectively change her state of mind. In fact, whenever she was cued by the signal of an uncomfortable feeling, she would begin to dissociate purely with the *idea* of approaching her computer. Recognizing that her state change occurred before she even touched the keyboard, Denise came to understand that it was not the shopping itself, and certainly not the dolls that the shopping would focus on, that gave her relief from her pain: It was the state change involved. The recognition of the power of her mind to create a state change allowed her to reexamine the "magic" of the Internet and begin exploring other, more healthful ways of creating that state change.

Like Denise, we can wean ourselves off the debt cycle by finding different pathways to a powerful, positive state change.

Spending is a thrill. It releases dopamine and kicks up a natural high. One of the secrets to getting out of the debt cycle is to train yourself to access that same sort of natural high through the act of *paying off debts*.

An unpaid bill generates a quiet disturbance. The awareness may be out of sight, but not out of mind. Using something that is not yours— i.e., someone else's money—can grow to become an oppressive cloud of preoccupation. Even when we depersonalize it by seeing it as money borrowed from a faceless institution or vague corporate authority, it is still someone else's money, and until you repay it, the lingering presence of unfinished business affects everything, even including those things you purchased with the money you pretended you owned. Emotional as well as financial interest accumulates on unpaid debt, putting your life out of balance.

In *Making Peace with Money*, author Jerrold Mundis describes the positive energy one can generate when repaying a debt by holding the check in one's hand and saying, "I bless this money. I return it to you. I wish you pleasure in using it." Mundis notes that through such practices, people have taught themselves to experience a significant level of fulfillment in returning borrowed money and paying outstanding debts.

The human organism thrills to the attainment of stasis. As Lao Tzu puts it in *Tao Te Ching*, "Returning is the way of the Tao." Completing the cycle of loan and repayment brings closure, and closure is a reliable path to fulfillment.

Seven Guidelines for Grounding Yourself in Financial Reality

You may have noticed that in the debt quiz above, not all questions were scored equally. Questions 11 and 12 each counted for a triple score, and question 13 counted quadruple. This is because questions 11 and 12 had to do with whether or not you overtly deceive those close to you about your debt reality, and 13 had to do with how closely you yourself are aware of your debt reality.

At its core, debt is a game of pretend. The only way out of debt is to call a halt to the game and look squarely at reality.

In Chapter 6 ("Your Brain on Money") we looked at ways to ground yourself, so as not to let the more emotional and reactive functions of your brain hijack your better judgment with regard to money. Here we'll take that one step further and look at a few ways to ground yourself in your financial reality.

Following are some steps you can take to ground yourself in the reality of your finances.

1. **Create a clear picture, on a single sheet of paper, of your total current debts.** This is an excellent first step toward financial health. In the debt quiz, knowing exactly how much you owe earns the most points of any single question.

   Take out every credit card statement, mortgage, loan statement, and any other statement of money owed and list the full balances owed on a sheet of paper, then add all the balances to arrive at a single number.

   Some people are able to do this in a half hour; for others, it may take hours or an entire day. If you have documents missing or don't have all the totals readily at hand, make the phone calls and do the research. Even if it takes a few days, commit to following through on every single debt until you have your entire debt picture nailed down on a *single piece of paper* and the totals added up to a *single number.*

   It's hard to slay a dragon if you can't see it.

2. **Start paying off your debts, beginning with those that carry the highest interest rates first.** Take that sheet you created in step 1 and sort those debts in order of priority. Those with the highest

interest rates are generally those you want to start paying off first. Once you've sorted them, rewrite the list on a new sheet to reflect this order of repayment. Keep this debt summary where you can find it, and rewrite it once a month with updated numbers.

This sheet is your marching orders. The point is to pay off each debt, one by one, down to zero. Note that paying the "Minimum due" does not count as an actual payment—that's barely covering interest.

3. **Identify your unique vulnerability.** Whether it is clothes, eating out, or electronic gadgets, identify whatever your particular hot buttons are, those areas where you're most commonly tempted to make impulse purchases. Recognize that these types of goods or services are for you as alcohol is to an alcoholic, and be on your guard when they present themselves.

4. **If you think it's necessary, cut up the cards and close the accounts**. Compulsive spending is caused by depression, anxiety, or other forms of mental and emotional stress. Compulsive spenders have to stop the addictive spending before they can proceed, just as alcoholics must stop drinking before they can begin to understand all the underlying reasons for their addiction.

It makes no sense to try to stop drinking or quit smoking as long as you have alcohol or cigarettes lying around the house. The same goes for credit cards. Be kind to yourself: Remove the temptation. Cut up the cards, and close the store accounts.

5. **Every time you face a spending decision, consult the big picture.** The big picture boils down to these two orienting and focusing questions:

   - What is in my (or our) best interest?
   - A year from now, will I be glad I've made this decision?

   Keeping the big picture in view doesn't mean that every decision will necessarily be correct. (Even the most seasoned and well-adjusted financial experts do not bat a thousand when it comes to their own financial choices.) But it will help keep you grounded and greatly improve the chances of your making the best decisions you can, in the circumstances.

6. **Commit to accurately tracking your cash flow every month.** The act of keeping track will automatically help you become more conscious about your spending.

    Don't make this complicated. The point is to have a clear picture of how much money comes in each month, how much goes out, and where it goes. Whether you keep a hand-written checkbook register, or keep track on your computer, it doesn't matter: Use whatever system seems easiest for you.

7. **Consult a professional to develop a plan for retiring your debt.** You may do just fine on your own, creating your debt summary and prioritizing your debt payment plan as described above. But if you feel you need to, don't hesitate to hire a pro. For a very reasonable fee, a certified financial planner or CPA can help you create a simple, practical plan that will chart your best path out of the woods.

    If you scored poorly on the Debt Quiz or believe you are seriously stuck in the compulsive spending cycle and/or debt cycle, consider Debtors Anonymous.

Seven Guidelines for Establishing a Healthy Money Life

1. **Remember that money is money.** Take a deep breath. Owing money does not "mean" anything about you or your value as a person, just as having a lot of money does not mean anything about who you are as a person. It's only money. Let go of whatever complexity and emotional drama you have attached to your

money, your spending, your debts, your possessions, your net worth, and all the rest. As crucial as it is that you deal with it responsibly and consciously, remember that it is only money.

A firm grasp of this fundamental principle—Money is simply money—is the foundation of all sound financial decisions and behaviors.

2. **Understand that internal satisfaction can transcend money.** Money means less when true inner peace exists; it becomes a simple medium of exchange, free from complex meanings or hopes of enhanced self-worth.

    We live in a society that tends to equate "success" with financial prowess. But many forms of success have no relationship at all to financial success. The most genuinely successful people typically find work in an area they enjoy and that is intrinsically motivating, and their financial success is in essence a byproduct of that larger *life* success.

    The German poet and philosopher Johann Wolfgang von Goethe, when asked for the secret of life, replied, "The secret of life is living."

3. **Know that there's also nothing wrong with money.** Be careful not to idealize poverty and rationalize the lack of success as somehow nobler than wealth. Money bestows on the possessor many choices not otherwise available. As Albert Camus put it, "It is a kind of spiritual snobbery that makes people think they can be happy without money."

4. **Learn how to balance money for today with money for tomorrow.** Money can be used constructively to enhance enjoyment and satisfaction in life. These joys should be balanced with the accumulation of money for future security.

5. **Create a financial plan that reflects your values and priorities.** If you don't know where you're going, any map will do. Money problems arise from falling prey to easy credit availability, but we only fall prey to easy credit when we lack a clear larger plan.

A financial plan doesn't have to be complicated; in fact it's better if it's not. The point is to identify your priorities in life, create some financial goals that support those priorities, and chart a general path for how you expect to get there.

6. **Seek out suggestions and advice from an expert.** The decision to seek consultation from people knowledgeable in specific areas is logically sound but emotionally difficult. Consulting someone who will mirror and agree with your own opinions is far easier than listening objectively to critical or contradictory information without responding defensively or remaining stubbornly attached to your original position.

   The point of consulting an expert is not to follow their advice and wholly abandon your own perspective, but to maintain your own viewpoint while staying open to what you can learn from theirs, and then using this new information to form a flexible and better-informed position.

7. **Go on a media diet.** The media is remarkably effective at fanning the flames of compulsive spending. The message the media gives you generally goes something like this: *You are fat, unfit, bad-smelling and unattractive, your life is boring, and you're in incredible danger—and the solutions to all these problems are just a purchase away.*

   Start noticing the choices you make, including what you buy and consume, based on what television, magazines, and other media tell you. Seek out one specific media source each week that you disagree with or dislike. Experience the difference from your previous perception.

   Start making your media choices conscious; exercise your prerogative to watch, read, and listen to only those specific media resources that you choose, and savor them well.

   Fasting is good for the soul: Consider giving yourself one fully media-free day per week.

Notes

1. http://www.federalreserve.gov/RELEASES/g19/Current/.
2. http://www.newyorkfed.org/aboutthefed/fedpoint/fed01.html.
3. "Borrowing to Make Ends Meet: The Growth of Credit Card Debt in the '90s." Demos (2003),
   http://archive.demos.org/pubs/borrowing_to_make_ends_meet.pdf.
4. Gary Weiss, "Don't Get Clobbered by Credit Cards!" *Parade*, August 10, 2008.

ten

INCREDIBLE DEALS AND UNBELIEVABLE OPPORTUNITIES: THE SECRET LANGUAGE OF SCAMS

It's a proprietary strategy. I can't go into it in great detail.

—Bernard Madoff, answering questions about his
trading approach, in *Barron's*, May 7, 2001

Three days before Christmas, on the evening of December 22, 2008, Rene-Thierry Magon de la Villehuchet told the cleaning crew in his Madison Avenue building that he was going to be working late, and wondered if they would mind finishing up and clearing out by 7 p.m. The workers obliged. When they returned the following morning, they found his office door locked. Inside, de la Villehuchet sat at his desk, a bottle of sleeping pills in front of him and a trash receptacle placed carefully by his side to catch the blood from the wrist he had slashed with a box cutter.

De la Villehuchet was cofounder of Access International Advisors, a distinguished investment firm that specializes in hedge funds and serves many of Europe's wealthy and powerful aristocrats. AIA had reportedly invested $1.4 billion with a well-known Manhattan fund manager, former NASDAQ chairman and prominent philanthropist by the name of

Bernard Madoff—the same Bernard Madoff who had been arrested earlier that month for engineering what has proved to be the greatest investment fraud in history.

In a letter to his brother Bertrand, de la Villehuchet said he felt personally responsible for the losses his company's clients had suffered, although it seems he was just as surprised by the revelations of Madoff's fraudulent dealings as anyone (in fact, the two men had never even met). As Bertrand told *The New York Times*, "He felt responsible and he felt guilty. Today, in the financial world, there is no responsibility; no one wants to shoulder the blame."

In popular films like *The Sting* and *Ocean's Eleven*, the con artist is often presented as a lovable rogue, a Robin Hood–like character who outwits his more thuggish and fat-cattish foes with a combination of rakish charm, gift of gab, and a healthy dose of good luck and Hollywood timing.

The tragedy of de la Villehuchet's suicide is a grim reminder that there is little that is charming or romantic about the genuine con game. In real life, fraud is the architect of misery.

Carlo's Coupons and Hamburgers from Uncle Sam

Carlo was only 21 when he arrived in the United States in 1903. Like so many immigrants of the day, he was short on cash (he had only $2.50 in his pocket) but long on ambition. Unfortunately, the ambition wasn't always tempered by morality, and Carlo soon found himself in trouble for everything from short-changing customers during his stint as a waiter to forging checks. He spent several years in prison in Canada and the United States before stumbling upon the legitimate business idea of selling advertising in a large business directory. The idea failed, but it was a good one, eventually turning up reinvented as The Yellow Pages.

Despite its failure, Carlo's business directory led unexpectedly to another brilliant idea. When a company in Spain wrote to inquire about a listing in his catalog, they happened to include an International Reply Coupon (IRC) that Carlo could use to buy U.S. stamps for his reply. Carlo had never seen an IRC before and was intrigued. After a little investigation, he realized that the coupons presented a business opportunity.

Inflation after World War I had decreased the U.S. dollar price of IRCs in Italy, which meant you could buy a dollar's worth of IRCs for far less than a dollar. Carlo's three-step plan was quite simple:

1. Send money abroad to buy International Reply Coupons.
2. Exchange the IRCs for stamps in the United States.
3. Sell the stamps in the United States at a profit.

This "buy low, sell high" strategy was completely legal and seemed eminently practical. There was just one hurdle: Carlo needed investors. He approached his network of friends and colleagues with an offer of a 50 percent return within 45 days (or 100 percent within 90 days) if they invested in his new entity, the Securities Exchange Company. When some invested and were repaid just as promised, word spread and more investors came knocking. By February, 1920, Carlo had made $5,000; less than six months later, he had made millions. At its peak, nearly 30,000 Bostonians were investing $250,000 a day in Carlo's enterprise.

But there was a problem. Stamps are cheap. In order to leverage his IRC system to generate returns in the millions of dollars for investors by selling stamps, Carlo's overhead would have to be massive. Financial analyst Clarence Barron calculated that it would take some 160 million of the postage coupons to support the operation on its current scale—yet there were only about 27,000 of them in circulation. An inquiry with the U.S. post office confirmed his suspicion: IRCs were not being bought in any real quantity, either at home or abroad.

The scam was exposed. In November of that year, Carlo—his last name was Ponzi—was sentenced to five years in prison for mail fraud, and the term *Ponzi scheme* entered our vocabulary.

Ponzi's strategy relied on two factors. First, he guessed (rightly) that many of his investors would continue to reinvest their principal and profits, meaning that he didn't have to actually pay back their money. Second, he counted on there being a constant influx of fresh income from new investors that he could use to pay back those earlier investors who *did* opt to cash out. It's this second tactic—paying back earlier investors with newer investors' money—that defines a Ponzi scheme, from Carlo's coupon deal all the way to Bernie Madoff's Wall Street billions.

Like Madoff's operation, Ponzi's scheme was elegant in its simplicity. He didn't offer complex financial deals, miracle science like water-burning engines, or grandiose promises of great wealth. Investors with as little as $10 could invest in his company for a promised return of 100 percent within 90 days. It was the embodiment of the American Dream, and people flocked to it. It seemed too good to be true, which is exactly what it was.

"I'll gladly pay you Tuesday for a hamburger today," so said the character named Wimpy in the Max Fleischer "Popeye" cartoons of the 1930s. It is that perennial hope that we can have it *now* and pay for it *later*— "later" being a euphemism for "never"—that feeds the Ponzi scheme. It fits perfectly within the essential modern American assumption that things will be better for our children's generation than ours—and better for *us* next week than today. Why should I worry about paying for that hamburger next Tuesday? Surely I'll be worth more then . . . won't I?

This monetary mythology creates some pretty strange scenarios. Consider the United States Social Security system. Few today are aware that the retirement age of 65 was established more than a century ago in Prussia, the precursor of modern Germany, by Otto von Bismarck. At the time, the promise of a guaranteed pension after age 65 posed no great risks to the government: people in the 1880s and 1890s rarely even reached that age. Today, so many are living well into their eighties and nineties that the same promise might well bankrupt us within the next generation.

Theoretically, the money you put into the system is money you should be getting out again some day; but it doesn't quite work out that way. The money deducted from your paycheck for Social Security does not pay for *your* benefits: It subsidizes the benefits of people who entered the system long before you did, and have now reached retirement age. For decades, this arrangement has managed to keep itself afloat, because there were always enough new employees paying into the system to pay out benefits to those who qualified for repayment. . . .

Wait—why does that sound so familiar? That's right: What started as a reasonable gesture of care-giving by the state has quite unintentionally metamorphosed into a massive government-led Ponzi scheme.

Why Do We Fall for Scams?

The Madoff scandal was to high-stakes investor fraud what the 2001 collapse of Enron was to corporate corruption. The fact that the lid came off Madoff Investment Securities just weeks after the precipitous stock market crash of September, 2008, much as Enron's collapse came only weeks after the September 11 attacks, helped to further sear both experiences into public consciousness. Yet while it is easy (and in some ways cathartic) to focus our wrath on such culpable figures as Bernie Madoff and Enron's Ken Lay, there is an uneasy undercurrent to the experience. The guilt and remorse that de la Villehuchet expressed to his brother, despite his own innocence in the whole affair, touches a chord that has been quietly thrumming inside all of us ever since the subprime meltdown first began unfolding:

"How could we have fallen for this?"

The unsettling truth about scams is that, unlike crimes such as assault, robbery, or homicide, they work only with our willing participation. It takes two to tango, so the saying goes, and so it is with the dance of the con.

Bonds buried in caves in the 1940s by the CIA to help Chiang Kai-shek fight the Communists . . . tropical islands available for personal ownership . . . leveraged contracts on agricultural fertilizer containers

. . . a library of 250 older but undiscovered films never before released for VHS or DVD . . .

These investment offerings all share two features in common: (1) they are all pure fiction: none of them exists or ever has; however, (2) there were at one point a lot of reasonable and wealthy investors *who believed they did*.

How do you create such a cult-like following? You offer an evocative promise that touches people's vague, hazy dreams and makes them appear vividly within reach. You paint a picture that enables people to see what they want to see. People project their own desires onto a promising story that crystallizes a fantasy of magical wealth. In a very real sense, it is not the scam artist who scams us, but it is we who allow ourselves to be taken in, fueled by a variation of that same *let's play pretend* impulse that lets us spend money we don't have to buy things we can't afford.

The dot-com frenzy of the late 1990s was not a scam, yet that same heady elixir of rapid growth and cult following fueled the same kind of mass lapse in judgment that allowed so many to lose so much to Carlo Ponzi 80 years earlier. Like every such explosion of collective financial naiveté, from John Law's Mississippi Bubble to the subprime-fed real estate boom of recent years, the dot-com frenzy was a sort of self-inflicted con game populated only by self-scamming marks.

Investment scams have grown so common that the North American Securities Administrators Association, a group representing state securities regulators, regularly publishes a list of Top 10 Investment Scams. In 1987, when the NASAA first studied how much investors lose to scam artists, they put the number at $40 billion a year. Today, according to the FBI, *insurance fraud alone* soaks up more than $40 billion in the United States. Despite massive media coverage and a far more financially literate public, pyramid and Ponzi schemes, swamp land in Florida, and "hot" stock tips still manage to dupe new investors.

After all these years, we still keep falling for the same old scams and rip-offs. Why? Because the con man's story seems to fit so well with the hopeful stories we tell ourselves. Cons work because *they tell us what we want to hear*.

Our Vulnerable Brains

As we discovered in Chapter 6, we are to some extent hard-wired to make financial errors, and those mistakes are not limited to legitimate investments and business opportunities. The same neurological weaknesses that make us vulnerable to "fire-sale pricing" on "brand new" furniture also makes us susceptible to too-good-to-be-true stories of old bonds buried in secret caves by the CIA.

The prefrontal cortex—the home of logic, level-headed decisions, and long-range planning—is the ideal resource for debunking a scam or outing a con. Unfortunately, our rational brain is often not consulted. Scams promise *big returns fast*, an image that readily evokes an immediate response in the limbic system and the emotionally oriented right hemisphere, completely bypassing our faculties of logic and long-range thinking. Instead of setting off warning bells, the promise of *big returns fast* excites us. American folklore idealizes the overnight success story, and no one, especially the emotional brain, wants to miss an opportunity when it seems to come along.

Because the higher and more sophisticated functions of the prefrontal cortex take time to develop, and also tend to wane with advancing age, the very young and very old are especially prone to this sort of emotional hijacking. Accordingly, young children are far more susceptible to advertising for candy, games, and theme park vacations—and seniors are often targeted as easy prey for hot stock tips, fast returns, fake condominiums, and bogus charities. In fact, the graying of America has created a bull market on fraud.

The Need to Believe

While examining a collection of antiquities in 2002, a French scholar made a discovery that rocked the world. An expert in ancient writings, the scholar had found an *ossuary*, a limestone box used to store the remains of the dead in ancient Jerusalem. On the box was inscribed the words: "James, son of Joseph, brother of Jesus."

The New Testament mentions several times that Jesus had a brother, who became the leader of the fledgling Christian movement in Jerusalem in the years following the crucifixion. This ossuary represented the most important physical evidence ever discovered to support the historical existence of Jesus, and international mayhem ensued. People flocked by the thousands to Toronto where the artifact was displayed, and Christian organizations around the world celebrated this irrefutable proof of the historical existence of Jesus.

The only problem was that the box was a forgery—and it wasn't alone. As it turned out, the bogus ossuary was just one in a long line of faked "historical" artifacts trafficked by a sophisticated, multimillion-dollar global forgery ring that had been scamming museum experts for a good 20 years.

How could such knowledgeable and discerning collectors be so consistently fooled, not once or twice, but continuously for two decades? In part, this was a sort of unconscious collusion, fueled by the deep emotional need of millions of people worldwide to validate their beliefs by the discovery of authentic physical evidence.

Inside even the most sophisticated of us is an urge we might describe as the *need to believe*. This has nothing to do with religion; it is a human impulse, pure and simple, and one we've known since childhood. Deep down, we would all really like to believe in Santa Claus, that kindly old grandfather who will magically bring us whatever we ask. And no matter how sophisticated we become as adults, we are still hoping to find Aladdin's lamp, that thing that, if we merely rub it, will produce an omnipotent genie who will grant our most cherished wishes.

Scams work because we are all susceptible to the fantasy of magical powers bringing immense return, of being "the lucky one," of running across someone who will let us in on something wildly lucrative that very few others know about. Education and sophistication are not always enough to overcome our innate need to believe in something too good to be true. This is why even seasoned Wall Street investors are susceptible to the same scams as people with much less financial and investment sophistication: for all their training, they are human.

The Need to Prove Our Worth

- "I'm not sure if you can afford this opportunity I'm about to present, but if you can, it will be the deal of a lifetime. Would you be able to come up with the funds if you had to?"
- "Maybe we should go over the numbers again because perhaps you don't understand the program. Smart people have known about it for years."

These two statements are both drawn from carefully honed scripts used by real-life scams. They represent the careful pitch used by the scam artist to tap into our need to feel worthy.

Most scam artists are highly skilled at reading people, and they know how to spot those who seek to prove their worth by being able to afford any product or investment they want. Self-doubt and insecurity often act as subtle markers of individuals inclined to buy more than they can afford. Typically having a want to be liked and admired, people of this type may feel embarrassed to tell the stockbroker that they really can't afford to purchase his or her current recommendations, and will often go scrambling for funds the moment they hang up the phone. These individuals may also succumb to a salesperson who insinuates that they can't really afford an item.

Some investors may be bullied into acting because they are especially susceptible to shaming or the fear of appearing stupid. A particularly eloquent, seemingly well-informed and knowledgeable promoter can make the investor feel embarrassed and want to compensate for his own perceived ignorance or inadequacies by agreeing with and following the advice of the salesperson.

Playing on greed and intimidation, such ploys work by making you feel embarrassed if you cannot come up with an amount of money. Your stated wish to consult a spouse, attorney, or investment advisor is turned against you as an indication of your own inadequacy: "Who wears the pants in your family? You seem like a guy who can make up his own mind."

If you hesitate, the scam artist quietly and sympathetically suggests that perhaps your reluctance indicates your inability to grasp the elegant simplicity of the program: Perhaps if we go over the figures again (he tells you as if speaking patiently to an especially slow child), you will get with the program. The final pitch to your greed is to evoke a sense of urgency, as if not acting *right now* would mean missing the train.

The Need to Be Special

One young professional woman described how she had heard of an investor who was doing extremely well. She called to ask if he might consider her as a client. She went to his office and was immediately impressed with its opulence and technical paraphernalia, including a ticker-tape machine and computers. She felt grateful to be accepted as a client—to be invited in, as the investor described, "to play with the smart money."

She later realized that she had ignored obvious warning signs. Had she done a little homework, she would have discovered that this "crack investment specialist" was not associated with the brokerage firm he claimed to be, and that he had in fact no successful track record in his investment arena. Recognizing these warning signs would have shattered the illusions that she initially desired, but she ignored them—and lost $28,000.

There is a particular appeal in getting "inside" information. It creates a sense of exclusivity, of being part of an elite group. Especially for those who have a hidden (or sometimes not so hidden) desire for specialness, the wish to be chosen and not be excluded is compelling.

Some investment schemes rely on the belief that those who have significant money are privy to investment opportunities not available to others. This myth of the privileged inner circle speaks of a secret banking system and arcane cabals of the mysteriously powerful, of being chosen for participation in what is otherwise reserved for the wealthy. "The big boys on Wall Street don't want people like us to know about deals like this."

These investors are more susceptible to scams that convince them they now have a chance to get in with the smart money. When a scam artist offers them a chance to become part of that inner circle, it appeals to both greed and specialness.

They are elated, because they feel they have been chosen. Unfortunately, as they soon learn, they *have*.

The Need to Belong

One of my patients, Melanie, became very excited when she spoke of a "hot tip" for a rumored takeover stock. As she told me:

> It's like fate loves me; fate is not ill disposed to me. If I win by a miracle, when there are insurmountable odds, fate is really smiling on me. It's so mixed up with exciting fantasies. And you feel so clever if you win, like at gambling, even if it is luck. And you get to explain your strategy and the reasons for your predictions when you pick a winning team. If I do well, I'm transformed from a drab woman to a savvy female sports forecaster or market sage. Until I miss betting on the right team or the stock that flies.

Further exploration revealed that the emotional core of this picture was not the big win, the cleverness, or the excitement but the *belonging*. When she described the appeal of gambling on football games, it turned out that her bets always had a specific end point, which was the Sunday game. Most important for her was the community of peers formed along with others who were betting on the same game.

Melanie created many "families" all her life to counterbalance the lack of cohesiveness and connectedness in her own chaotic family. As a child, she felt ineffective at obtaining emotional responses from her parents. Because of her vulnerability and sensitivity, Melanie was especially susceptible to not getting affirmation, love, and bonding with others in the usual ways.

As an adult, her gambling behavior and stock market gambling offered affirmation and bonding. If the stock did well, a whole group of people brought together by the broker would benefit. If it didn't do well, Melanie still had the experience of being together with a group of people. To her, this was more important than the actual money she made. She said, "It's like the guys at the ice house who get together and celebrate on Monday night if we've won a big bet: It's a communal thing."

The Need to Be Taken Care Of

Phoebus Vincent Smith, a new parishioner at the United Christian Fellowship Church in Palmdale, California, said he wanted to make blacks like himself rich through savvy investments. He offered to take care of those in the congregation. Bishop Edwin Derensdourg, believing he would help his parishioners who had limited experience with putting money to work, invited Mr. Smith to address the men's group at the church, and became the first of the congregation to invest.

Within six months, the pastor's investment had paid back thousands of dollars, and he was driving a Rolls-Royce—a gift from Mr. Smith. So far, so good; in fact, so *very* good. Nearly a thousand church members invested close to $2 million with Mr. Smith. A few months later, all the money disappeared.

Some con artists tap into people's wish to be taken care of by ties within tightly knit groups, such as the recent rise in faith-based scams. The scam artist exploits the bonds of trust that pastors have with their congregations; once the pastor is taken in by the fraud, the entire church becomes vulnerable.

The Federal Trade Commission organized a "church scam summit" in North Carolina because so many churches in that area had become victims of consumer fraud. The most common characteristic among those who had been defrauded was a belief that what happened to them was beyond their control. They regarded the transaction passively, and, often on the basis of little information, wrote a check for a significant amount to someone they didn't know. Studies showed that the same people were far more careful in examining the references of candidates for the post of office secretary (who made less in three years than the amount of the one investment).

These investments were not viewed as making a conscious choice but as turning over money to someone who would then take care of them and their money.

Susceptibility to Impulse

"This offer will probably be completely subscribed by tomorrow. If you're not in by then, it's gone."

Con artists use scripts like this one, setting immediate all-or-nothing deadlines to capitalize on our susceptibility to impulse. Further emotional charge is added by appealing to confidentiality and secrecy.

In addition to rapid gains, some scams appeal to a higher purpose, such as to save the environment, feed a starving nation, or prevent disease.

These investment victims combine impulsiveness with an inability to consider consequences or a disinterest in doing so. They are usually shocked to find themselves in the middle of a scam, simply because the possibility never occurred to them.

The Desire to Put One Over

Scam artists know that investors who don't discuss their investments with others place themselves at risk. This self-isolation insulates the investors, making them far more vulnerable to their own willingness to "see what they believe." Later, the victim's shame and embarrassment at making a foolish decision keeps the mistakes hidden.

Game recognizes game. The perpetrator sees a bit of a cheat in the victim, then exploits it. The victim wants to go directly to the bonus round, to get a free ride or win big without methodical saving and investment. This is why you don't hear of a scam involving a 9 percent annualized return: There's nothing so great about that. The mark is someone who wants to make a mark out of someone else—who wants too much for nothing.

In the television show *The Sopranos*, Uncle Junior alludes to this when he tells another character about how he and his brother created a con he calls the "executive game."

> You know, your father and me started that game over 30 years ago. We were talking one day about how the credit card companies work their angle. How they didn't care what you bought, as long as you didn't pay all at once. They juice you to death and you thank them for letting you have a card. And you'd rather be juiced than pay all at once. It's a certain kind of player—that's why we call it the *executive* game.

This "victim greed" mixes a concoction of hope, wish, entitlement, and ignorance, sometimes joined by grandiosity and magical thinking. The pot-of-gold lotto fantasy of being the one chosen out of 35 million is a version of what is sometimes called *rainbow thinking*.

Scam, Soak, Repeat

While it may seem contrary to logic and common sense, people who have been cheated once are no less likely to be cheated again. Some firms even compile and sell "sucker lists" of people who have bought by telephone, sometimes including information on income and investment tastes in previous scams.

What drives the sucker to repeat? Why would a victim burned by one fraud not have heightened awareness the second time around?

- Some people continue to invest as a way of denying to themselves that they have been schemed.
- Some attempt to recoup their losses by continuing a high-risk and potentially high-reward investment, figuring that "lightning never strikes twice in the same place." This old saw, alas, is even less true for fraud than it is for lightning.
- Some repeat victims have misplaced trust in a particularly believable scam artist.
- Some maintain hope for what will come. "If I can find a legitimate firm, I can make money in this."
- The embarrassment of victimhood creates a vulnerability to attempt to compensate for both the loss of face and capital, lessening clarity of judgment in the face of a "new opportunity." Embarrassment and shame then make it difficult to admit, even to oneself.
- Some scam artists specialize in "forced teaming," an approach based on expressing sympathy with the victim's past fraudulent losses, sometimes specifically mentioning an earlier fraud, in order to disarm the investor and establish camaraderie—and trust. After making a direct tie-in to a previous scheme, the scam artist will note, "Yeah, we know those guys: We put them out of business."

Variations on a Theme

There is just one problem with incredible deals and unbelievable opportunities: All too often, they *seem* so credible and believable.

The ability to create an illusion is present in every successful seller.
A very successful and scrupulously honest bond trader once told me,
"Actually I don't sell bonds. I sell stories. It's important to me to include
everything I know in the story, but I always know that *it's the story I am
selling*." This is true of salespeople, entertainers, novelists, politicians—
and, alas, swindlers.

Here are some variations of the fraud story: dialects in the secret language of scams.

Soft Scams

Soft scams misrepresent genuine products, companies, business connections, or information. Charitable gift annuities offered by little-
known organizations with sketchy information can be fraudulent.
Independent insurance agents enticed by scam artists offering high
commissions may sell securities that promise high returns with little or
no risk.

On August 8, 2000, a news release distributed through the business
news service Internet Wire announced that the CEO of Emulex Corporation had resigned and the company was under investigation by the
Securities and Exchange Commission (SEC). The next morning, the
company's stock plummeted from $103 to $45 during the first 16 minutes of trading, creating a phenomenal decline in market value of $2.2
billion, before NASDAQ officials halted trading on that stock.

As it turned out, none of the news was true: The company was fine,
the CEO was not going anywhere, and as far as the SEC was concerned,
Emulex had not even an outstanding parking ticket. The release was a
fake, put into circulation by an Internet Wire employee in order to create exactly the panic it did. The scam artist had sold short his Emulex

shares and cashed in when the price fell. Investors lost more than $100 million in one day.

Hard Scams

Unlike soft scams, hard scams revolve around nonexistent companies or products.

A Florida investment firm named Hammersmith Trust, a "prime banking" scheme promising as much as a 1600 percent annual return, scammed wealthy individuals out of at least $100 million. David Gilillan, the head of Hammersmith Trust (one of eight individuals who was eventually sent to prison), impressed wealthy and sophisticated investors with his outstanding knowledge of international finance. As he spoke of obscure international banking vehicles and secret insider trading, those who were on hand to listen concluded that he was a financial genius.

Potential investors recruited to the inner circle heard a pitch that sounded legitimate, though highly speculative. Gilillan convinced them to leverage international bonds with a guaranteed return of 30 percent per month. Later, they learned that not one dime was ever invested in anything.

Even after the FBI and U.S. Customs agents executed a search warrant and confiscated all paperwork, computers, and office documents, Hammersmith principals still managed to take in new money.

The Bad Investment Scam

Bad investment scams involve actual products but with high risk and inappropriate investments. Assured of high return with little or no risk, investors purchase questionable oil and gas partnerships, equipment leasing of pay phones, ATMs, or Internet kiosks.

Uniprime Capital Acceptance, a small Las Vegas automobile dealership, had publicly traded shares at about a dollar. One day it made an announcement that would be staggering for any company: They had discovered a cure for AIDS.

Not surprisingly, the first question people asked was, how on earth does an auto dealership come up with a cure for a dreaded disease? It turned out that Uniprime had a small subsidiary, New Technologies and Concepts, and the doctor who headed this operation had been quietly working on his intravenous treatment for 15 years at a hospital in Spain.

Internet chat rooms took off with the news, which had huge implications for the health and well-being of humanity—and profit for its makers. Uniprime was called "the greatest stock ever," and likened to "buying Microsoft at a nickel." The stock vaulted to $5 a share and a market valuation of $100 million.

Like most stories too good to be true, it wasn't. The "doctor" was a con man, and during the 15 years that he was supposedly testing his revolutionary treatment, he was actually doing time in a Colorado prison. The closest he had ever been to the medical profession was during a stint as a janitor in a nursing home.

The Affinity Scam

Trust is an essential part of scam success, and nothing works better to increase trust than to emphasize a similarity between the mark and the scam artist. Solicitors in affinity scams target select groups by demonstrating a common background—similar religion, ethnicity, or professional membership, for example. Some salespeople affect the accent of the region of the country where they are calling in order to foster a sale. If the potential victim is from a small town, then—Whaddya know!—so is the scammer. If the mark used to work at Raytheon, then so did the broker.

Identity Theft

Identity theft, the assumption of someone else's identity by lifting their Social Security number, credit card, bank account, or other critical information, has become increasingly common in recent years.

An Atlanta man posing as a jury administrator for the court system would call wealthy business owners and say, "You've forgotten to respond to a summons for jury duty and face a penalty. I can straighten it out for you right now, if you just give me some basic information." That basic information was all he needed to start spending money under his mark's identity.

A credit card scam that sounds like the real thing involves a caller who identifies himself "from the security and fraud department at Visa." He provides his badge number as proof. "Your card has been flagged for an unusual purchase pattern, and I'm calling to verify." Adding the issuing bank's name as confirmation, he asked, "Did you purchase an anti-telemarketing device for $385.50 from a marketing company based in Nevada?" With a "no" response, he is prepared to "issue a credit to your account." He will launch a fraud investigation and assign a control number. In order to "verify you are in possession of your card, to make sure it hasn't been lost or stolen, please read the three-digit purchase code from the back of the card." This code enables the con artist to make purchases over the telephone or online.

The Internet Scam

Money scams and identity theft cases run rampant on the Internet. Scam artists use the Web as a highly effective tool for illegal activities, and any employee in a company who uses the computer with Internet access is vulnerable, regardless of the understanding of these issues at an executive level. Following are a few examples.

Prolific spammers. A young man named Jeremy Jaynes generated hundreds of thousands of emails a day pitching software, work-at-home schemes, and pornography. Jaynes worked out of his Raleigh, North Carolina home with the help of 16 high-speed lines—an Internet capacity that would normally serve a company with more than 1,000 employees. While he received responses on only about one out of every 30,000 emails he sent, that was enough to net him up to $750,000 per month.

Phishing scams. In this scam, simple seemingly legitimate emails, purportedly from large and well-known organizations, seek to obtain personal information. In one typical phishing scam, an email warns Citibank customers of a possible security threat, and directs them to a site where they can update their debit card PINs. Rather than belonging to Citibank, however, the site routed the information to a Web server in Bremen, Germany.

Debt capital offer. Small business owners receive an email from a financial representative indicating that their business can qualify for a low-interest business loan by completing a questionnaire. The information gleaned from the filled-out questionnaires is used to gain access to funds.

Fake website. This ploy lures someone to a fake website and asks for personal information pretending to confirm its accuracy. For example, an email seemingly from eBay notifies the user that his account has been placed in restricted status until his personal information is updated.

Office supply routine. A caller contacts a secretary and claims to represent its office supply company, and then requests the model and serial numbers of office printers for warranty purposes. Later an email offer, evidently from a well-recognized office supply company and mentioning their specific printer models, offers a deep discount on bulk purchase supplies. When payment is received by credit card, the supplies never materialize.

The Pyramid Scheme

First cousin to the Ponzi scheme, the pyramid scheme relies on investors recruiting others to join a program, usually without a product. The classic example is the chain letter that asks you to add your name to the bottom of the list and send copies on to five people you know, tucking a few dollars into each envelop. Most recently, pyramid schemes have taken the form of "gifting clubs" or "giving programs," indicating that some of the money contributed will be donated to charity and that you will receive a tax-free gift when it reaches a certain amount, such as $10,000.

Another variation, "The Dinner Club," paralleled the four courses of a dinner party. Eight new people, the "appetizers," filled the bottom row, paying $5,000 each to the "dessert" person at the top of the tree. These bottom-rung individuals advanced to the "soup and salad" level and then to the "entrée" rung as new people joined. At the "dessert" course (if the scheme was still intact by this time), eight new people at the bottom would give $5,000 each for a total of $40,000. The plan worked perfectly at first, but it soon collapsed under its own weight when there were no new participants willing to pony up the $5,000 to become appetizers.

The Uncanny Forecaster Scam

The ability to accurately predict the future has been impressing scam victims for centuries; today the fortune-teller of the past has been reinvented for the stock market.

Someone identifying himself as a broker calls or writes, offering an investment tip. "This is a stock that is going to do very well in the near term," goes the scripted line. "I don't want you to buy the stock or even think of investing any money with me. After all, you don't even know me. Just keep an eye on this stock."

When you watch the stock and it goes up, he contacts you again and offers a second tip, a stock he predicts will take a beating. This script is, "I don't want you to short it, but just notice how it does." When this stock goes down, you're hooked for his third call. He has an investment opportunity, a sure-fire stock that he urges you to buy, and when he receives your suggested investment of $10,000 to $25,000, both he and your money vanish.

How was he able to make his forecasts with such uncanny accuracy? How did he know what was going to happen? He didn't; he was simply playing the odds. Out of a hundred people, he tells 50 that the stock will rise, and the other 50 that it will fall—and only bothers calling back the 50 who happened to receive the right "forecast." He divides this remainder again into two groups for his second forecast, again telling half it will go up and half it will decline. After the second call plays out, at least some of the 25 who have seen him be right twice out of two times will now be impressed, excited, and vulnerable.

Seven Guidelines for Staying Unscammed

1. **Work with professionals.** Ask for references on any group or broker you're considering investing with—and call the references. Invest only with a registered broker who answers all your questions.

    Get a professional second opinion on any investment you have any questions about.

2. **Know when to hang up the phone.** Ignore unsolicited telephone calls from brokers or salespeople from unknown firms. Never give out or even verify personal financial information to unsolicited callers, even if they claim to represent your bank or credit card company.

    This holds true for unsolicited emails, too.

3. **Watch your credit cards.** Shred or carefully store any receipts or invoices that display your credit card number. Review credit card statements for bogus charges.

4. **Take the time to look twice.** There is a space between urge and action: This is where judgment resides. Notice, respect, and honor that space: Fill it with homework, an investment game plan, and consultation with experts.

    Haste makes waste—and sometimes disaster. Don't let yourself be pressured into a decision before you're fully ready to make that decision. An investment is not an emergency decision. Allow yourself to sleep on it.

5. **Notice when you are vulnerable.** Vulnerable situations make someone more susceptible to scams. Greater vulnerability occurs during times of identifiable crisis, such as divorce, job loss, a death in the family, or economic downturn. Fear of insufficient funds in retirement, too, fosters greater susceptibility.

   Confront the illusion that somebody is going to take care of you. It is the hardest one to let go. You will pay for your illusions, and it is important to know exactly what they cost.

6. **Be wary of hearing what you want to hear.** Every seller—the legitimate as well as the bogus—knows that you have dreams and would love to develop your fantasies. In listening to a pitch about a stock or a deal, you *want* to hear how well it will do.

   But listen to what isn't being said. Keep the big picture in focus—the worst-case outcome as well as the best-case, along with the mid-range of reasonable expectations.

   If it all sounds really good, consult someone who is not inside the fantasy that you and the seller have created.

7. **If it seems too good to be true, it's probably too good to be true.** Never buy an investment on the basis of a "hot tip" or because the investment is offered to "only a select group of people."

   Ask yourself why you are the lucky one. All of us wish that someone would hand us something. If an offer is too good to be true, it usually isn't true. If it were truly "risk-free," they wouldn't need to say it.

   Invest only in something you understand and can explain in one sentence.

Part III

Writing a New Money Story

eleven

HOW MUCH IS ENOUGH?

Just a little bit more.

—John D. Rockefeller, then the richest man on earth,
in reply to a reporter who asked, "How much money is enough?"

R on came to me because of an earth-shattering event in his life: He
had run out of wall space.

Ron was an accomplished architect; he was also a goal-setting
machine. Pick a target, and he could hit it. Years before, he had decided
he would feel comfortable and secure if he could only fund his retirement plan. Before long, he had accomplished exactly that. He then
upped the ante and decided he also needed to pay off the mortgage on
his home—which he promptly did. Then he decided to do the same
with his vacation property. *Check.* Next Ron decided he needed to put
together a net worth of $5 million. *Done.*

With each accomplishment, Ron told himself that the next success
would make him feel complete. He had long ago met his goal of annual
earnings of $400,000, but higher monetary targets seemed to offer new
hope of contentment, so he pushed on. Happiness, he was sure, was
only a goal away. Dozens of goals later that happiness still eluded him.

The event that had precipitated Ron's visit to my office was his recently
being given a national award in architectural design. When the actual
award arrived, as he had done so many times before, he hung the hand-
some plaque in his office—only this time the new award filled the only

remaining space on his wall. Every vertical surface of his office was now utterly and completely filled with awards and medals, as was his over-stuffed trophy case. There was simply no more room.

For some, running out of room for trophies might be an annoyance, or a point of pride, or perhaps an amusing benchmark. For Ron, it was a life crisis. Why? Because even though he had covered every inch of his wall with awards testifying to his success, *it was not enough.* What brought Ron to my office was the sudden, terrifying realization that he had no clue how much was enough—indeed, that for Ron, it seemed there was no such thing as enough.

It made me think of Alice and the Cheshire Cat:

> "Would you tell me please, which way I ought to go from here?" asked Alice.
> "That depends a good deal on where you want to go," said the Cat.
> "I don't much care where—" said Alice.
> "Then it doesn't matter which way you go," said the Cat.
> "—so long as I get *somewhere*," Alice added as an explanation.
> "Oh, you're sure to do that," said the Cat, "if you only walk long enough."[1]

Ron had walked awfully far, yet he still didn't really seem to be getting anywhere.

Why this endless quest for more? Why is "enough" so elusive? Because it isn't really the money we're after. As we've seen throughout this book, for most of us money is not simply money, but a symbol for something else. If it's that something else we really seek, then the acquisition of money can never possibly satisfy, any more than you could satiate the need for food by tearing a few pages out of *Gourmet* or *Bon Appetit* and eating them.

What happens instead is that our pursuit of money slips off the edge of reason and into the murky territory of addiction.

"Just One More Try . . ."

Ricky Brumfeld had recently undergone back surgery when she played her very first Las Vegas slot machine in July, 1997. She knew there was scant hope of a big win, statistically speaking, but she hoped that perhaps the excitement might take her mind off the relentless ache, at least for a short time. Yet she was scarcely prepared for the events that unfolded. It was the Fourth of July, and Ricky was about to experience an unusual sort of Independence Day. In an amazing stroke of beginner's luck, she won $3,700 her first time out—but that wasn't the half of it. To her astonishment, Ricky discovered that when she played the slots, she experienced complete emancipation from her back symptoms. It was as if she had taken a morphine injection straight to the hip: The pain was simply *gone*.

She quickly became consumed by the machines. She fell into jealous rages when she felt her favorite machine rewarded a less devoted player with a jackpot. By the following Easter, Ricky had lost more than $100,000 in cash and credit card debt. She stopped playing only when she was arrested on child abuse charges for leaving her two children locked in a car in the casino parking lot while she hit the slots. "I knew it was really wrong to do that," said Ricky, "but the urge to go into the casino was stronger than my instincts as a mother."[2]

Lest we think too badly of poor Ricky, her descent into this wretched state did not spring purely from some inherent weakness or character flaw; indeed, her behavior was simply what the casino environment had been scientifically designed to produce. For no one has studied the psychology and neuroscience of addictive behavior more avidly nor with more attention to its application than slot machine manufacturers. These contraptions, both in the design of the machines themselves and in the software that runs them, are engineered using the latest and most sophisticated findings of behavioral psychology in order to manipulate the human brain and its insatiable craving for *more*.

Anthony Baerlocher, the chief game designer at International Game Technology, describes scenarios in which a slot machine dispenses a number of small payouts initially to provide positive reinforcement to keep the players playing. Once someone hits a couple of small jackpots, they are hooked. A slot machine called "The Price is Right" dispenses these small payouts while nibbling at the player's stash. The most successful slot machine he has designed, "Wheel of Fortune," works by creating near-misses, such as landing just one click past the "250 times bet," thus evoking the fervent hope that spurs the player to continue playing: "I was so close!" The device takes in more than a billion dollars per year.

Antigambling activists have called slot machines "the crack cocaine of gambling." No other form of gambling manipulates the human mind so specifically and completely. Over 40 million Americans annually play slot machines in the United States. This figure continues to grow. By the end of the 1980s, casinos were legal in two states. Today they are legal in more than 30. The casino industry is driven by slot machines, which in the United States rake in an average of $1 billion per *day*.

"Please, Sir, I Want Some More…"

Addiction is often seen as a condition or disease—something we "have." But addiction is really a *process*, a quest for something tangible that can regulate our mood and self-esteem, at least temporarily. While the range of things we can become addicted to is virtually endless—from money and work to sex and drugs, online pornography to off-track betting—the process for each is the same.

The initial components of addiction include *dependence* and *tolerance*. The element of dependence is what most of us think of as constituting addiction. But it's that second component—tolerance—that really cinches the addictive deal, because it means that over time, more and more of the thing is needed to continue experiencing that same high and avoid the uncomfortable effects of withdrawal. This is why we want more, and more, and more.

Addictions happen because the addictive behavior—smoking, for example, or drug use—produces long-term physical changes in the reward pathways of the brain that make it more receptive to the effects of that particular behavior. In fact, research indicates that the changes in function and structure of brain neurons induced by repeated drug use can last up to several *years* after the last use of the actual drug.

What's more, those pleasure pathways become highly sensitized not simply to the behavior, but even to the *promise* of the behavior. The mere sight of a drug or its associated paraphernalia elicits an anticipatory shudder of pleasure prior to the warmth and sensation of the rush, along with its clarity and relief. The alcoholic starts to feel the pleasure associated with drinking just from the sight of a favorite bar, or the feel of a glass in hand. A cocaine user's brain starts to light up just from looking at a photograph of coke lines on a mirror.

For Ricky Brumfeld, the enhanced release of dopamine and serotonin triggered by playing the slot machine was enough to numb her back pain, and over time, just the sights and sounds of the casino floor would activate those same neural pathways. For Ron, the mere sight of all those plaques and trophies sufficed to evoke the thrill of professional accomplishment—until he ran out of wall space.

Money cannot be expected to fill emotional needs or resolve ancient conflicts, but oh, how we try. Some individuals do manage to maintain a lifelong illusion that money will some day equal happiness and self-validation; they continue to look for "the big deal" or to feel that it's only a matter of "a little more time" until money answers their quest.

Consider the case of James Trainor. Dubbed the "kissing bandit" by the media, Trainor was in the process of robbing a bank in central Florida when he stopped in his tracks and stood still long enough to kiss a stack of bills. Unfortunately for James, the spot he chose for his pantomimed declaration of undying love happened to be smack in front of a security camera. Trainor was soon apprehended, his arrest further facilitated by the fact that he had made no effort to disguise himself.

Loving money enough to rob a bank and kiss the cash for the camera takes more than just a personal budget deficit. It takes an addiction—a money story gone completely off the rails.

Midlife Crisis

Midlife, the time stretching generally from the mid-forties to the mid-fifties, is a time of impending or threatened loss of beauty, perpetual energy, vigor, and potency. Money can come to seem the magic that will reverse all these losses. The less developed and more vulnerable our inner core of identity, the greater our reliance on attaining possessions is likely to be, and the greater the allure and magic attributed to money.

At midlife, even individuals with a strong sense of self inevitably reexamine the meanings of work, love, money, and success. Those who reach this point with some unfinished business in the forming of their own identity may increasingly seek an identity in work or in money.

I often see people who are in middle age and have done all the right things and achieved great rewards but are still vaguely dissatisfied. They want to change something external—career, spouse, or location—and hope that the change will fix what's missing on the inside. They hope that a change in setting will bring about a change in character. When they make all sorts of changes externally and find that they are not the answer, they experience a midlife crisis: a painful revelation that they've not only failed to achieve *enough*, but that they've completely lost touch with what *enough* looks like.

What's the cost of this addiction? An ad for Rolls-Royce asks "What Does a Rolls-Royce Cost?" and answers its own question with these responses:

- The years without a holiday;
- The school sports days you never saw;
- The friendships you had to leave behind;
- Risking your health for the health of the business;
- Late nights in the office when your contemporaries were in the pub;

- Missing your children's first steps into the world;
- Demanding excellence in everything you do.

The ad concludes that a Rolls-Royce costs "more than most are prepared to give." But as Ricky Brumfeld demonstrated, while we may not think we are prepared to give up everything for money, sometimes *we are*.

In extreme cases, a drug addict or alcoholic will go to any lengths to acquire more of the substance, stealing or even killing to get a fix. The addiction to money is no different. In Chapter 9 we looked at some of the questionable behaviors that can accompany the debt cycle, causing otherwise honest people to do some dishonest things, such as lying about bills or concealing receipts. In Chapter 10 we explored the darker territory of fraud and scams. But the compulsion for money can take people to even darker territories than mere fraud. The insatiable quest for more can drag one over the ethics line into petty theft and its burly cousin grand larceny, to embezzlement, abuse, assault, and murder.

Such infractions are comparatively rare, of course: Most of us keep our money compulsions within the realm of socially acceptable behavior. But while we may not literally kill one another for money, too many of us commit the quiet crime of smothering our families and ourselves, an asphyxiation of happiness and fulfillment, if not of actual oxygen.

Hi Ho, Hi Ho, It's Off to Work We Go

Remember Mike, the successful businessman we met briefly in Chapter 2, who said he "felt most alive" when nailing down a big business deal? Whenever Mike completed a major business project, he would immediately start working on the next. In fact, he would quickly get rid of the money he'd made on the first deal, so he would *have* to start working on the next one without delay. Mike was driven by an almost obsessive need to create new challenges constantly—and was utterly incapable of enjoying the fruits of his labors.

"I used to work my ass off to make half a million on a deal," Mike told me, "but then I'd make myself miserable by focusing totally on the lousy thousand dollars that I *didn't* make."

Mike explained that he always felt he was running from something. He recognized that he was afraid of failing—but he was even more afraid of losing that fear, because if he did, he might also lose his driving motivation to succeed. Mike told me he was afraid to enjoy the moment, because if he did, he might start to lose his ambition. Mike was running from something, all right: He was running from *the present*. He was fiercely engaged in making a living, but walled off from actually living.

Top producer, deal chaser, heavy hitter, hard charger, go getter . . . we have so many terms to describe a person like Mike, but there's one that really calls it like it is: Mike is a workaholic.

Mike is not alone. Millions of Americans work more than 60 hours a week. A full one-third of Canadians identify themselves as workaholics. Many of these people view work as the only area in which they can establish and maintain their identities and enjoy feelings of importance, validation, and affirmation. Others use work to counteract underlying feelings of inadequacy and ineffectiveness. In either case, the workaholic cannot rest.

Individuals who are truly addicted to work don't necessarily find much pleasure in the work itself, and indeed, success is often an anticlimax. As in Mike's case, accomplishment brings only frustration and disappointment, along with the drive to do more. Something is still missing; they want *more*.

Here is how one woman, a specialist in her profession, described it to me:

My work reassures me. When I feel overwhelmed, I turn to my work, which I know well, and I feel calmed. I became an achiever because it's something I could do that would exist in time and space and become objectively real. My work gives me pats on the back.

She described how work provided continuity and stability in her life. When disruptions occurred in her personal life, she immersed herself even further in her work to reestablish her internal sense of order. She remembered that even as a child, when she became upset, she would retreat to her room to engage furiously in her childhood version of "work."

Work addictions are made more destructive by the fact that we often don't acknowledge them as addictions. Indeed, they are consistently rewarded by society and our peers. The labels of "super mom," "family provider," and "star performer" can all hide a story of slow death by paycheck.

The Darker Side of Excellence

There is something about work that makes it unique among all addictive behaviors: Rather than frowning on it, society condones and even admires it. Of all the things to which one may become addicted, money and work carry the most social approval, which makes them perhaps the most readily justifiable—and therefore most comfortably deniable—of addictions.

It's easy to rationalize an addiction to work when it's phrased as "giving my kids every opportunity." It's not that hard to live with the destructive consequences of a money addiction when society tells us that it makes us better parents, spouses, or friends. Our desire for more money, once justified, is integrated seamlessly into our money story, where it is reinforced by our peers, our colleagues, our employers, and our culture. That justification blurs the lines between ethics and excess. It absolves us of guilt for trading family time for a more expensive car or a larger home. After all, isn't it the promise of unlimited reward for hard work and dedication that has brought people to this country for centuries? *Hey, I'm only being a good citizen!* Thus the obsession with professional accomplishment becomes not merely acceptable but a testament to character and a badge of civic honor.

Make no misunderstanding: Excellence is an admirable pursuit, and hard work in the pursuit of a compelling goal is a noble path to tread.

What turns the pursuit of excellence to the dark side of the force (to use George Lucas's memorable phrase) is when we link our own self-esteem to production of demonstrable *evidence* of our excellence.

We often measure this evidence in terms of money and material acquisitions—but not always. We may also find the external evidence in the acknowledgment of others, in applause, accolades, or, as in Ron's case, wall plaques. Or we may find it in the sense of honor and pride we ascribe to our efforts themselves. There are plenty of workaholics who struggle financially, pointing not to their bursting bank balances but to their impeccable history of thankless hard work as their badge of pride and evidence of self-worth. In Arthur Miller's *Death of a Salesman*, the title character Willy Loman spends the entire drama desperately trying to tabulate the measure of his self-worth in terms of his reputation, his sales record, his son's accomplishments, and his sterling family values—all of these progressively revealed to be essentially bankrupt—and finally comes to the dark conclusion that his only genuine worth lies in redemption of his meager life insurance policy.

This is the dead end of the workaholic path, and the only way off that path is the realization that genuine worth can never be found in external rewards or symbols, but only in the internal experience of that worth.

Neither money, the things it buys, nor the work that generates it, can be expected to fill emotional needs, resolve long-running conflicts, or bestow fulfillment. Those people who manage to maintain the lifelong illusion that money will some day equal happiness and self-validation live out those lives in continual pursuit of "the big deal," urgently repeating the slot machine players' mantra—*next time, next time, next time*—in an effort to stave off the existential depression that swallows Willy Loman when they realize that the next big deal will never arrive.

Quiz: Are You a Workaholic?

Working long and hard hours and deriving great satisfaction from one's work does *not* make someone a workaholic. A true workaholic may not even especially enjoy working, but *has* to work: It is something he or she cannot do without, just as an addicted smoker cannot manage going a day without cigarettes.

Consider the following questions in relation to your work and your feelings about your work identity:

1. When you leave work at the end of the work day, do problems, projects, phone calls, appointments, and meetings follow you home and encroach upon your private time?
2. When you are away from your work, do you find yourself replaying conversations at work, reassessing decisions, and reexamining work details?
3. Do you sometimes find it difficult to enjoy any activity that is not connected with work?
4. When you are not at work or not able to work, do you feel anxiety, depression, or other types of discomfort that might be described as symptoms of withdrawal?
5. Have you convinced yourself that success in your line of work necessitates a dedication bordering on the obsessive—that working the hours you work isn't really your preference, but "the job demands it"?
6. Do you take setbacks, feedback, or criticism of work projects personally?
7. Do you see what you do for work as being who you *are*?
8. Are you seeking to prove your worth, whether to someone else or to yourself, by the work you do?
9. Do you believe that only extreme effort and accomplishment will fully demonstrate your true value?
10. Is work an escape from doing things you would rather avoid, such as meeting family obligations or facing family conflicts?
11. Do others close to you complain regularly about your work hours or about your never being around?
12. Has anyone close to you ever described you as a workaholic?

Quiz: Are You Addicted to *Less*?

As the anorexic illustrates, the story of addictive behavior is not always one of *more*: It can also manifest as the relentless pursuit of *less*. The flip side of money addiction is addiction to poverty—the relentless opposition to wealth. A *yes* answer to any of the following questions suggests that you may share some of the attributes of the confirmed poverty addict.

1. Do you believe it is more virtuous or admirable to be poor than to be rich?
2. Do you believe being poor is more spiritual than being wealthy?
3. When you have an influx of money, do you tend to spend it quickly and/or impulsively and return rapidly to a familiar state of poverty?
4. Do you often refrain from making needed repairs on your car or your home, or from getting medical care for yourself (such as regular checkups or dental cleaning), because you don't feel you can afford to spend the money?
5. Is it more comfortable for you to spend money on others than on yourself?
6. Do you undercharge for your work or your skills?
7. Is it uncomfortable for you to collect on fees that people owe you for your work?
8. Does it seem like whenever you are about to get ahead financially, some crisis happens in your life that gets in the way and stops your progress cold?

Six Guidelines for a Healthy Relationship with Work

1. **Get clear on the purpose of your work.** Sure, you work to make a living and pay the bills. But that's only work's wrapping, not its core. Examine whether you are doing what you do for someone else's response or approval, or for your own benefit and the

satisfaction of your own ideals. No matter what your job, position, or career, make sure that at its heart, you are doing what you do for your own satisfaction.

2. **Create clear boundaries.** Establish a clear boundary between your work life and your private life: each day, each weekend, and for designated vacation periods. Setting and respecting this boundary allows you to be fully present for both work and private life.

3. **Leave work at work.** Assess the amount of time you spend talking about your work with family and friends, and the amount of time you spend associating only with friends from work or people in the same line of work. Being caught up in war stories may represent an inability to establish boundaries for work or a habit of identifying your work as who you are.

4. **Focus each day's work on productivity goals rather than work ethic goals.** Make a conscious shift from holding yourself to an "X hours per day" standard to a "job well done" personal satisfaction standard. You can do this even if your present job requires you to work a set number of hours: Instead of simply "putting in your hours," view each day's work as a quest to create personal satisfaction with what you've created in that given day.

5. **Create clear financial goals.** As part of your simple financial plan (discussed in Chapter 9), create specific, measurable money goals for your investments and retirement. Give each investment a clear purpose: for college, for retirement, for a new home, for a "rainy day" emergency fund, etc.

6. **Accept the fact that you have a life.** One way to assuage the guilt or discomfort you might feel in taking more time off from work and relaxing is to reframe this time as a necessary component of your work. This is not sophistry or rationalization: In order for you to be maximally effective when you *are* at work, it's crucial that you make time for play and a private life. Having a better life *away* from work will also create a better life *at* work.

Writing a New Script

Just as the anorexic girl wants to lose "just five pounds more" and persists in losing those five pounds over and over until she is on the brink of death, a flawed money story can lead us to some frightening places. They may seem as innocuous as Ricky's Fourth of July holiday in Vegas or Mike's extra hours at the office, but they are the starting points for spending "just five dollars more" or "just five minutes more" in an endless downward spiral.

The case of the anorexic who continues to lose "just five pounds more" is a good starting point for examining our escape route from money addictions. For those with eating disorders, food is far more than simple nutrition. A host of symbolic meanings—nurturance and comfort, the physiological regulation of calmness and relaxation, control and protest, the emotional significance of abundance versus starvation—are tied to every meal, every *bite*. These meanings are hitchhikers that grab their ride on the nutritive elements of a meal. They create a *food story*, with its own drama, its own characters, and its own plotlines. Recovery for an anorexic isn't about eating. It's about *rewriting*, creating a new and successful food story.

For someone with an eating disorder, in other words, the path to health is not simply to eat more, it is to change one's relationship with food. The anorexic is cured not when she eats appropriately and gains weight, but when she uses food ultimately as simple nutrition and nothing more.

The same is true for money and work addiction. Our "cure" comes when we can leave our money hitchhikers at the side of the road and continue the journey with money as simple currency. For food, money, or work to become simply themselves and nothing more, your sense of self must be complete and not regulated by using one of these to supplement or prop it up.

So How Much *Is* Enough?

A passage in one of Schumann's piano sonatas is marked *so rasch wie möglich*, meaning "as fast as possible." A few bars later, he adds *schneller—*

"faster"—and a bit later, *noch schneller*: "still faster!"[3] This may be Schumann's sense of humor at work. It's not so funny in the context of our money story. How can we want more when we already want it all? The ancient Greek philosopher Epicurus spoke volumes of wisdom when he wrote, "Nothing is good enough for the man for whom enough is too little."

How do you know how much is enough? Being able to answer this question means having a sense of "good enough" *inside*, which in turn means feeling a kind of internal affirmation of one's own worth. When you equate love and self-esteem with money, fame, and power, you're setting yourself up for failure. You can create a story with the most elaborate setting—a mansion, a jet, and all the trappings—but bringing that story to life still won't create that sense of self-worth. It cannot grow from the outside in; it cannot be *bought*.

Much of our challenge with money stems from our difficulty in making one small distinction: We fail to differentiate what we *have* from who we *are*. Do you remember the brief quiz in Chapter 1 that illustrated the relativity of financial goals?

1. My current annual income is $_____.
2. In order to insure happiness and contentment financially, with no more money problems and worries, my annual income would need to be $_____.

If you're like most people, the second number will tend to be about twice the size of the first. So far so good: We've got a goal, and goals are great. But what happens when we *reach* that number? Rather than finding the predicted contentment in that number, most of us do exactly what Ron was doing: We now set a *new* number, usually about twice the size of the number we've just reached—and on and on it goes. The more we earn, buy, have, and spend, the more we want to earn, buy, have, and spend. It's that endless cycle known fondly as the *rat race*.

Making peace with our moving target isn't about learning how to aim better, or creating a fixed target that doesn't move even after we hit it. Creating financial targets (goals) is an important part of writing a new money story—but finding peace lies not in the target, but in the shooter. Your new money story begins with determining not what it is you want to *have*, but who it is you want to *be*.

You're probably wondering what became of Ron and his wall of awards. After we took a long, hard look at Ron's money story, he sat down and examined his personal and professional priorities with the goal of bringing them into alignment. Before long, he had worked out a strategy: Rather than taking on every new business project that came his way, he would choose only those architectural projects that he could do uniquely well, and that he felt passionate about.

In other words, he shifted from a *work ethic* to a *productivity ethic*: The goal of each work day shifted from "putting in 12 to 14 hours" to "feeling satisfaction with the day's accomplishments."

This transition resulted in Ron working more happily, making even more money, and increasing his personal time. He devoted some of his excess time to funding and organizing Big Brother events. Ron found more money, more time, and more accomplishments—and he also found more contentment.

Notes

1. *Alice's Adventures in Wonderland*, Lewis Carroll.
2. "The Chrome-Shiny, Lights-Flashing, Wheel-Spinning, Touch-Screened, Drew-Carey-Wisecracking, Video-Playing, 'Sound Events'-Packed, Pulse-Quickening Bandit," by Gary Rivlin, *The New York Times*, May 9, 2004.
3. Sonata No. 2 in G minor (1838), Op. 22.

twelve

THE HEART OF THE MATTER

*I can remember when Wilbur and I could hardly wait for
morning to come to get at something that interested us.*

—Orville Wright, from *The Miracle of Kitty Hawk*

When Gary first came to me for some executive coaching, he
wasn't entirely clear on what he was looking for. In fact, even
after he told me his story, he still wasn't sure why he had come to my
office in the first place.

What he did know was that his business was suffering. Gary was a
physician who ran a specialty medical practice, and as with Paul, the
physician we met briefly in Chapter 7, the shift to managed care had
increased his overhead cost. Gary painted a pretty dismal picture of his
situation. His malpractice insurance alone had increased by $20,000
the previous year. "If it goes up that much again," he said, "I'll have to
close my doors within six months."

Gary finished his story and gave me a hopeless look. I acknowledged
his frustration and then began asking a few questions about his work
and his life. I inquired about his personal and professional passions, and
he drew a blank.

Passions? There were none that he could think of.

What did he do that excited him? I asked. He frowned. He couldn't
really remember doing *anything* that excited him particularly, at least

not lately. Over the past few years, he had become engulfed in the downward spiral of his financial picture. His only goals were around survival. His story had swallowed him. Gary had not felt truly alive in a very, very long time.

Sadly, Gary's experience is not all that uncommon. In 2005, a study by Harris Interactive of nearly 8,000 adults found that 33 percent of workers felt that they were at a dead end in their current jobs, and even more (42 percent) believed they were "trying to cope with feelings of burnout." Fewer than half (44 percent) of the respondents said they were glad that they had chosen to work for their current employers.[1]

In short, a good number of us hate our jobs. We dread waking up on Monday morning—and Tuesday, and Wednesday through Friday. If it weren't for the addiction that drives us to consume more, many of us might never make it to work at all. Living on autopilot, we go through the motions, paying the bills, doing our jobs, getting from day to day, week to week, with little to look forward to on the horizon. Like Gary, we become swallowed by our stories—not only our money stories, but our work stories and our life stories.

Fortunately, it doesn't have to end there.

The wonderful thing about your story is that it's not carved in stone, inscribed on a clay tablet, or published in a book sitting on a musty library shelf. Your story is a living, breathing thing—and you are the one writing it. And because you are writing it, you can change it.

The Spark of Passion

After some discussion, Gary finally mentioned one specific subspecialty procedure that he enjoyed. I asked him to tell me more about it, to explain how it worked, and what results it produced. As he began talking about the process, his body posture and mood began to shift. He became more eager and animated and sat up on the edge of his seat. We'd hit on something special: a *passion*.

I asked Gary how many other physicians at the large metropolitan hospital where he worked also did this procedure.

"Actually," he said with a modest measure of pride, "no one, not at my hospital, anyway. There is just one other physician in the city who knows how to do this procedure."

Not only did he love this specialized niche, but for each procedure he did, he received a significant direct payment. Even better, the procedure was immensely beneficial to his patients; it was not an "enhancement" process but a necessary medical procedure that changed their lives. It was something Gary was truly inspired to do.

He currently performed one of these surgeries per month, on average. I asked him what he would envision as a stretch goal for performing this operation. He thought about it, and then said, "Well, doing one a week would be wonderful—but honestly, if I could do *two or three* a week, that would be amazing!"

And there it was: Gary had found the heart of his work story. Changing people's lives with this procedure—a highly skilled procedure that only one other doctor in his entire city was capable of performing—was a passion that, if Gary could fully tap into it, would give him a completely renewed vigor for his practice, his profession, and perhaps, even his life. We set about planning a strategy for him to reach his goal, Gary's passion clearly evident as we talked. We started by working out a plan to locate referral sources, both locally and regionally, and to educate them about his expertise.

It would perhaps be a bit dramatic to say that the man who walked out of my office that day was a different person from the man who had walked in an hour earlier. But that's how it seemed—and it *was* dramatic.

As Gary put his plan into action and began developing his new professional story, he felt an exhilaration that had been missing for years. He began seeing other possibilities in his practice, as well, and developed a keen interest in approaching things differently and seeing things in a new light. He developed professional and nonprofessional alliances throughout the region. After an initial warm-up at Toastmasters, he presented his work and findings to a nationwide group of colleagues, and he hired a consultant to help him develop a plan to market his sub-specialty procedure internationally, too.

Within four months from the day of our meeting, Gary was performing two or three of his signature procedures per week.

The Pursuit of Happiness

There is a deep-rooted mythology in our culture that says, the most successful people are the most driven, the ones who work nonstop, typically sacrificing their family lives and even their health in the relentless pursuit of top achievement. We've got those images of the wealthy, wretched Scrooge and the happy, impoverished Cratchit family etched into our brains, and the either/or lesson that goes with it: *You can lead a happy life, or be wealthy and successful in business, but not both at the same time.*

The problem with this "truth" is that it simply isn't true. Success and happiness are not mutually exclusive—quite the opposite, in fact.

In one of the longest running studies of its kind, Harvard psychiatrist George Vaillant studied a group of individuals over several decades to discover that contrary to popular belief, those who enjoy the best marriages and the most intimate friendships are also most likely to become extremely successful in their professions and corporate world.

Vaillant observed that the key factors in living long and healthy lives included the role of play and creative activity; the benefits of forming new friendships and social networks; and the importance of intellectual curiosity and lifelong learning.

Many of the successful people in his study were so certain of themselves and their goals that they actually preferred to preside over their own smaller businesses than to grow wealthy as an executive in someone else's larger company. Wealth took a back seat to passion. As Vaillant said in an interview with the *Harvard University Gazette*, "You can add life to your years, instead of just years to your life." And for those in the study, it seemed that adding life to their years added dollar signs, too.

Six Guidelines for Finding Your Passion

What is it that you do uniquely well and enjoy doing more than anything else? Perhaps like Gary you have something you do better than anyone else around you. Or perhaps there is something you so completely enjoy that it galvanizes you and brings out the best in you. What is your passion?

For many of us, a first introspective glance may reveal little to energize us. But remember, that's how Gary felt when he began rewriting his story. Disengagement and depression surrounding work needn't be permanent. Somewhere in there, there is *passion*—a spark to put to the tinder of work and fan into flames.

Finding your passion starts with making a shift in how you see and interact with the world. You can use these strategies to start your quest:

1. **Get curious.** Embrace the fact that you don't know, and begin to ask, "Why?" Develop a hunger to understand the new, unknown, and unfamiliar.

2. **Engage.** It's tough to find passion without leaving the house. Passion is directed energy and revealing it requires that you create opportunities to engage in new activities, meet new people, and get out of your comfort zone. Join a club or a team. Say *yes* when you might normally have said *no*.

3. **Get out of the details.** Gary's passion was right in front of his nose, but with the pressing specter of his rising costs and his deflated spirit, he couldn't see it. Passion requires that you take a big-picture view of things. Create some contemplative space for yourself. Practice the "media diet" we explored in Chapter 9.

4. **Think back to when you were a kid.** At one point in time, we all felt passion. Children have boatloads of it by default, but over time it has a way of slipping away. Spend some time mentally revisiting your childhood. Reflect on times when you were at your most engaged, vibrant, and alive. What did you love? What *did* you want to be when you grew up?

5. **Recruit help.** Like Gary, you might need extra help finding your passion. It might be a professional or it might simply be the insight of a close friend or partner who can tell you when they've seen you really come alive. Seek a professional coach, mentor, or a mastermind group. Share your quest—you won't regret opening up.

6. **Move on.** An old dog lies half-asleep on the porch of a general store, moaning and groaning in the sun. After watching him go on like that for a few minutes, a customer asks the store owner, "Why is your dog acting that way?"

    "Oh, him," drawls the man, "that's Homer. Homer's fussin' cause he's lyin' on a nail."

    "Well, why doesn't he move?"

    "'Cause it ain't hurtin' him bad enough."

    When Gary first came to see me, he was lyin' on a nail: He had become so absorbed in his story of financial hardship that he couldn't seem to focus on anything else. It's easy to get into a rut of telling our story over and over, either to ourselves or to whomever will listen: the boyfriend or girlfriend who left us, the no-good spouse who ruined our life, the cheating business partner, the lousy boss, the job we can't stand but can't quit, the government, the economy, the weather . . .

There may be some truth (or even a lot of truth) to any one of these stories. But they're stories. And you get to choose which story you'll spend your time telling—*and living*—with a fresh choice every day, every hour, and every minute.

There are times when you just need to move on—when you need to get off the nail you've been lying on before you can see clearly enough to find your passion.

Ideals, Needs, and Wants: The Power of Alignment

Leslie consulted me because she wanted to expand her business, but felt stuck. An acknowledged expert in a niche area, Leslie supervised the work of consultants who worked for her. Although she worked successfully on behalf of her clients, her income did not match her recognized expertise, and her own needs were not being met.

As with Gary, we focused initially on what Leslie did uniquely well and what her primary passion was. But for Leslie, something was still missing.

I sent her an "Inventory for Ideals, Needs, and Wants," a document I use in executive and mentor coaching, and asked her to select from a prepared list the three ideals and three needs that best represented her core self. Here is what she chose from the list:

Ideals

- Creativity
- Mastery
- Teaching others

Needs

- Autonomy
- Self-enhancement

Wants

- To be taken care of

We immediately recognized a disparity between Leslie's *want* to be taken care of, her *needs* for autonomy and self-enhancement, and her *ideals* of mastery, creativity, and teaching others. Her wants, needs, and ideals were not in synchrony, nor were they aligned toward her goals.

Leslie was aware that throughout her life, money had resonated with emotional issues. Money had been the language of care and love in her family, seemingly the tangible evidence that her parents loved her, confirmed by a will that promised significant inheritance. She also recognized that she had continued the storyline: making substantial money now meant she was taking care of herself; therefore professional success also meant that she was giving up her wish of being taken care of by someone else. The impossible had become accessible, though now by her own efforts.

The solution was for Leslie to consciously shift an old *want*: rather than wanting to be taken care of by someone else, she could fulfill that same desire by appreciating her new capacity to take care of herself.

The result of our work was that Leslie worked happily at doing what she did uniquely well—consulting with individuals and families in her specialty area. She also leveraged her time and income by training and licensing people in her program.

We've all felt the mismatch of needs and values in our lives at some point. One of our highest values might be *family*, but a need for *accomplishment* might keep us at the office long past the start of a soccer game or family outing.

Needs and ideals form core themes of personal story plot. Like Leslie, becoming aware of your unique blend of these elements will help you identify the misalignment of your current story and begin creating a new one that works.

Know Your Ideals

Your ideals are your internal standards of excellence. They are your core values, your personal model of what has genuine worth. When we live up to our ideals, we feel a sense of worth and esteem. When we don't, we feel shame and lack of fulfillment. Your ideals resonate with the core essence of who you *are*.

There are dozens of possible ideals, and by definition they all have value. (For example, who *doesn't* value health, happiness, or kindness?) The key here is to identify those few that are your key guiding priorities, those core ideals that are most important to you, those which you most passionately believe in. Your core ideals may shift or evolve as you progress through life, but they will not stray too far from the "home base" of who you are.

From the list below, choose the three ideals that are most important to you. Be honest. Choose values that inspire you, not those you think you *should* value, that society tells you to value, or that you see others holding as valuable.

This list is not exhaustive; feel free to add others. You may find it easier to work through the list choosing more than three, and then go back over it again to narrow down your list. Once you've finished, fill in the three blanks at the bottom with your chosen three top ideals.

Achievement	Growth
Adventure	Happiness
Beauty	Health
Catalyze	Honesty
Charity	Independence
Connectedness	Individuality
Contribute	Influence
Creativity	Intimacy
Dignity	Justice
Discovery	Kindness
Family	Knowledge
Feel	Leadership
Freedom	Learning
Generosity	Mastery

Peace	Winning
Pleasure	Other:
Power	_____
Self-esteem	_____
Sensitivity	_____
Spirituality	_____
Success	_____
Teaching	_____
Truth	_____

My top three ideals, in order of most to least important, are:

1. _____

2. _____

3. _____

Four Guidelines for Living Your Ideals

Once you've clarified your ideals, consider ways you might begin to incorporate them into your life. For example:

1. **See how they apply.** Consider the different areas of your life, one by one—your career, life as a spouse, as a parent, a sibling, a friend, and any other areas—and explore how each of the top three ideals you've identified here applies to or reveals itself in each of these areas.
2. **Honor your order of priorities.** Recognize and honor the hierarchy of ideals when making decisions. For example, the immediate needs of your child might supercede a desire to learn and be creative.
3. **Appreciate the price.** Each ideal carries with it a price tag, so to speak; that is, there is a personal cost involved in being committed

to upholding and honoring that ideal. For example, there will inevitably be sleepless nights and boring moments involved in raising a child.

4. **Live your ideals.** Think of yourself as a tigress and your ideals as your cubs: they are your life, and you will do anything and everything to protect them. If you feel you have not been entirely true to your ideals or protected them with that kind of fierce integrity, then choose this moment as your time to reclaim them.

If you are unclear about any one of the ideals you've identified, spend additional time focusing on it, and if you feel it's necessary, rewrite that list until it rings unquestionably true for you.

Know Your Needs

Unlike our ideals, which are standards of value to which we aspire, a need is an essential requirement that we must actually have present in our lives, a necessity for mind, body, or spirit. Early in life, our needs consist of physical nurturance, empathic attunement, attachment, effectiveness, exploration, assertion, feeling and tension regulation, and sensory needs. In adulthood, our needs become adult versions of these same basic needs, all providing for physical requirements, comfort, identity, affirmation, love, communication, safety, and sexual/sensual needs.

Consistently meeting your own needs results in a sense of effectiveness and optimum functioning, like the satisfaction of having completed a task or project, knowing you have given it everything you had. Frustrated or unmet needs create the opposite feeling, of constant discomfort and ineffectiveness. For example, when the basic need for connection is derailed or nonexistent, we feel an emotional disharmony. A need may be most obvious when it is not met.

As with ideals, each of us is unique and has a particular set of needs that we value more highly than the others. From the following list of needs, choose the three that are most important to you. This list isn't exhaustive; feel free to add other needs.

Acceptance	Physical activity
Accomplishment	Recognition
Acknowledgment	Safety
Actualization	Security
Care	Simplicity
Certainty	Strength
Comfort	Time alone
Communication	Other:
Control	_____
Duty	_____
Effectiveness	_____
Empathy	_____
Harmony	_____
Nurturance	_____
Order	_____

My top three needs, in order of most to least important, are:

1. _____

2. _____

3. _____

When your needs and ideals are in synchrony with each other and are combined with a clear vision and defined goals, all of your efforts go in the same direction. It will feel right and result in mastery.

A discrepancy can exist for organizational systems as well as for individuals. For example, corporate *ideals* might include teamwork, leadership, caring for and promoting the creativity of employees, innovation, and realizing human potential. Corporate *needs* include productivity and the bottom line of profit and loss. When the core ideals of a corporation parallel its core values of an individual within that corporation, both grow.

Your Wants

"You can't always get what you want," sang the Rolling Stones, "but if you try some time, you just might find, you get what you need."

They were right about that, too: you don't always get what you want, even though you sometimes do get what you need—and they're often not the same thing.

Wants or desires are not fundamental constructs like needs or values. A want can be replaced with another want, and fantasies are readily interchangeable—but one need cannot substitute for another need.

While ideals and needs both spring from the very essence of who we are, wants are far more circumstantial. A particular want, for example, may arise as the temporary manifestation of an unmet need from the past, such as the unmet need for affirmation as a child resulting in adulthood in the relentless pursuit of validation, accolades, and accomplishments. While needs are universal, wants are tied to experiences uniquely personal and with their own particular histories.

Unsatisfied wants may result from not having a defined goal (not having a definition of *enough*), or from trying to satisfy a past want in present time. While you can get sick if you don't get enough of a need, you can also get sick if you get *too much* of a want. You can never get enough of what you don't need.

Here's the thing about desires: If the ones you have don't serve you, *you can choose new ones*. Like your money story, your wants are not carved in stone nor cast in your DNA. And choosing desires for yourself that are in alignment with your needs—and even better, with your ideals as well—is a recipe for satisfaction.

Using Ideals and Needs to Make Decisions and Evaluate Goals

Conflicting needs, wants, and values hinder our performance and drive us to invest time, money, and energy in things that don't fulfill us. Accordingly, it makes sense to weigh every significant decision you make against the considerations of your ideals, needs, and wants, *before* you make the decision.

- If the decision meets all three, it is a *yes*.
- If the decision is in alignment with your ideals and needs, but seems to be in conflict with a particular want, it is a *maybe*. Examine this particular want to see if it is significant enough to nix the decision. Since wants are more transitory than ideals and needs, a sound decision may overrule a want.
- If the decision opposes or does not meet one of your needs or ideals, then the decision can be "No" or "On hold."

This alignment of ideals, needs, and wants can be applied to establishing direction and goals in all significant areas of life: home, career, relationships, way of being, business, personal success, financial plan, and spiritual development.

We live in a culture that is often very goal-oriented. There is nothing wrong with being focused on a goal—as long as the goal aligns well with your ideals and needs. If it does not, then you are working at cross purposes and cannot possibly win, because if you win, you lose.

I use a process for making and following through on important decisions and goals that I call the Ideals and Needs Decision Tree.

Ideal + Need → Goal → Commitment → Fulfillment → Self-validation

Before adopting a goal as your own, examine it closely to see whether or not it is in synch with your top ideals and needs. If it does align well with your ideals and needs, then move to *commitment*.

Once you have committed to the goal, then be loyal to yourself by *fulfilling* that commitment, not simply because you said you would, but because that goal is an integral expression of your ideals and needs, and thus its full-out pursuit—not only its final accomplishment, but the journey along the way as well—also serves as an essential *validation* of your genuine worth.

Because the goal is aligned with your ideals and needs, it is a consonant expression of who you are.

Defeat from the Jaws of Victory

Politicians seem to fulfill various roles in our lives. They watch out for the common good; they attend to all manner of logistics in the managing of the social order; and they lead us in times of trouble. And they do one more thing: Now and then, they flame out in entertainingly spectacular fireballs of scandal and self-destruction.

Hardly a season goes by without some new political drama of disgrace and disrepute—and we seem to love it. The term *schadenfreude* (literally, "the joy of sorrow") describes the pleasure we derive from another person's misfortune, and it seems to be one of the duties of politicians, as well as movie stars, pop stars, and top athletes, that they satisfy our *schadenfreude* from time to time.

I don't think it's an entirely perverse impulse on our part: Perhaps we need these dramas as cautionary tales, examples to remind us, "There but the grace of God go I." That way lies the path of self-sabotage, and it is a frighteningly real possibility for all of us. Literature and film are replete with famous characters who seem to snatch defeat from the jaws of victory, falling into catastrophic harm's way just as their most profoundly hoped-for wishes are about to come to fruition. Shakespeare's Lady Macbeth and Ibsen's Rebecca West both suffer grave illnesses almost the moment they know a major wish is about to be fulfilled. In *The Horse's Mouth*, Joyce Cary's irascible painter, Gulley Jimson, finds a unique route out of success: He paints his most elaborate masterpiece on a wall scheduled for demolition and personally bulldozes the wall as soon as the mural is completed.

Those who have the opportunity, intelligence, and imagination to succeed, and yet do not live up to their potential, or suffer when they do, are victims of their own internal obstacles, rather than any external impediment to success. It is as if they cannot tolerate their own success. Why would someone recoil from the very thing they have sought so long and for which they have striven so hard? Could it be that there is a core conflict between their core ideals and their needs—or between their true ideals and their stated ideals?

Success Is a Mindset

Success has less to do with skills or intelligence than with a mindset. Success is not necessarily about hard work, a product, or a service, though these may be necessary components. Success is less about what you do and more about how you do it, with what quality of enthusiasm and passion, and, especially, with how aligned it is with your core ideals.

Your assumptions and beliefs drive your behavior. Coming to the end of the past is not enough: You need to have a purpose, a dream consistent with your internal ideals in order to have hope. Getting over the past and creating a future, although related, are not the same thing. To create new possibilities, you have to focus on the future. The past, though seemingly only a step away, is a place to which you can never return. Focus your energy on where you are headed rather than where you've been.

Hope follows and is actualized by well-aligned goals and plans. Hope is the confident expectation that something good can and will be created. If there is hope in the future, it adds to the present as you move toward that which you picture in your mind. Pinpoint focus and laser precision of that picture allow the pathway of the plan and the flexibility of strategy to have a context and meaning.

If you follow a solution or strategy that someone else has recommended for you without first fitting it to your ideals and your situation, you will be trying to wear a suit tailored to someone else. If you want to change your life, your performance, and your career, you must first change the story you're telling—in other words, the story by which you are *living*.

Aristotle viewed money as having two functions: *as a means to an end*, and *as an end in itself*. He felt the latter was fraught with danger, and he was right. When we make money our purpose, we remove everything from the equation that fills us with passion. When money is our main purpose for going to work each day, life is lousy.

To be clear: There is absolutely nothing wrong with being wealthy, or wanting to be. But wealth is not the substance of success, but rather its side effect. When it comes to your career, the goal cannot be wealth—but the reward certainly can be.

The heart of the matter is simply this: *that your heart is in the matter*. The key to genuine success lies in *alignment*. To achieve happiness as well as financial success in your career and in your life, all of you must be going in the same direction. The inside and the outside must match: Your motivation, passion, strategies, and goals must be consistent with each other and, even more importantly, with who you *are*.

When you invest your time, passion, energy, and money in your core ideals, success is the inevitable result. The constant study of and immersion in that which reflects your core ideals serves to amplify your power, influence, and capacity to achieve great things. It builds your career, enriches your life, and makes you more of who you truly are. Genuine success of this kind serves to realize your full potential as a human being, and at the same time, creates a life worth living.

Notes

1. http://www.harrisinteractive.com/harris_poll/index.asp?PID=568.

thirteen

WRITING A
NEW MONEY STORY

*I left the woods for as good a reason as I went there. Perhaps it seemed
to me that I had several more lives to live, and could not spare any
more time for that one. It is remarkable how easily and insensibly we
fall into a particular route, and make a beaten track for ourselves. . . .
The surface of the earth is soft and impressible by the feet of men; and
so with the paths which the mind travels. . . . I learned this, at least,
by my experiment: that if one advances confidently in the direction of
his dreams, and endeavors to live the life which he has imagined, he
will meet with a success unexpected in common hours.*

—Henry David Thoreau, from the Conclusion to *Walden*

Major James Nesmeth spent seven years as a prisoner of war in
North Vietnam. During the time he was imprisoned, he was
confined in isolation and allowed no physical activity. In order to preserve his sanity, Major Nesmith decided to practice his golf game.

Of course, he could not play golf physically, not in any literal sense:
He was locked up in a five-by-five cage. But, he reasoned, there were
no limitations of time or space inside his head. He could create the perfect golfing environment in his mind, and practice his game in the pri-
vacy and comfort of his own visualized world.

In his imagination, he evoked a picture of the ideal country club and placed himself at the club, experiencing everything in great detail. He saw himself dressed in golfing clothes, smelled the fragrance of the trees and grass, and as he began to play, he felt himself make each stroke with his entire body. Every day, for seven years, Major Nesmith played a full 18 holes in his mind while his body sat in his five-by-five cage. Taking a full four hours or so to walk himself through every step of the "course," he never hooked, sliced, or missed a single shot or putt. After all, he was making this up, right? So why not make it up *perfect*?

Before joining the Army and shipping out to Vietnam, Major Nesmeth was an average weekend golfer, barely breaking 100. After he was released from his captivity and made his way home, he eventually got out onto a real grass-and-air golf course. His first day out on the links he shot a stunning score of 74. He had taken a full 20 strokes off his game—without once laying a hand on a club.

Master of Your Story

James Nesmith's golf game changed so dramatically for one reason only: That was how he had programmed his brain to see it. He literally made up a new story, and the story calls the shots.

A vision crystallizes possibility into a fundamental, articulated idea. A vision gives hope a shape and form, allowing you to program your future while at the same time rehearsing it. As Nesmith's story so vividly illustrates, you program a message for success in your mind by creating the experience of having achieved it.

Recent positron-emission tomography (PET) scans of the brain have confirmed that the brain assimilates a mental picture similarly, regardless of whether the stimulus derives from the optic nerve or—like Major Nesmith's seven years of golf practice—from the imagination. In other words, the brain does not distinguish between a mental image and a physical image.

Following are several other fascinating findings from this new area of research.

- Thoughts and visualization bring about actual physical changes in the brain.
- When you repeatedly hold a vision of successfully attaining a goal, the act of visualization etches the experience more strongly into the neural networks and neuronal pathways.
- Mental visualization of a complex movement can actually improve performance.

Visualization crystallizes possibility into an articulated idea—the experience changes the brain. A vision serves as a guide and inspiration to design ways to realize it—to live into it.

When you program your system with a visualized goal, you create structural tension in your brain—cognitive dissonance—the difference between where you are and where you visualize and affirm. Your brain then strives to resolve this tension by actualizing the goal, in several ways: by bringing your creative ideas toward that end; by helping you to see potential resources in your environment that you had not previously noticed; and by providing you with heightened motivation to take action on those new perceptions.

Your life is the manifestation of your beliefs. Change begins when you recognize that the story you're living is the story you are writing.

The Pull of the Familiar

Jenny's debt story began with a credit card that she used only rarely, for emergencies. Gradually, the card became a way she rewarded herself when she felt entitled to have nice things. She eventually got a second card, and then a third, and before long she was juggling five cards, paying the minimum on each with another. Her debt cycle was in full swing, occupying much of her waking time and sapping much of her energy.

Jenny finally sought debt counseling, and by following the program her counselor laid out, she became almost debt-free. Oddly, though, as she was nearly out of debt, she relapsed, purchasing her way deep into the red again. Before long she was back to five cards, juggling away, and absorbed by a new mountain of debt.

Jenny was in the same old story once again. Did she really think it would have a new and different ending?

Why is repetition so compelling to intelligent people, even when it makes no sense? Why do we keep walking the same path over and over, as if "trying harder" will make the critical difference—when we know very well where it is almost certain to lead? The path to debt, to plateaued careers, failed relationships, and even failing health may or may not be paved with good intentions, but it is often strewn thick with what seems like senseless repetition.

One reason we keep making the same mistakes over and over is that *our brains like it*. There is something secure and familiar about repetition. We repeat the same story because we know what the outcome will be. Predictability masquerades as effectiveness. The pull of the old grasps hands with our fear of the new to form a powerful force that holds us back from the possibility of our better futures.

Jenny felt like a fish out of water when her major obstacle was not in place. It was as if she *needed* the obstacle in place to anchor her, to provide a focus for feeling bad, a feeling to which she had grown accustomed throughout her life. Feeling good was an unfamiliar story for her, a new territory of experience with no familiar landmarks. Getting debt-free generated an anxiety of the unfamiliar, and she reverted to her old story to recover the comfort of the familiar.

Jenny's experience reflects a critical truth: It can be difficult to the point of impossible to simply let go of an old story—without first writing a new one. *The new story* is the crucial missing link in the process of self-change.

Long-standing habits and accustomed behaviors are like a daily commute. Though repetitive, it is familiar, and therefore it is easy. Changing the pattern is like choosing to dive off the path, to enter suddenly into uncharted territory with no assuring landmarks.

In fact, this is what is literally happening in the brain as a grooved neuronal pathway and network—the default mode—is changed to reflect new experience. New choices generate the creation of entirely new neural connections and pathways. We don't simply look for a new path: We forge that path in synapses and axons.

In coaching work, Jenny learned to couple her anxiety and trepidation with a new interpretation: that it represented progress. As she gave up the debt habit, she developed a new model of feeling good and seeing herself in a positive way.

The Power of Choice

At the University of Hertfordshire in the United Kingdom, a researcher named Ben Fletcher devised a study to get people to break their usual habits. Each day the subjects picked a different option from poles of contrasting behaviors—lively versus quiet, introvert versus extrovert, reactive versus proactive—and behaved according to this assignment. For example, an introverted person would act as an extrovert for an entire day. Twice a week, they also had to stretch themselves to behave in a way entirely outside their usual life pattern, such as eating or reading something they would never have done.

Here was the odd thing: After four months, Fletcher's subjects had lost an average of eleven pounds of body weight! They had not gone on diets, adopted any exercise regimens, or done anything that was aimed at affecting their weight, but lose it they had. What's more, even six months later, despite the fact that the study was over and they had all returned to their usual routines for half a year, nearly all of them had *kept* off the weight.

What on earth could have created such a remarkable and unexpected change? After reviewing his study carefully, Fletcher concluded that when people are required to change their routine behavior, it makes them actually *think* about decisions rather than simply choosing a default mode out of habit. In having to process certain decisions actively, they ended up extending their decisionmaking abilities to other choices in their lives, such as what to eat and what not to.

This is the power of story-busting. Once you begin to examine your previously unexamined choices, you begin a constructive cycle of self-determination. As you exercise the mental muscles of self-reflection, you awaken your capacity to more thoughtfully make active choices in your life, deciding which choices and behaviors are in your best interests—which ones further the storyline you wish to be living, and which do not.

E.B. White, Pulitzer Prize–winning editor of the classic writing handbook *The Elements of Style* and author of such beloved children's books as *Stuart Little* and *Charlotte's Web*, wrote a single sentence about writing that has served as a lifeline for every writer who followed: "The best writing is rewriting." Ernest Hemingway put it a little more bluntly: "The first draft of anything is crap." Though expressed differently, both statements mean essentially the same thing: *You don't have to get it right the first time*. And thank heavens; because this is true not only for novels and short stories, but also for the chapters of your life.

Your money story is the manifestations of your beliefs. You are always free to change your mind, always free to change your beliefs, including core assumptions about who you are.

What Is Your Existing Money Story?

What gives our money stories such power over us is that typically, they are entirely unexamined and unspoken. For most people, they will remain so for the rest of their lives—but not for you. The only reason the language of money is secret is that we *keep* it a secret. It's time to let the cat out of the bag and examine your money story in the light of day, so that if you don't like what it says, you can change it.

There are three essential steps to writing a new money story:

1. Identify clearly your existing money story.
2. Identify which parts of that story you want to keep and which you want to change.
3. Craft a "money mission statement" to guide your new money story.

To help you identify your existing money story, let's revisit the inquiries and self-reflections we've explored throughout this book. If you haven't already taken the time to answer these questions for yourself, you may want to do so now before going on to the later portions of this chapter.

Chapter 1: Money Talks—But What Is It Saying? *(Page 12)*

- My current annual income is $_____.
- To be happy and content, my annual income would need to be $_____.

Chapter 2: What Money Means *(Pages 17, 34–35)*

- To me, money means (answer with a single word): _____.
- What were your most recent purchases of more than $100?
- What did each purchase mean to you? What did each make you feel?
- If they didn't give you that feeling, would you have still bought them at that price?

Chapter 3: The Cost of Money *(Pages 39, 44)*

- List five things you value.
- Which of these would you willingly trade for money?
- What in your life are you compromising right now for money?

Chapter 4: Your Life Is a Story *(Page 59)*

- My life story is a (tragedy, comedy, drama, adventure, etc.): _____.

- In my life story, I play the (choose a word or phrase to describe your role): _____.

Chapter 5: Your Money Story *(Pages 66, 74-79)*

- What is the greatest annual income I can reasonably expect to earn? $_____.
- What is the greatest annual income my money story will allow me to have? $_____.
- What are the beliefs that form the premise of your money story?
- Can you track when in time you made the original decision that led to each view or belief?
- Can you see the connection between the original decision and the view or perspective you now hold?
- What have been the three most significant experiences with money in your life?
- What feelings made each one so significant?
- What do those experiences say about you and your money story?

Ghost of Money Past

- What childhood experiences, attitudes, and ideas about money can you remember?
- When you were growing up, what ideas and attitudes were you presented with regarding money, its use, and its importance?
- How did your parents feel about and behave with money?
- How did they feel, talk about, and behave toward those who had more money than they did?
- How did they feel, talk about, and behave toward those who had less money than they did?
- What did your parents tell you about money?
- Was this consistent with how you saw them behave about money?

Ghost of Money Present

- What do you now believe about money?
- What do you use money to express or do:
  - for yourself?
  - for or to others?
  - as reward for obedience or performance?
  - to enhance growth?
  - to create opportunity?
  - for control (such as buying for your family what you really want yourself)?
  - for punishment (for example, by withholding)?
  - to manipulate behaviors or attachments?
- What statements do your money behaviors make about your sense of who you are?
- Does your money and its pursuit connect you with others, or separate you?

Ghost of Money Future

- Do you use money to advance your sense of freedom? Of your creativity? Of your power? Of your authority? Of your self-worth?
- How fully and honestly do you speak with your spouse or partner about money, finances, spending, goals, savings, and debt?
- How open with your children are you about money details?
- What do you tell your children about money?
- How consistent is this with how they see you behave about money?

Chapter 7: Bubbles and Bubble Baths *(Page 124)*

Quiz: What Is Your Investing Mindset?

- Do you seem to consistently lose money on investments?
- Do you feel paralyzed or afraid when it comes to investing money?
- Do you feel overwhelmed by the prospect of learning more about managing and investing your money?

- Do you expect or allow other people to make money decisions for you, even if they are not experts?
- Do you respond to financial gains with depression or feelings of guilt?
- Do you respond to financial losses with self-recrimination or feelings of anger or futility?
- Is it painful for you to admit mistakes or to cut your losses?
- Do you have trouble putting aside thoughts of "what might have been if only" you had purchased investments earlier or sold them earlier?
- Do you resist seeking suggestions and advice, even differing opinions, to judge a prospective investment or business decision?
- Do you feel you are fully able to make all your own financial decisions by yourself—despite consistent evidence to the contrary?

Chapter 8: Spend, Baby, Spend! *(Pages 132, 142–145)*

Quiz: Are You a Compulsive Spender?

- Do you go shopping, whether in person or on the Internet, to escape feeling bored, empty, defeated, angry, or scared?
- After a setback or disappointment, does it feel like spending money will help you feel better?
- Do you shop or spend money in a way that creates conflicts for you, or between you and others?
- Do you spend impulsively and later wish you hadn't bought the items?
- Have your spending habits created chaos in your life?
- Do you buy things with your credit cards that you wouldn't buy if you had to pay cash?
- When you shop or make a purchase, does your mood change?
- When you spend money, do you sometimes feel a secret thrill, as if you're doing something taboo, dangerous, or defiant?

- Do you think about money that you don't have, money you wish you had, or money you owe, and then still go out to shop?
- Do you compromise your life or leisure to adjust to your shopping debts?
- Are you unable to fully enjoy what you purchase because you feel bad, guilty, ashamed, or embarrassed about your purchases?
- Do you make purchases to enhance your self-esteem?
- If no one else noticed or observed that you had bought certain items, would you be significantly less likely to buy them?

Money Exercise for Couples

- What are the three things you have done with money that make you feel the proudest?
- What are the three things you have done with money that make you feel the most embarrassed or ashamed?
- What are the three smartest money choices you've ever made?
- What are the three worst mistakes you have made with or about money?
- What are the three best money investments you have made?
- What are the three worst money investments you have made?
- What are the three things most important to you that you've bought with money?
- What are the three things most important to you that you've traded for money?
- What are the three most important things that money will buy for you?
- What are the three things that money will not buy for you?
- What are the three things you would agree to give up in your life for more money?
- What are the three most important things you would do with more money?

Chapter 9: Into Thin Air: The Secret Language of Debt
(Pages 159-160)

Debt Quiz

- Do you routinely make minimum payments on credit card balances?
- Are the balances on your credit card statements gradually increasing every month?
- Do you have a balance on one or more cards of more than 50 percent of the credit limit for that card?
- Do you often use cash advances on your credit cards to pay other bills?
- Do you routinely "play the float" on cards (juggle payments between cards) in order to pay bills?
- Do you regularly have past due bills, rent, or mortgage payments?
- Do you have little or no savings?
- Have you been denied credit or had a credit card purchase declined during the last quarter?
- Have you had one or more checks bounce during the last quarter?
- Have you had one or more notices or phone calls from a collection agency in last quarter?
- Do you ever hide, misrepresent, or neglect to mention a debt to your spouse or other family member?
- Do you ever hide a bill or credit card statement from your spouse or other family member?
- Are you unable to state, offhand and without sitting down to go through your records, the exact total amount of money you presently owe?

Chapter 11: How Much Is Enough? *(Pages 204–206)*

Quiz: Are You a Workaholic?

- When you leave work at the end of the work day, do problems, projects, phone calls, appointments, and meetings follow you home and encroach upon your private time?

- When you are away from your work, do you find yourself replaying conversations at work, reassessing decisions, and reexamining work details?
- Do you sometimes find it difficult to enjoy any activity that is not connected with work?
- When you are not at work or not able to work, do you feel anxiety, depression, or other types of discomfort that might be described as symptoms of withdrawal?
- Have you convinced yourself that success in your line of work necessitates a dedication bordering on the obsessive—that working the hours you work isn't really your preference but "the job demands it"?
- Do you take setbacks, feedback, or criticism of work projects personally?
- Do you see what you do for work as being who you *are*?
- Are you seeking to prove your worth, whether to someone else or to yourself, by the work you do?
- Do you believe that only extreme effort and accomplishment will fully demonstrate your true value?
- Is work an escape from doing things you would rather avoid, such as meeting family obligations or facing family conflicts?
- Do others close to you complain regularly about your work hours or about your never being around?
- Has anyone close to you ever described you as a workaholic?

Quiz: Are You Addicted to Less?

- Do you believe it is more virtuous or admirable to be poor than to be rich?
- Do you believe being poor is more spiritual than being wealthy?
- When you have an influx of money, do you tend to spend it

quickly and/or impulsively and return rapidly to a familiar state of poverty?

- Do you often refrain from making needed repairs on your car or your home, or from getting medical care for yourself (such as regular checkups or dental cleaning), because you don't feel you can afford to spend the money?
- Is it more comfortable for you to spend money on others than on yourself?
- Do you undercharge for your work or your skills?
- Is it uncomfortable for you to collect on fees that people owe you for your work?
- Does it seem like whenever you are about to get ahead financially, some crisis happens in your life that gets in the way and stops your progress cold?

Chapter 12: The Heart of the Matter *(Pages 218–222)*

List your top three ideals. Then, list your top three needs.

Four Inquiries for Honing Your New Money Story

The following four questions will help you identify which parts of your money story you want to preserve, which you want to change, and which you want to toss out onto the editing room floor.

1. **What do you want to *keep* or *enhance*?**
   The important thing about your money story is to discern what works and what does not. The components that work don't need fixing. The ones that don't work need to be changed, revised, or tossed.

   No matter what your situation, the chances are excellent that not every aspect of your money story is broken. You may, for example, struggle with debts you can never seem to get free of, yet be quite successful at investing. Even if you have some dysfunctional or deeply ingrained negative money patterns, not all your money beliefs are necessarily unproductive or destructive. As you write your new money story, you want to make sure you don't throw out the baby with the bathwater.

In what areas of your financial life have you felt successful? What accomplishments are you most proud of? What are you good at when it comes to money? As important as it is to be honest about your weaknesses and failings, it is equally crucial to be forthright about your strengths.

Choose three areas of your existing money story that you'd like to keep or enhance:

a. _____

b. _____

c. _____

2. **What do you want to *let go*?**

For any belief or behavior, there comes a point when you must ask yourself, "Does it work?" For the things that don't serve us, we need to find a way to release them.

This is not always easy, and it takes honest reflection. Unfulfilled hope—the persistent sense of "what might have been"—is sometimes the most difficult goodbye. But it's time for honest reflection: If there are elements of your money story that simply aren't working, it's time to thank them for their time, shake their hands while looking them in the eye, and tell them a kind but firm, "Goodbye."

F. Scott Fitzgerald once said that in the process of creating good writing, you have to "murder your darlings." Sometimes the aspects of ourselves that we most need to let go of are those we happen to be especially fond of or attached to. But remember the question to ask in the unblinking light of day: *Is it working?*

Review your money beliefs and behaviors. If you could eliminate three of them from your life, which ones would have the most impact?

a. _____

b. _____

c. _____

3. What do you want to *avoid*?

There are some things in the world that can't be changed. They're a part of life, and you may simply need to avoid them. An alcoholic can't eliminate alcohol from the world, but he can make a decision to stay out of bars.

Recognize what you can and can't determine. Disengage from battles you cannot win. For example, if you're trying to change another person, you'll probably be about as successful as if you were seeking to single-handedly reverse the earth's axial spin.

Those things you may want to avoid are not limited to bars, casinos, and credit cards. You can also decide to avoid such nonproductive, energy-draining activities as arguing with others or complaining about your job.

What three things can you avoid that will positively rewrite your money story?

a. _____

b. _____

c. _____

4. What do you want to *change*?

There are also beliefs and behaviors that may not work, but which you still might be able to use to your advantage. When a problem or difficulty recurs, rather than simply trying to get around it, get past it, or get over it, realize that it's only there because that's the way you wrote the story. If you created it, why not consider creating something else instead?

For example, if you feel intimidated by investing, you might change your fear of the unknown into an intention to become more informed, with a commitment to take action on that new information.

What are three behaviors or beliefs that you could change, reverse, or leverage to help you toward financial success?

a. _____

b. _____

c. _____

Create a Money Mission Statement

Financial success is a journey, and it requires a roadmap. In the guidelines in Chapters 6, 7, and 9, we talked about creating a simple financial plan. A mission statement is something more basic than a financial plan: It is the bedrock upon which your financial plan is built. Your money mission statement captures in a single sentence the essence of what you are seeking to create with money. If your life were a movie, this sentence would be on the poster.

A mission statement springs from four elements: ideals, purpose, strategies, and goals.

Ideals are the core values that motivate and guide you, such as helping people, mastery, being your own boss, putting family first, making a difference, expressing yourself, and so forth. They come first, because they define what's important to you.

Purpose is what you intend to accomplish: to be successful, to make money, to be happy, to retire early. It's the destination and the reason for making the trip—the *why*. Why make more money? Why retire, or make a million dollars, or capture more market share, or buy a sports car, or buy a summer home? A compelling purpose engages your passion.

Strategy involves *how* you intend to serve your purpose: develop certain skills, minimize expenses, engage a financial advisor, set aside time to meditate, implement a plan to do what you do uniquely well.

Goals are not the endpoint of the journey: They are signposts along the way. Let's say your purpose is to travel the world, and your strategy is to retire early so you can do that. You'll need to achieve some interim goals, such as funding a retirement plan, increasing your savings or earnings, creating a network of friends in different countries, etc.

We are always reaching our goals, consciously or not. Making your goals explicit and tangible will help ensure that you reach the ones you intended to reach. Effective goals are those that are SMART: Specific, Measurable, Attainable, Realistic, and Time-bound.

Your Money Mission Statement: Worksheet

Ideals: List your three most important ideals, in order of priority, that will guide your financial decision making:

1. _____

2. _____

3. _____

Purpose: Why do you want *x* amount of money in your life? How will it serve you?

_____

_____

_____

Strategy: How will you realize that purpose? What steps will you take?

_____

_____

_____

Goals: What are your SMART goals?

1. _____

2. _____

3. _____

For each goal, identify the next two or three steps you will take to move yourself toward that goal, and set a timeline for each.

Your Money Mission Statement: One Sentence

In one sentence, what is your mission statement regarding your money?

_____

_____

_____

Making the Story Real

Earlier we spoke about new findings from PET scans, and the extraordinary power of a held vision to etch itself physically into the complexly grooved surface of the brain. This research has also shown that there are several key elements to a successful visualization that vastly assist the process.

Repetition

The neural networks dedicated to your vision must be renewed and repeated regularly, or they will fade, just as muscle tissue will soften and dissipate if the muscle is not used regularly.

Integration

Consciously incorporate this new vision into an ongoing larger story of you and your life. A vision cannot exist in isolation: Don't just *see* the vision, *live* it.

Specificity

The more detailed your visual image, the more specifically etched your brain will be about achieving the goal.

Written Articulation

Write it down. Research on memory tells us that a new idea or fact lasts an average of 40 seconds in short-term memory before it's gone — unless you write it down to review. Read each one at the beginning and the end of each day.

Major Nesmith did not have the luxury of being able to write his vision on paper, but he certainly fulfilled the other three conditions in a big way: His vision was extremely specific, it was integrated into his picture of his life, and he repeated it faithfully every single day for seven years.

That is exactly what you need to do. Picture yourself having just succeeded at your goal, at a specific time in the future, such as one year from now. Create this success experience specific to time, place, and experience, using all five senses. Hold the energy of the precise outcome you've just achieved, the goals met, and the feelings the experience brings. Imagine the details of the scene of your success inside and outside, engaging all senses, thoughts, feelings, and bodily experience along with details of the scene.

For example, for a successful business transaction, include the values and needs fulfilled, the impact this deal will have on others, the money you have made from it, and the particulars of what you are doing in the moment, right down to the feeling of sitting down in a pair of leather-bound chairs and shaking someone's hand. Believe it or not, Major Nesmith's brutal environment actually brought with it a very particular benefit: Like it or not, he was forced to sit quietly and spend time thinking, without distraction.

While sometimes a job can feel like it, you are probably *not* living in a five-by-five metal cage. Therefore, to take 20 strokes off your game and carve a new vision of success into your brain, you'll need to take the time and make the discipline to put yourself in that quiet place of solitude every day.

At the beginning and end of each day, carve out a few moments to play your vision. The vision comes first and initiates the experience.

How to Talk to Yourself About Money

Your words reveal your internal model of reality. In crafting your mission statement, you'll want to use only language that supports your success.

This applies a hundredfold to the language you use every day. Nobody has more influence on your beliefs and assumptions than you yourself. Others may tell you "the market's down" once, or twice, or 10 times in a day—but you may well repeat that belief *a thousand times or more* per day. Your dad may have said "Money doesn't grow on trees!" a few dozen or a few hundred times in your childhood—but that's nothing compared with the hundreds of thousands of times you may have reaffirmed that belief to yourself.

For example, if you say you will *try* to reach a goal, you may be protecting yourself from anticipated failure. *Trying* speaks of a less than full commitment, a potential diversion to other alternatives against failure. The phrases *I'll try, I should, I ought to, I know I need to,* are those of the not-yet-committed. Such word choices provide a built-in "out." When you hear someone say, "I'm going to try to quit smoking," you know that he or she will continue to smoke.

There is perhaps no factor more important to your success than the story you tell yourself, and the language you couch it in can make all the difference.

Use Specific, Concrete Terms

"More" is not a goal: It can never be reached. Abstract terms and goals can impede precise action. Nonspecific terms generalize and universalize experiences, and therefore have little or no power to evoke a specific focus and invoke a particular action. Wanting to *be happy*, to *change*, or to *be comfortable with money* defy goal-planning and strategy.

Again, express your goals in terms that are Specific, Measurable, Attainable, Realistic, and Time-bound. Concrete goals include dates, amounts, and other tangible measurements that describe *specifically* what you are going to do and the results you intend to bring about. Abstractions such as *freedom, security*, and *happiness* are wonderful to hold for yourself—but they are *ideals*, not *goals*.

Use Active Language

Active language—*I will, I do, I am*—reflects an active position and ownership of initiative. Passive language—*I'll try, I hope, If I'm lucky*—results from beliefs about fate, luck, destiny, victimhood, entitlement, or hope. The language of this position makes the creator both subject and victim: *My fear took over, The market beat me up this week. . . .*

Pressure words—*should, have to, ought to, need to, must*—indicate an external point of reference and carry the implicit suggestion that you are not in charge of your destiny but at the mercy of external forces. Use language that reflects the fact that you are taking authority over your life: You are the author of your story.

Use Positive Language

Rather than stating what you don't want or want to avoid, frame your plan and criteria in positive terms: what you *do* want, what you *will* do. Let go of words that describe limitation, such as *impossible, can't, don't,* or *shouldn't.* These reveal an assumption of constraint and a presupposition of failure.

When you talk about money, you are talking about *yourself.* Your money story reveals you and your relationship not just to money but to yourself. How well you understand yourself and what you do with that understanding determines your money story. Change your money story, and you change your life.

fourteen

LIVING A NEW MONEY STORY

Try not. Do. Or do not. There is no try.

— Yoda, in *The Empire Strikes Back* (1980)

A group of penguins got together to discuss something that had been bothering them for some time. They knew they were birds, and birds, they reasoned, are supposed to be able to fly. They had seen other birds fly from time to time. But none of *them* were flying. In fact, they couldn't remember ever having seen a penguin fly. So what was stopping them from achieving their potential? None of them had an answer—so they decided they would attend a motivational seminar to help them achieve their full potential.

The big day finally came, and all the penguins shuffled into their auditorium seats, eager to hear what the seminar presenter had to say. After a few announcements, the speaker was introduced, and then he began to address the room.

"I see all you penguins here in our audience today," he said. "And I feel your pain. I understand your frustration. But I'm here to tell you, today, *you will fly*! The only thing that's holding you back is yourselves. All you need is the belief that you can fly, and the determination to follow through on that belief and make it happen.

"Now, here's what I want you to do," he continued, and he began to flap his arms as he spoke. "Follow after me, and do exactly as I'm doing." He encouraged them to flap their wings, visualize themselves in flight, and repeat a series of empowering affirmations about flying. The penguins just sat and stared. Finally, one penguin stood up and began to flap his wings. He flapped harder and faster—and before long, he rose off the floor and began flying around the conference room! When the others saw what was happening, they were thunderstruck . . . and then, one by one, they joined in, and soon the room was filled with penguins flying around and honking gleefully back and forth to one another. It was a remarkable sight.

At the end of the training, they were so grateful, they gave the speaker a standing ovation that lasted a full five minutes.

When the seminar was over, the penguins walked home.

In the last chapter, you wrote some words on paper. You chose those words with care and they represent great meaning and significance—but still, your "money mission statement" is words on paper: an outline of your story, not the story itself. The truth about your money story is that it's not something you write on paper, it's something you paint onto the canvas of your life. It is not really something you write; it is something you *live*.

My most fervent hope is that you will not put down this book and then walk home, like the penguins at the motivational seminar, but that, having read it, you will *fly*.

Financial Intelligence

According to Warren Buffett, the world's most successful investor, "Investing is not a game where the guy with the 160 IQ beats the guy with a 130 IQ. Once you have ordinary intelligence, what you need is the temperament to control the urges that get other people into trouble in investing."[1]

Buffett's observation is supported not only by his exceptional track record but also by research. One of psychology's open secrets is that IQ, school grades, and SAT scores do not accurately predict how well one will do in life. *People skills* correlate with financial success far more consistently than IQ skills. What Buffett calls "ordinary intelligence," combined with a common-sense ability to integrate that basic knowledge with the realities of human behavior, both in ourselves and in those around us, is a far greater prerequisite for leading a successful life than more academic kinds of intelligence.

Internationally known psychologist and *New York Times* science reporter Daniel Goleman coined the term "emotional intelligence" to describe just this sort of common-sense intelligence, and he offers compelling evidence that this "EQ" often supercedes IQ in life importance. His message struck such a chord that his 1995 book on the subject, *Emotional Intelligence: Why It Can Matter More than IQ*, sold more than 5 million copies in 30 languages. According to Goleman, emotional intelligence consists of these basic qualities:

- Self-motivation
- Persistence in the face of stress and frustrations
- Self-regulation of moods and feelings
- Empathic attunement to others
- Managing distress to not occlude reason
- Impulse control and delay of gratification

Buffett is right: Successful investing is not so much a matter of *intellectual intelligence* as it is one of *emotional intelligence*, coupled with a solid grounding in simple principles of financial common sense (such as those we explored in our chapters on investing, spending, and debt). The combination of these two, emotional intelligence and basic financial common sense, is the real key to *financial success*.

We might call this *financial intelligence*.

The wonderful thing about financial intelligence is that it can be learned, and it takes no exceptional inborn talent or rare attributes to hone to a keen edge. Let's look at some of the essential aspects of financial intelligence, as hinted at in Dr. Goleman's definition.

Delayed Gratification

A classic study at the Stanford campus school illustrates the impact of practicing delayed gratification. In the study, groups of four-year-olds were given a chance to have one small marshmallow immediately or a number of larger marshmallows if they waited about 15 minutes while the tester left the room. Some children grabbed the small marshmallow immediately. Others went through an agonizing quarter-hour, waiting for the tester to return and distracting themselves by covering their eyes, sleeping, or actively engaging each other.

The subjects were then tracked, and in follow-up studies many years later, the researchers found that those who had been able to delay gratification at age four were more confident, self-assertive, and successful as adolescents. For example, those who delayed gratification had an average SAT score 210 points higher than those who did not delay gratification. In fact, the ability to delay gratification was found to be *twice* as predictive of SAT tests than was IQ.

The ability to delay gratification is not only a predictor of later success traits; it also has direct and significant application in our financial lives. Chronic overspending and excessive debt are direct symptoms of an inability or reluctance to delay gratification. We didn't want "starter homes," we wanted the dream home, and we wanted it *now*—and thus the world was introduced to the miracle of subprime mortgages.

In the investment world the promise of immediate gratification, such as a hot stock tip, can override a carefully drawn plan. A surging market or incipient bubble can sweep investors and their emotions into its force far more readily when they have diminished capacity for delayed gratification.

> **Recommendation:** To develop strong financial intelligence, strengthen your capacity to delay gratification. Think about what you want to buy, research it, visualize it—and wait.

Optimism

Optimism, the anticipation of the best possible outcome, motivates; pessimism, its opposite, derails and demotivates. Those with a greater personal store of optimism are better able to sustain their focus and endeavors and are less susceptible to the distractions of anxiety, setbacks, or frustration. The more optimistic among us navigate our lives with less anxiety or emotional distress. (It's important to note that examining worst-case scenarios and downside possibilities offers valuable assessments, and is *not* the same thing as pessimism.)

The staying power and success of those who maintain optimism was demonstrated by Martin Seligman in an extensive study of insurance retailers. About 75 percent of life insurance salespeople quit within the first three years. The optimists in his study had a 37 percent greater success than those less optimistic. The explanation given was that optimistic salespeople experience setbacks just as often as everyone else does—but for them, a simple "no" is not a defeat, nor is it taken personally, but is seen simply as one more step in the process of getting to a *yes*.

The ability to sustain this sort of positive, constructive emotional frame can be applied to any and every aspect of daily life.

Optimism is not the same as *hoping*. "Some day" fantasies idealize the future and push optimism over the edge of reality into the domain of rabbits' feet and wishing wells. A counterpart to denial, the unrealistic "someday" ignores reality. It keeps us in persistent search for the "perfect person" or "perfect deal" to provide everything we ever wanted or needed. It makes us think the $50 stock that tanked to $5 will come back . . . someday. Optimism brings out our persistence and best efforts, while hope untethered to pragmatism renders us a prisoner of rose-colored fantasies.

RECOMMENDATION: To develop strong financial intelligence, strengthen your capacity to maintain a positive outlook and visualize your preferred outcome. Use your reason and sense of facts to research best-case, worst-case, and mid-range projections—and keep your emotional eye fixed on the brightest horizon.

Emotional Control

It is feelings rather than fact that determine most of our decisions. Financial decisions often result from unexamined feelings.

A feeling of safety exists when remaining within a crowd, and anxiety exists as an outlier. Safety in numbers often preempts the insecurity of going against the crowd. Validation, acceptance, approval, and connection all exist within crowd momentum. These emotions hold powerful influence over otherwise intellectual decisions of money and investing. We love stocks when they are expensive and hate them when they are cheap. Stock prices reflect expectations about growth, and those expectations can make investors' view of reality quite elastic. In bull markets, investors expand their time horizon to extend further into the future, while discouraged investors in a bear market shorten their time horizon to as little as six months. These changes in perspective have far more to do with feeling than objective reality.

Bubbles, such as the tech boom of the late 1990s (or the tulip boom in the early 1600s), are the most highly visible examples of emotional investing, but the majority of *all* mistakes and losses in investing result not from bad information or bad financial strategy, but from emotions untempered by reason. At times of stress or dramatic events, our rational and strategic decisions about money and investing are preempted by our emotions.

Emotional intelligence isn't about having "smarter" feelings, it is about having the ability to manage one's feelings at times when they are at their strongest and to integrate them along with reason and other faculties into one's decisions. The moment when we need the rule of reason most—during times of pressure or crisis—is exactly when we abandon them most readily. Most investors fail because they get too excited at the top and too fearful at the bottom.

RECOMMENDATION: When financial decisions present themselves, identify, articulate, and acknowledge your feelings. Then, set them to the side. Consider them, but only as minority partners to the decision.

Capacity to Ignore the Herd

Warren Buffett has distilled his "secret" down to 12 words: "Be greedy when others are fearful, and fearful when others are greedy." Baron Nathan de Rothschild said much the same thing in the late eighteenth century when he coined one of the most famous adages in the world of finance: "Buy at the sound of cannons, sell at the sound of trumpets." Over two centuries apart, both financiers were giving us the same advice: *Be a contrarian.* (Remember Groucho Marx's opening number from *Horse Feathers?* "Whatever it is, I'm against it!")

A contrarian is defined as one who takes a position opposite to the prevailing trend. If everyone is buying stocks, the contrarian sells to lock in gains; if market sentiment is bearish, the contrarian buys. A true contrarian sells at the highs and buys at the lows, countering all prevailing market sentiment and emotional inclination.

While being contrarian sounds good in theory, it is nearly impossible to practice. Scrully Blotnick, Ph.D., studied contrarian theory in investing as a columnist for *Forbes* magazine. He surveyed various groups of people to see who subscribed to contrarian thinking and investing. Nearly 90 percent of the people he interviewed considered themselves as being contrarian investors—yet if this were true, that would have left only a 10 percent "majority" for them to oppose!

True contrarians are in fact quite rare. Reason says, "Buy low and sell high" in order to take profits and cut losses. However, in practice this is virtually impossible to do, because it is extremely difficult emotionally to sell off a stock when it has been escalating rapidly, or to buy it when it has been plummeting. Emotions ride the bandwagon. Most investors cannot follow a Buffett-like strategy because they get excited at the top and depressed at the bottom.

Actually, what characterizes savvy investors like Buffett is not really a black-and-white equation of simply doing the opposite of what everyone else is doing. Put more accurately, it is the capacity to *ignore* what everyone else is doing and assess the situation dispassionately. These highly skilled individuals have the ability to *supercede their emotions* and remain objective, even at times when the majority are succumbing to stages of panic or greed. It's not a better grasp of facts and figures but their highly developed sense of emotional intelligence that underlies their success.

When asked how he was able to profit so significantly from the French stock market panic of 1871, Baron de Rothschild's son, Nathaniel, replied, "When the streets of Paris are running with blood, I buy." His rare ability allowed him to distance himself from crowd momentum, and at the same time to observe it as a marker for decisions.

> **Recommendation:** "Keep your eye on the ball and your head in the game." Focus on the facts of the situation, without distraction, and remember the big picture, your purpose, and your plan.

Can We Talk?

As important as it is, if you want to live a truly successful money story, financial intelligence alone is not enough. And the operative word in that sentence is *alone*.

In Chapter 13 we looked at some key principles in how to talk to ourselves about money. Equally important is to learn how to talk about it *to each other*. "No man is an island, entire of itself," wrote the poet John Donne. We do not live our money stories in isolation. For most of us, the bulk of our money decisions, and certainly our most significant ones, are choices we will make in concert with at least one other person.

The problem is, *we don't really know how to talk about money*. Like sex and death, money is a perennially taboo subject in our culture. We skirt around it, make jokes about it, refer to it obliquely, or avoid it entirely. We tell half-truths about it, get defensive about it, worry about it but refuse to name that anxiety for what it is, and make up stories about it. The one thing we so often *don't* do is simply talk about it: Tell the truth, the whole truth, and nothing but the truth. In fact, the inability to communicate well about money is one of the most common causes of marital conflict and relationship discord, right up there with the inability to communicate well about sex.

By now, we've thoroughly covered the idea that money can represent many different forces and issues in our lives. However, some money issues really *are* about money. And knowing how to talk about these genuine money issues is nowhere more important than in your primary relationship.

In our quest to live a healthier, more productive and fulfilling money story, one of the single most powerful things we can do is learn how to communicate about money openly, honestly, and productively. And note: Each of these three conditions—*openly*, *honestly*, and *productively*—is distinct; they are not three words for the same thing.

The following guidelines will help establish clear, effective communication around money. And when that happens, you'll be amazed at how much stronger, more enjoyable, and more fulfilling a relationship becomes.

Seven Guidelines for Effective Money Conversations

1. **Communicate from a base of empathy.** Each person has a distinct point of view. Communication is not the triumph of one viewpoint over another. It is the establishment of a common ground for understanding different points of view, in order to create a mutual, collaborative agreement or plan.

    Requiring that someone else respond to you in one particular way renders that person and their response inauthentic.

    Developing empathy with another is predicated on first doing so with yourself. If you are not genuinely aware of how you are experiencing the world, you cannot become similarly aware of another person's perspective. Empathy is a way of listening to yourself or to another person with resonance of an entire experience of feeling, thinking, perceiving, and behaving.

Another term for this is *rapport*. Rapport derives from the old French word *rapporter*, meaning to *bring back* or *carry back*. Establishing rapport with another is to travel into that person's sphere, to step into their shoes, and bring back a sense of who they are and how they are experiencing the world.

2. **Seek to understand—not to change.** Much of the difficulty in relationships comes from our thinking we can change someone else's behavior or attitude. The only person you can change is you. The impulse to change another's behavior usually springs from some dissatisfaction in an aspect of ourselves. Seeking to have another person live an unexpressed part of yourself can be both unsatisfying and addictive. Attempting to change someone else's personality, attitude, style, or mode of processing won't work, and will only derail the process.

   What someone believes is more important than what they know. Learn your partner's belief system, because these assumptions drive behavior and filter what is heard.

3. **Clarify with questions.** A large corporation's executive team huddled around a tape recorder, listening to the most recent presentation by their company's CEO. They played the recording, rewound it, and played it again, and again, and yet again. A junior officer walked in and saw them all sitting around the machine, looks of bewilderment on their faces. She asked them what was going on.

   In his speech, they explained, the CEO had indicated that the organization should "embrace more color." They each had a different idea about what he had meant by this directive: a change in dress? Or in racial makeup? Perhaps, in office decor, in language, in marketing message, in their logo and letterhead? They were combing through the speech, parsing each word, looking for clues as to what the CEO had in mind.

   "Has any of you picked up the phone and asked him?" she asked. No one had thought of that.

Socrates taught us that asking questions is a far more effective way to engage with others than providing answers. The detail may contain the feeling and the important aspects that otherwise would have to be assumed.

4. **Reflect back what you hear.** When discussing an emotionally charged subject such as money, reflect back to the other person what you hear them saying before responding with your own thoughts and feelings. This reflection insures that you correctly registered what was said, and more importantly, what was *meant*, and it also provides the other party the opportunity to clarify their own expression, if necessary.

   It also communicates your sense of respect and regard for the other person: It says that before launching into your point of view, you want to make sure that you have correctly grasped theirs. And by the way, this has the happy fringe benefit of better positioning your partner to then hear your point of view.

5. **Listen between the lines.** Yogi Berra once said, "You can see a lot by watching." You can also hear a lot by listening. The truth is always conspiring to assemble itself before us, if we will just get ourselves out of the way and pay attention. We are always communicating, and there are many languages; some even use words.

   Feeling invisible to another creates a unique sense of being eclipsed, the pain of not being seen by another. Eclipsing is when one body in the solar system passes in front of another, rendering it invisible, as if it disappears. People do this, too. While eclipsing may masquerade as rivalry or jealousy, it is significantly more powerful.

   Listen literally and closely to what someone says, and you will see constant clues about what is wanted and needed. Truth and reality are perception.

6. **Acknowledge the different roles you each have adopted.** No two people are alike, and no two halves of a relationship are identical. Be aware of the distinct roles you have each taken on within your

relationship. These may reflect your gender, your differing income levels, your differing skills or native abilities around money (e.g., perhaps one of you is naturally better organized and more easily handles bills), differing roles in child rearing, and so on.

Acknowledging these roles doesn't mean they are fixed or immutable; it simply means being clear about how you've agreed, implicitly or explicitly, to function together at this point. If you want to change that, you can discuss it; if you're happy with how it is, the "don't fix what ain't broke" principle may apply. In any case, it's impossible to genuinely assess how your distinct roles are working when they live in the murky realm of the assumed and unexplored. Talk about it.

It's particularly important to acknowledge the income and work differences and potential of you and your spouse, and the implications this has for the balance of power in your relationship. There are almost always differences; don't ignore them.

Be aware too of the rules, stated or unstated, by which male and female roles are chosen and rewarded in the family, and of such jobs as who makes decisions, who handles financial matters, and who handles the daily matters of life, including household, children, and chores. Clarify how each of you is validated or invalidated, empowered or eroded in areas of work and money.

7. **When communication breaks down, step up.** Everyone fails to empathize with another at times. Despite our best intentions, we mess up. We're only human. Most important in a relationship is the repair of such an empathic rupture, because then true understanding can occur. At times the most important thing may not be what you have done, but what you do after what you have done.

When an important relationship is derailed by communication lapse or unintended thoughtlessness, it's often useful to set aside an attachment to being "right." To forgive another is to free yourself.

25 Guidelines for Living Your New Money Story

In the end, your actions are the language in which your money story speaks. Whether you choose to buy or not, to save, to invest, or to decide not to decide, your money behaviors will be the final expression of your beliefs, and will determine your financial success.

Some of the following guidelines are restatements of suggestions you've encountered earlier in this book; some are new.

1. **Keep your money mission statement always visible and in focus.** Your money mission statement defines the essence of your financial goals and the principles and ideals underlying them. It proclaims the meaning, use, and value of money to you, including short- and long-term plans. Keep this statement where you can see it often — on your desk, on your wall, on your computer — and review it periodically, refining it as needed, to make sure that it accurately orients your decisions with your purpose and philosophy.

2. **Have a plan.** Create a strategy and a fully informed, well-structured financial plan, with provisions for saving and investment that are in alignment with your money mission statement, based on facts rather than on emotions. Periodically review your plan to make sure it reflects your purpose, your values, and your most up-to-date information and advisements from counsel you seek and trust.

3. **Stick to your plan.** In times of trauma, crisis, or circumstances beyond your control, stick to your plan.

    In times of elation, unexpected growth, and great success, stick to your plan.

    When you are most prone to overreact, stick to your plan.

    When you recognize procrastination or failure to act or react, stick to your plan.

    When your plan isn't working well, review whether you are fully executing the plan; if you are, then review the current validity of your plan. Once you are satisfied that your current plan is solid—then stick to your plan.

4. **Seek out suggestions, critique, advice, and expertise.** Consult with people knowledgeable in specific areas. At times this may be difficult emotionally, when it would seem easier to consult (read collude) with someone who will mirror your views and agree with your opinions. The search for validation aims to maintain your comfort zone and avoid change. Consulting a mirror for advice is what the wicked queen does in *Snow White*. Leave the mirror for touching up makeup; for your plan, consult objective experts.

   Seek those expert in areas other than your own, and those with different points of view. Listen from another's perspective, while not abandoning your own. Use that new information from a flexible and informed position.

   In addition to a financial advisor and other experts in specific fields, consider using the services of a coach, mentor, or mastermind group; they can provide invaluable perspective on how (and whether) your actions, decisions, and ideals are all in effective alignment, and if they are not, can help you reassess and realign.

5. **Estimate expenses in detail.** Studies at the Robert H. Smith School of Business at the University of Maryland found that people spend less when they have to estimate expenses in detail.

   Don't *ballpark* what your life and the things in it will cost. This is not a ball game, it's your life. Get down to hard numbers.

6. **Establish priorities.** Prioritize plans and pursuits based on core ideals and needs. Money and finances must be balanced with family, work, health, friendships, leisure, making a difference in your community, and taking care of yourself. Neglect or imbalance in one area may generate overcompensation in other areas.

   Priorities are not static; they are not something you can figure out on a weekend and then set aside for the rest of the year. (Remember the penguins.) You will likely reconfront, refine, and even redefine priorities every day, and make decisions based on your fresh answers to the fundamental question: What is *really* important?

7. **Align your internal ideals with your financial goals.** Your ideals, the internal model of who and what you are, generate the unspoken assumptions on which you operate. Clarify your external goals to be certain that they are consistent with your ideals.

   The clarity and consistency of your principles and goals can be called on at times of emergency or confusion to help bring the big picture into focus. Be certain there is a fit between your internal and external goals, that what you want to accomplish is consistent with your ideals. This consistency can provide an organizing structure and direction to your ambition.

8. **Distinguish needs from wants.** A *need* is an essential requirement, a necessity for mind, body, or spirit. You can get sick if you don't have enough of what you need: nutrition, touch, rest, or security. A need can be satisfied.

   You can also get sick if you have too much of what you *want* (for example, Mexican food, alcohol, sexual freedom, solitude).

   Wants (wishes and desires) are replaceable with other wants, but a need cannot substitute for another need. And you can never get enough of that which you don't need.

9. **Determine what is good enough.** The pursuit of perfection results from not having a standard of what is *good enough*. "More" is not a goal. More money, like perfection, is a quest never satisfied. For perfectionists, failure may even be a relief, ending the relentless and impossible pursuit of perfection. The undefined pursuit of "more" is a guaranteed plan for failure.

   As playwright Neil Simon said, "Money brings some happiness. But after a certain point, all it brings is more money."

   Having an endpoint lets you know when you arrive, when you can feel satisfaction, when you can experience effectiveness and mastery at reaching a goal.

10. **Know what reaching a goal will do and what it will not do.** Monetary wealth can provide pleasure, luxury, and financial security, but it may not make your marriage better. It is important to know what achieving a goal *will* do, so that you have the clarity to distinguish what it will *not* do.

    A common mechanism for keeping hope alive is stopping short of a goal so there is no need to confront the illusion that reaching the goal will provide all the hoped-for solutions. Reaching a goal will not undo the past, or make other troubles go away.

11. **Don't invest with your heart.** Never fall in love or hate with a stock—it won't love you back. It doesn't even know that you own it. Invest in the stock or bond of a company that you genuinely want to own, not in a "hot trend" or "good story." Remember that if someone tells you it's "a sure thing," it isn't.

12. **Don't use credit cards.** Numerous studies have shown that people spend significantly more (on average, 23 percent more) when using credit cards than when paying with cash or check. Credit cards make money an abstraction, as well as relegating payment to a future time. Pay in cash.

13. **Consider the opportunity cost of your purchase.** Before you spend significant money on an item, calculate what it would be worth in five years if you were instead to invest that same money. And in 10 years.

14. **Consider the absolute value rather than the anchor price.** Seventy-five percent off a jacket that's overpriced by 300 percent is not a deal. A "sale price" is meaningless if it is anchored in an inflated initial price.

15. **Consider the actual product and what you will do with it if purchased.** Will you *really* use it? For how long? One year from now, what choices will you be glad you've made?

16. **Be suspicious of being "special."** Special offers or other indications that you are in a select group—an inner circle of

unique consideration—will make you buy more than you need. Special, exclusive, unique offers induce a desire to respond with gratitude—and with purchase. Be suspicious of special offers.

17. **Simplify your symbolism.** Designer brands are marketed to symbolically represent quality, desirability, and the experience of having arrived. The symbolism of specialness adds cost. The qualities that we attribute to brands create a relationship with the brand that results in both desire and the commitment to pay more. Ask yourself whether you'd pay the same amount for a product if the logo were changed and nothing else.

18. **Leave emotions at home.** Emotions hijack the logical brain, and along with it, reasonable decisions. Stress may seek relief through buying, hoarding, or purchasing out of other emotional needs such as insecurity or a desire to win approval.

    Make financial decisions independently of emotional decisions and distinguish between the two. Worry about the right things.

19. **Shop alone.** The social contagion of shopping with friends induces a relaxation of usual constraints, as well as the desire to impress friends with a purchase.

20. **Remember that you have the right to say "No."** Don't hesitate to say "No." And don't hesitate to say *yes* either when you are clear about what you want and need. The other person in your interaction also has a right to say *no* or *yes*. Don't hesitate, for example, to make a simple request for a fee for service equal to its value.

21. **You have to be free to say *no* before you can be free to say *yes*.** Unless you are free to say *no*, *yes* has no meaning.

22. **Disengage from "what might have been."** Getting what you always wanted in the past may not feel as good as you expected, because it's no longer the past. If you attempt to reenter an old story and acquire what you missed in the past, it won't work. "If only" fantasies erode the power of today.

To keep a goal just out of reach maintains the "someday" fantasies associated with it. "I'll lose the 10 pounds, and then I'll be happy." The weight-loss goal must remain elusive, or the hope of happiness contained in the loss of the last 10 pounds would be exposed as illusion. The unattainable becomes addictive.

It is difficult to sell a stock that has declined significantly. The sale makes a reality of money loss rather than a theory of paper loss. The sale also banishes the hope of future gains.

You have to relinquish a past position in order to move ahead. When you let go of the past, you reclaim your aliveness (and effectiveness) in the present.

23. **Keep the big picture in mind.** A study by the Joseph Rowntree Foundation found that wealthy Londoners do not feel rich, because they never mix with people less affluent than themselves. When you take a good look at the global neighborhood and realize that half of humanity lives on less than $3 a day, it puts things in perspective. According to University of California sociologist William Domhoff, "In the United States, just 20 percent of the people own a remarkable 85 percent of the wealth, leaving only 15 percent of the wealth for the bottom 80 percent."[2] It's good to keep the big picture in mind.

The big picture consists of your own ideals and principles, and objectively organizing your life and decisions according to what you believe to be in your best interest. Whenever you might be caught up in details or in the grip of emotion, stop and ask, "What is in my best interest?"

The next right step may not always be clear, but you can almost always be clear about what the next right step *isn't*.

24. **Strike while the iron's cold.** A study from UCLA found that when purchases were interrupted by a conscious break in the buying process, purchasers became more objective and discerning about the need to buy. Neuroscientists at Emory University found that this delay disrupted dopamine release. A drop in dopamine

after you buy is called "buyer's remorse." That same drop *before* you buy is called "coming to your senses."

There are few true emergencies in life. Most decisions involving money really do allow time for consideration. Weighing different factors, gathering data, and perhaps consulting experts works best to make most decisions. Rarely does any legitimate crisis demand that these steps be skipped.

In between urge and action lies a gap: Impulsivity erases that gap, while emotional intelligence seeks it out. Create a contemplative pause—a space of time between choosing something and paying for it. Postpone all decisions based on impulse, frustration, or anger until you have regained objectivity.

Calling a *time out* is a useful maneuver for emotionally charged matters. "Let me think about that, and I'll get back to you," *is* a decision. A wise mentor once told me, "Never speak more clearly than you think."

25. **You'll never do anything important or fulfilling that will feel comfortable at first.** Growth and progress always feel uncertain in the beginning. At the point of jumping in the pool for the first time to learn to swim, you can either proceed despite your discomfort or abandon your task and immediately stop the anxiety. Anxiety signals that you are moving ahead into a new experience—it is not an indication of danger or inability. You have to proceed despite anxiety in order to master the task.

If worrying about the future fills the present, both are diminished. A plan is only a guideline, not a certainty. The capacity to endure uncertainty is the essence of growth.

The only familiar territory is behind you. Danish philosopher Søren Kierkegaard said, "Life can only be understood backwards, but it must be lived forwards."

Growth and change are hard. In fact, the only thing harder is *not* growing or changing.

"There is a path through the money minefield," we said back in Chapter 1. "Finding that path starts with a simple question: What *is* money?"

The answer to that question turns out to be, *money is simply money*— nothing more and nothing less. When you let go of whatever layers of meaning, drama, emotion, and complexity you may have draped around money, it loses its mysterious power to control you, and instead becomes what it was meant to be: a powerful force you can use to shape the life that you envision.

The truth about the secret language of money is that it is only a secret if we conspire to keep it that way. Blow off the dust of past experiences and the cobwebs of emotional attachments; set your money out in the air and sunshine where you can see it for what it is. Owning your money, rather than letting your money own you, goes hand in hand with taking ownership of your story.

This is your life; these are your dreams and goals; these are your relationships; these are your ideals, values, and purpose. This is your money, and it can mean whatever you tell it to. Money is the language of enterprise and harnessed energy, the language of trade and service, ingenuity and aspiration, a language that has the capacity to tell an infinite number of stories.

This is *your* story, and you get to write it, tell it, and live it as you choose.

Notes

1. "Emotional IQ Just as Important as Brainpower for Buffett," by Alex Markels, *U.S. News & World Report*, August 6, 2007.
2. G. William Domhoff, *Who Rules America? Power, Politics, and Social Change*, New York: McGraw-Hill, 2006. Updated 2009 figures available from WhoRulesAmerica.net at http://sociology.ucsc.edu/whorulesamerica/power/weath.html.

INDEX